SKETCHES

OF THE

PHILOSOPHY OF APPARITIONS;

OR,

AN ATTEMPT TO TRACE SUCH ILLUSIONS TO
THEIR PHYSICAL CAUSES.

By SAMUEL HIBBERT, M.D. F.R.S.E.

SECRETARY TO THE SOCIETY OF SCOTTISH ANTIQUARIES,

&c. &c. &c.

———————— " I' the name of truth
Are ye fantastical, or that indeed
Which outwardly ye show?"—*Macbeth.*

THE SECOND EDITION, ENLARGED.

TO

SIR WALTER SCOTT

OF ABBOTSFORD, BART.

PRESIDENT OF THE ROYAL SOCIETY OF EDINBURGH,
&c. &c. &c.

SIR,

AMONG the pages of your various works, are many incidental notices of early and prevailing superstitions, from the perusal of which I have often experienced a more than common degree of interest, on account of their intimate connexion with the history of the Human Mind. You have, indeed, yourself occasionally adverted to the importance of investigating the mental principles to which certain popular illusions may be referred: in most respectfully, therefore, inscribing to you this little volume, in which such an attempt has been made, I beg that it may be considered as a sincere testimony of gratitude for the pleasure and advantage which I have frequently derived from your literary labours.

I have the honour to be,

SIR,

Your most obedient and

Very faithful servant,

S. HIBBERT, M.D.

Edinburgh, 29th March, 1825.

PREFACE.

In the winter of 1823, I had the honour of reading an Essay on Spectral Impressions to the Royal Society of Edinburgh. Whatever interest it excited was rather due to the subject, than to the degree of success with which a theory of apparitions could possibly be discussed in the limits of a short paper. This consideration, therefore, among others, has given rise to the present volume.

The plan of this work may now be briefly stated :—

In the first place, a view is given of the various opinions, ancient as well as modern, which have been entertained on the subject of apparitions. The hypothesis, however, which I have myself preferred, is, that apparitions are nothing more than ideas, or the recollected images of the mind, which have been rendered more vivid than actual impressions.

An explanation is next rendered of the particular morbid affections with which the production of phantasms is often connected.

It is also pointed out, that in many ghost-stories of a supposed supernatural character, the ideas, which by disease are rendered so unduly intense as to induce spectral illusions, may be traced to such fantastical objects of prior belief as are incorporated in the various systems of superstition, which for ages have possessed the minds of the vulgar.

But if apparitions are really to be considered as ideas equalling or exceeding in vividness actual impressions, there ought to exist some important and definite laws of the mind which have given rise to this undue degree of vividness. These laws, accordingly, form the subject of a long investigation.

Another object of this dissertation was to have established, that, in every undue excitement of our feelings, (as, for instance, when ideas become more vivid than actual impressions) the operations of the intellectual faculty of the mind sustain corresponding modifications, by which the efforts of the judgment are rendered proportionally incorrect. But the reason which I assign for being obliged to suspend such an intention, is, "that an object of this nature cannot be attempted but in connexion with almost all the phenomena of the human mind. To pursue the inquiry, therefore, any farther, would be to make a dissertation on apparitions the absurd vehicle of a regular system of metaphysics."

This work is not addressed to any particular class of readers. As we live in an age exceeded by no previous one for the desire of information, and as there is a general interest excited on the subject of apparitions, which are properly regarded as unexplained phenomena, I have not thought fit to fashion this discourse to the exclusive taste either of metaphysicians or physiologists; but, on the contrary, have so endeavoured to treat it, that, without any previous study of the sciences which it involves, it may be fully understood. Yet the reader ought by no means to flatter himself, that he will be enabled to comprehend the laws which give rise to phantasms without any mental exertion on his own part. The phenomena, which for ages have puzzled the most learned men in the world, are not to be thus easily dealt with.

I shall, lastly, remark, that the illustrations

which appear in the course of this work are not more numerous than the treatise requires; my object being not only to render the principles that I have inculcated as intelligible as possible, but to direct the attention of the reader less to the vulgar absurdities which are blended with ghost-stories, than to the important philosophical inferences that are frequently to be deduced from them. The subject of apparitions has, indeed, for centuries, occupied the attention of the learned; but seldom without reference to superstitious speculations. It is time, however, that these illusions should be viewed in a perfectly different light; for, if the conclusions to which I have arrived be correct, they are calculated, more than almost every other class of mental phenomena, to throw considerable light upon certain important laws connected with the physiology of the human mind.

S. H.

CONTENTS.

PART I.

SKETCHES OF CERTAIN OPINIONS, ANCIENT AND MODERN, WHICH HAVE BEEN ENTERTAINED ON THE SUBJECT OF APPARITIONS.

	Page
CHAP. I. The Opinions entertained regarding the Credibility of Ghost-Stories,	3
II. The Reference of Apparitions to Hallucinations, &c.	15
III. The Opinions entertained that a Ghost was a material Product, *sui Generis*,	18
IV. The Opinions entertained that Ghosts were external Ideas, or Astral Spirits,	25
V. The Opinions entertained that Ghosts were attributable to Fancy or Imagination,	31
VI. The Opinions which attribute the supposed Influence of Fancy to the direct Operations of the Soul,	38
VII. The Notions entertained that Ideas, by their Action on the Nerves, gave rise to Spectral Impressions,	44
VIII. The Opinions that Spectral Impressions were the Result of a false Judgment of the Intellect,	46
IX. The Devil supposed to be a Cause of Ghosts,	48

PART II.

THE PARTICULAR MORBID AFFECTIONS WITH WHICH THE PRODUCTION OF PHANTASMS IS OFTEN CONNECTED.

CHAP. I. The Pathology of Spectral Illusions,	61
II. Spectral Illusions resulting from the highly-excited States of particular Temperaments,	72

CONTENTS.

Chap. III. Spectral Illusions arising from the Hysteric Temperament, - - - 81
IV. Spectral Illusions occurring from Plethora; for instance, from the Neglect of accustomed periodical Blood-letting, - - - 86
V. The Spectral Illusions which occasionally occur as Hectic Symptoms, - - - 91
VI. Spectral Illusions from Febrile and Inflammatory Affections, - - - 94
VII. Spectral Illusions arising from Inflammation of the Brain, - - - 99
VIII. Spectral Illusions arising from a highly-excited State of Nervous Irritability acting generally on the System, - - - 112
IX. The Spectral Illusions of Hypochondriacks, 117
X. Certain less frequent Morbid Sources of Spectral Illusions, - - - 119

PART III.

PROOFS THAT THE OBJECTS OF SPECTRAL ILLUSIONS ARE FREQUENTLY SUGGESTED BY THE FANTASTIC IMAGERY OF SUPERSTITIOUS BELIEF.

Chap. I. Explanation of the Mode in which the Ideas which are suggested by various Popular Superstitions become recalled in a highly-vivified State, so as to constitute the Imagery of Spectral Illusions, 125
II. Remarks on the Apparitions of Good Spirits, recorded in Popular Narratives, - 138
III. General Remarks on the Apparitions connected with Demonology, - - 160
IV. General Remarks on the Apparitions of Departed Spirits, - - - - 191

PART IV.

AN ATTEMPT TO INVESTIGATE THE MENTAL LAWS WHICH GIVE RISE TO SPECTRAL ILLUSIONS.

Chap. I. General Object of the Investigation which follows, 241
II. Indications afforded by Mental Excitements, that Organs of Sensation are the Medium through which past Feelings are renovated, - 244

CONTENTS.

	Page
CHAP. III. The various Degrees of Excitement, of which Ideas, or the renovated Feelings of the Mind, are susceptible,	258
IV. An Inquiry into those Laws of Mental Consciousness which give rise to the Illusions of Dreams,	272
V. Phantasms may arise from Ideas of which the Mind might otherwise have been either conscious or unconscious,	282
VI. The Effect of Morbific Excitements of the Mind when heightened by the vivifying Influence of Hope and Fear,	295
VII. The Illusions which Hope and Fear are capable of exciting independently of the Co-operation of Morbific Causes,	305
VIII. Mental Excitements distinguished as partial or general,	311
IX. General Mental Excitements considered as the Result of Morbific Causes co-operating with moral Agents,	315
X. The frequent Effect of general Morbific Excitements in rendering the Mind unconscious either of pleasurable or painful Feelings,	319
XI. The Influence of any prevailing moral Disposition may be so increased by a Morbific Excitement, as to be productive of Spectral Impressions of a corresponding Character,	323
XII. When moral Agents which exert a pleasurable Influence are heightened in their Effects by the Co-operation of Morbific Excitements of a similar pleasurable Quality, the Mind may be rendered totally unconscious of opposite or painful Feelings,	340
XIII. When moral Agents which exert a painful Influence are heightened in their Effects by the Co-operation of Morbific Excitements of a similar painful Quality, the Mind may be rendered totally unconscious of opposite or pleasurable Feelings,	347
XIV. Proofs that, during intense Excitements of the Mind, no less than during Syncope and Sleep, the Causes which exclusively act upon Organs of Sensation eventually extend their vivifying Influence to the Renovation of past Feelings,	353
XV. When Morbific Causes of Mental Excitement exert to their utmost Extent their stimulating	

	Page
Powers, they often change the Quality of their Action, as from Pleasure to Pain, or from Pain to Pleasure,	361
CHAP. XVI. When Causes act acutely upon Organs of Sensation, and are unremittingly prolonged, they occasionally change the Quality of their Action; as, for instance, from Pain to Pleasure. Ideas likewise partake of this Change of Excitement,	367

PART V.

SLIGHT REMARKS ON THE MODIFICATIONS WHICH THE INTELLECTUAL FACULTY OFTEN UNDERGOES DURING INTENSE EXCITEMENTS OF THE MIND, - - 377.

PART VI.

SUMMARY OF THE COMPARATIVE DEGREES OF FAINTNESS, VIVIDNESS, OR INTENSITY SUBSISTING BETWEEN SENSATIONS AND IDEAS, DURING THEIR VARIOUS EXCITEMENTS AND DEPRESSIONS.

Introduction,	391
CHAP. I. The various Excitements and Depressions connected with the Sleeping and Dreaming States,	393
II. The Order of Phenomena observable in extreme Mental Excitements, when Sensations and Ideas are conjointly rendered more vivid,	409
III. The Images of Spectral Impressions differ from those of Dreams in being much more vivid,	429
NOTES,	441

DIRECTIONS TO THE BINDER.

FORMULA (contained in a Tabular View) of the various comparative Degrees of Faintness, Vividness, or Intensity, supposed to subsist between Sensations and Ideas, when conjointly excited or depressed,—*to face page* 392.

Wood Cut of Grotesque Carvings over the Door of the Cheetham Library, Manchester,—illustrative of the Demonology of the Middle Ages,—*to face page* 172.

PART I.

SKETCHES OF CERTAIN OPINIONS,

ANCIENT AND MODERN,

WHICH HAVE BEEN ENTERTAINED ON THE SUBJECT OF

APPARITIONS.

PART I.

CHAPTER I.

THE OPINIONS ENTERTAINED REGARDING THE CREDIBILITY OF GHOST-STORIES.

"We thinke that to be a lie, which is written, or rather fathered upon Luther; to wit, that he knew the devill, and was verie conversant with him, and had eaten manie bushels of salt and made jollie good cheere with him; and that he was confuted, in a disputation with a real divell, about the abolishing of private masse."—*Scot's Discovery of Witchcraft.*

To give a regular history of the various opinions entertained in successive ages relative to apparitions, would form the copious subject of a large volume; a selection of them, therefore, is all that will be here attempted.

There is perhaps no age of history in which the idle attempts to reconcile the wild incidents of spectral impressions have not induced many learned people to reject the whole, or most of them, as fabulous, or as the coinage of rank impostors. Hence, probably, the ridicule which apparitions incurred from Lucian, and hence the doubt which, in the 16th century, Reginald Scot entertained relative to Martin Luther's visions, a few of which were certainly fabrications. It is, indeed, certain, that many stories of apparitions are either gross forgeries, or are attributable to the tricks of jugglers. The devils which Benvenuto Cellini saw, when he got into a conjurer's circle, are, by Mr Roscoe, the learned translator of his life, referred to the effects of a magic-lantern. Granting, however, that this was the case, the excited state of Cellini's mind would greatly contribute to aid the deception practised upon him.*

It must thus be instantly kept in view, that however numerous ghost-stories may be, there are comparitively few which are to be depended upon. If they had their origin in true spectral illusions, they are, at the same time, grossly exaggerated, while other narratives are nothing more than the device of rank impostors. As specimens of this dubious kind of visions may be adduced, the popular narratives published in the commencement of the 18th century, one of which relates, how one Mr John Gairdner, minister near to Elgin, " fell into a trance on the 10th of January 1717, and lay as if dead, to the sight and appearance of all spectators, for the space of two days; and being put in a coffin, and carried to his parish, in order to be buried in the church-yard; and when

---

* See Note 1st at the end of the volume.

going to put him in his grave, he was heard to make a noise in his coffin, and it being opened, he was found alive, to the wonderful astonishment of all there present; being carried home and put in a warm bed, he in a little time coming to himself, related many strange and amazing things which he had seen in the other world." Another choice production of this kind narrates, " how Mr Richard Brightly, minister of the gospel near Salcraig, at several times heard heavenly music when at prayer, when many persons appeared unto him in white raiment; also how, on the 9th of August, at night, as he was praying, he fell into a trance, and saw the state of the damned in everlasting torment, and that of the blessed in glory; and being then warned of his death by an angel, how he afterwards ordered his coffin and grave to be made, and invited his parishioners to hear his last sermon, which he preached the Sunday following, having his coffin borne before him, and then declared his visions;—and how he saw Death riding in triumph on a pale horse, —of the message he had given him to warn the inhabitants of the wrath to come, and of his dying in the pulpit when he had delivered the same; lastly, of his burial, and of the harmonious music that was heard in the air during his interment;" the truth of all which was certified by the signatures of Mr William Parsons, two ministers, and three other honest men. A third pamphlet describes what " was revealed to William Rutherford, farmer in the Merse, by an angel which appeared unto him as he was praying in his corn-yard, who opened up to him strange visions unknown to the inhabitants of the earth, with the dreadful wrath that is coming on Britain, with an eclipse of the gospel, and the great death that shall befall many, who shall be suddenly snatched away before these things come to pass; also the glorious deliverance the church will get after these sad times are over; with the great plenty that will follow immediately thereafter, with the conversion of the heathen nations, and with meal being sold for four shillings a boll:—the truth of all this being attested by the minister of the parish, and four honest men who were eye and ear-witnesses."*

Truly ridiculous as such pretended visions are, and unworthy of the smallest degree of attention, there are however some narratives on record, which require a more serious notice. Of this kind is the curious account written many years ago by Nicolai, the famous bookseller of Berlin,—a narrative which Dr Ferrier very properly characterizes as " one of the extreme cases of mental delusion which a man of strong judgment has ventured to report of himself." It is, indeed, a case which affords correct data for investigations relative to the belief in apparitions; on which account I shall take the liberty of transcribing the narrative in this essay, however frequently it may have appeared before the public.

"Individuals who pretend to have seen and heard spirits are not to be persuaded that their apparitions were simply the creatures of their senses. You may tell them of the impositions that are frequently prac-

---

* Preface to the Memorials by the Rev. Mr Robert Law, edited by Charles Kirkpatrick Sharpe, Esq. Edinburgh, A.D. 1818.

tised, and the fallacy which may lead us to take a spirit of our imagination by moonlight for a corpse. We are generally advised to seize the ghosts, in which case it is often found that they are of a very corporeal nature. An appeal is also made to self-deception, because many persons believe they actually see and hear where nothing is either to be seen or heard. No reasonable man, I think, will ever deny the possibility of our being sometimes deceived in this manner by our fancy, if he is in any degree acquainted with the nature of its operations. Nevertheless, the lovers of the marvellous will give no credit to these objections, whenever they are disposed to consider the phantoms of imagination as realities. We cannot therefore sufficiently collect and authenticate such proofs as shew how easily we are misled, and with what delusive facility the imagination can exhibit, not only to deranged persons, but also to those who are in the perfect use of their senses, such forms as are scarcely to be distinguished from real objects.

" I myself have experienced an instance of this, which not only in a psychological, but also in a medical point of view, appears to me of the utmost importance. I saw, in the full use of my senses, and (after I had got the better of the fright which at first seized me, and the disagreeable sensation which it caused) even in the greatest composure of mind, for almost two months constantly, and involuntarily, a number of human and other apparitions;—nay, I even heard their voices;—yet after all, this was nothing but the consequence of nervous debility, or irritation, or some unusual state of the animal system.

"The publication of the case in the Journal of Practical Medicine, by Professor Hufeland of Jena, is the cause of my now communicating it to the academy. When I had the pleasure of spending a few happy days with that gentleman last summer, at Pyrmont, I related to him this curious incident."

The narrator now explains the state of his system at the time; but this important part of the account not being at present connected with our subject, it will be noticed in its proper place.

"In the first two months of the year 1791, I was much affected in my mind by several incidents of a very disagreeable nature; and on the 24th of February a circumstance occurred which irritated me extremely. At ten o'clock in the forenoon my wife and another person came to console me; I was in a violent perturbation of mind, owing to a series of incidents which had altogether wounded my moral feelings, and from which I saw no possibility of relief; when suddenly I observed at the distance of ten paces from me a figure,—the figure of a deceased person. I pointed at it, and asked my wife whether she did not see it. She saw nothing; but being much alarmed, endeavoured to compose me, and sent for the physician. The figure remained some seven or eight minutes, and at length I became a little more calm; and as I was extremely exhausted, I soon afterwards fell into a troubled kind of slumber, which lasted for half an hour. The vision was ascribed to the great agitation of mind in which I had been, and it was supposed I should have nothing more to apprehend from that cause; but the violent affection had put my nerves into some unnatural state; from this arose further consequences, which require a more detailed description.

"In the afternoon, a little after four o'clock, the figure which I had seen in the morning again appeared. I was alone when this happened; a circumstance which, as may be easily conceived, could not be very agreeable. I went therefore to the apartment of my wife, to whom I related it. But thither also the figure pursued me. Sometimes it was present, sometimes it vanished, but it was always the same standing figure. A little after six o'clock several stalking figures also appeared; but they had no connexion with the standing figure. I can assign no other reason for this apparition than that, though much more composed in my mind, I had not been able so soon entirely to forget the cause of such deep and distressing vexation, and had reflected on the consequences of it, in order, if possible, to avoid them; and that this happened three hours after dinner, at the time when the digestion just begins.

"At length I became more composed with respect to the disagreeable incident which had given rise to the first apparition; but though I had used very excellent medicines, and found myself in other respects perfectly well, yet the apparitions did not diminish, but on the contrary rather increased in number, and were transformed in the most extraordinary manner."

Nicolai now makes some very important remarks on the subject of these waking dreams, and on their incongruous character. Of these observations I shall not fail to avail myself on another occasion. The narrative then proceeds after the following manner:

"The figure of the deceased person never appeared to me after the first dreadful day; but several other figures shewed themselves afterwards very distinctly; sometimes such as I knew, mostly, however, of persons I did not know, and amongst those known to me, were the semblances of both living and deceased persons, but mostly the former: and I made the observation, that acquaintance with whom I daily conversed never appeared to me as phantasms; it was always such as were at a distance."

"It is also to be noted, that these figures appeared to me at all times, and under the most different circumstances, equally distinct and clear. Whether I was alone, or in company, by broad day-light equally as in the night-time, in my own as well as in my neighbour's house; yet when I was at another person's house, they were less frequent, and when I walked the public street they very seldom appeared. When I shut my eyes, sometimes the figures disappeared, sometimes they remained even after I had closed them. If they vanished in the former case, on opening my eyes again, nearly the same figures appeared which I had seen before.

"I sometimes conversed with my physician and my wife, concerning the phantasms which at the time hovered around me; for in general the forms appeared oftener in motion than at rest. They did not always continue present—they frequently left me altogether, and again appeared for a short or longer space of time, singly or more at once; but, in general, several appeared together. For the most part I saw human figures of both sexes; they commonly passed to and fro as if they had no connexion with each other, like people at a fair where all is bustle; sometimes they appeared to have business with one another. Once or twice I saw amongst them persons on horseback, and dogs and birds; these figures all appeared to me in their natural size, as distinctly as if they had existed in real life, with the several tints on the uncovered parts of the body, and with all the different kinds and colours of clothes. But I think, however, that the colours were somewhat *paler* than they are in nature.

"None of the figures had any distinguishing characteristic, they were neither terrible, ludicrous, nor repulsive; most of them were ordinary in their appearance,—some were even agreeable.

"On the whole, the longer I continued in this state, the more did the number of phantasms increase, and the apparitions became more frequent. About four weeks afterwards I began to hear them speak: sometimes the phantasms spoke with one another; but for the most part they addressed themselves to me: these speeches were in general short, and never contained any thing disagreeable. Intelligent and respected friends often appeared to me, who endeavoured to console me in my grief, which still left deep traces on my mind. This speaking I heard most frequently when I was alone: though I sometimes heard it in company, intermixed with the conversation of real persons; frequently in single phrases only; but sometimes even in connected discourse.

"Though at this time I enjoyed rather a good state of health both in body and mind, and had become so very familiar with these phantasms, that at last they did not excite the least disagreeable emotion, but on the contrary afforded me frequent subjects for amusement and mirth; yet as the disorder sensibly increased, and the figures appeared to me for whole days together, and even during the night, if I happened to awake, I had recourse to several medicines."*

Such is the curious case of Nicolai, in which it would not occasionally be very difficult to explain why certain mental images, to the exclusion of other objects of his waking visions, should have acquired an undue degree of vividness. Frequently, however, it would be impossible to trace any correspondence which the particular complexion or disposition of his mind might have with the quality of the phantasms that were the offspring of his wild imagination. The uninteresting recollections incidental to each train of thought, as well as the lively objects of his grief, appear to have alternately assumed an embodied form. From this circumstance, then, arises the suspicion, that there were not only causes of a moral description,

---

* Memoir on the Appearance of Spectres or Phantoms occasioned by Disease, with Psychological Remarks. Read by Nicolai to the Royal Society of Berlin, on the 28th of February, 1799. The translation of this paper is given in Nicholson's Journal, vol. vi. p. 161.

but also some morbid condition of the body, which might have contributed to render the ideas of his mind of such a high state of intensity, that they became no less vivid than actual impressions.

After these remarks, the general object of this Dissertation may admit of an easy explanation. An essay seriously written, with the view of confuting all the superstitious absurdities connected with the popular belief in apparitions, would, no doubt, in this philosophic age, be considered of the same importance as the publication of arguments, how weighty soever they may be, intended to weaken the confidence which some very well-disposed persons still choose to entertain on the subject of dreams, or upon the relation which is supposed to subsist between them and future events. At the same time, the utility of an inquiry into the *rationale* of our dreams has never been doubted, as every proper theory connected with a speculation of this kind must necessarily involve the successful investigation of certain primary laws of the human mind, by which our various states of mental feelings are governed. A similar argument applies to those embodied phantasies, which, under the general name of Apparitions, are the sportive images of what may, with the greatest propriety, be styled *our waking dreams*. To explain, therefore, the physical causes of such mental illusions, and, in connexion with this elucidation, to point out the origin of the popular belief in apparitions, is an attempt which precludes any notions that may be urged against it on the score of insignificance. The inquiry necessarily involves an accurate and extensive knowledge of the laws of thought, and a capability of applying them to cases, where, from the co-operating influence of certain constitutional and morbid causes incidental to the human frame, the quality and intensity of our mental states undergo very remarkable modifications. In this point of view, a theory of apparitions is inseparably connected with the pathology of the human mind.

But, before entering into an independent investigation of this kind, it may be proper to inquire, What have been the opinions hitherto entertained on the subject by such philosophers as have been the least desirous to contemplate it with the superstitious feelings of the vulgar? A few of these opinions will be explained in the First Part of this work.

CHAPTER II.

THE REFERENCE OF APPARITIONS TO HALLUCINATIONS, &c.

> "Now, whilst his blood mounts upward, now he knows
> The solid gain that from conviction flows,
> And strengthen'd confidence shall hence fulfil
> (With conscious innocence more valued still)
> The dreariest task that winter-night can bring,
> By church-yard dark, or grove, or fairy ring;
> Still buoying up the timid mind of youth,
> Till loit'ring reason hoists the scale of truth."
>
> BLOOMFIELD.

It has long been common to refer apparitions to hallucinations. For instance, a person, prior to an epilepsy, may see every thing crooked. In some affections of vision, objects are greatly magnified: thus, a gentleman whom I know in Edinburgh saw, about twilight, a cow magnified to ten or twelve times its original size, grazing on a field, like some of the Brobdingnag cattle described by Swift.

Many ghost-stories, however, admit of still more familiar explanations, of which I shall give a few instances. The first is from the Statistical Account of Scotland, published by Sir John Sinclair.

"About fifty years ago, a clergyman in the neighbourhood, whose faith was more regulated by the scepticism of philosophy than the credulity of superstition, could not be prevailed upon to yield his assent to the opinion of the times. At length, however, he felt from experience, that he doubted what he ought to have believed. One night, as he was returning home at a late hour from a presbytery, he was seized by the fairies, and carried aloft into the air. Through fields of æther and fleecy clouds he journeyed many a mile, descrying, like Sancho Panza on his clavileno, the earth far distant below him, and no bigger than a nut-shell. Being thus sufficiently convinced of the reality of their existence, they let him down at the door of his own house, where he afterwards often recited to the wondering circle the marvellous tale of his adventure." Upon this story, I find, in Mr Ellis's edition of Brand's Popular Antiquities, the following comment is made:—" In plain English, I should suspect that spirits of a different sort from fairies had taken the honest clergyman by the head, and though he has omitted the circumstance in his marvellous narration, I have no doubt but that the good man saw double on the occasion, and that his own mare, not fairies, landed him safe at his own door."

Other explanations of ghost-stories are referable to optical mistakes of the nature of external objects. The phenomena connected with the Giant of the Broken * are known to every one. To the same class of *pseudo-apparitions* belong the Fata Morgana, and the Mirage or Water of the Desert.

Sometimes, when the mind is *morally prepared* for spectral impressions, the most familiar substances are converted into ghosts. Mr Ellis gives a story to this

---

* Note 2.

effect, as related by a sea-captain of the port of Newcastle-upon-Tyne. "His cook, he said, chanced to die on their passage homeward. This honest fellow, having had one of his legs a little shorter than the other, used to walk in that way which our vulgar idiom calls, ' with an up and a down.' A few nights after his body had been committed to the deep, our captain was alarmed by his mate with an account that the cook was walking before the ship, and that all hands were on deck to see him. The captain, after an oath or two for having been disturbed, ordered them to let him alone, and try which, the ship or he, should first get to Newcastle. But, turning out on farther importunity, he honestly confessed that he had like to have caught the contagion; for, on seeing something move in a way so similar to that which an old friend used, and withal having a cap on so like that which he was wont to wear, he verily thought there was more in the report than he was at first willing to believe. A general panic diffused itself. He ordered the ship to be steered towards the object, but not a man would move the helm! Compelled to do this himself, he found, on a nearer approach, that the ridiculous cause of all their terror was part of a maintop, the remains of some wreck floating before them. Unless he had ventured to make this nearer approach to the supposed ghost, the tale of the walking cook had long been in the mouths, and excited the fears of many honest and very brave fellows in the Wapping of Newcastle-upon-Tyne."

It is quite unnecessary to give any more illustrations of this kind, which might, indeed, be multiplied to almost an indefinite extent.

CHAPTER III.

THE OPINIONS ENTERTAINED THAT A GHOST WAS A MATERIAL PRODUCT, *SUI GENERIS.*

> " These were their learned speculations,
> And all their constant occupations
> To measure wind and weigh the air,
> And turn a circle to a square;
> To make a powder of the sun,
> By which all doctors should b' undone;
> To find the North-west Passage out,
> Although the farthest way about;—
> If chemists from a rose's ashes
> Can raise the rose itself in glasses?"—BUTLER.

IN very early times, we find philosophers inclined to doubt if apparitions might not be accounted for on natural principles, without supposing that a belief in them was either referable to hallucinations, to human imagination, or to impositions that might have been practised. At length Lucretius attacked the popular notion entertained of ghosts, by maintaining that they were not spirits returned from the mansions of the dead, but nothing more than thin films, pellicles, or membranes, cast off from the surfaces of all bodies like the exuviæ or sloughs of reptiles.

An opinion, by no means dissimilar to that of the Epicureans, was revived in Europe about the middle of the 17th century. It had its origin in Palingenesy, or the resurrection of plants, a grand secret known to Digby, Kircher, Schot, Gafferel, Vallemont, and others. These philosophers performed the operation of Palingenesy after the following manner:—They took a plant, bruised it, burnt it, collected its ashes, and, in the process of calcination, extracted from it a salt. This salt they then put into a glass phial, and mixed with it some peculiar substance, which these chemists have not disclosed. When the compound was formed, it was pulverulent, and possessed a bluish colour. The powder was next submitted to a gentle heat, when its particles being instantly put into motion, there then gradually arose, as from the midst of the ashes, a stem, leaves, and flowers; or, in other words, an apparition of the plant which had been submitted to combustion. But as soon as the heat was taken away, the form of the plant, which had been thus sublimed, was precipitated to the bottom of the vessel. Heat was then re-applied, and the vegetable phœnix was resuscitated;—it was withdrawn, and the form once more became latent among the ashes. This notable experiment was said to have been performed before the Royal Society of England, and it satisfactorily proved to this learned body, that the presence of heat gave a sort of life to the vegetable apparition, and that the absence of caloric caused its death.

Cowley was quite delighted with the experiment of the rose and its ashes, and in conceiving that he had detected the same phenomenon in the letters written with the juice of lemons, which were revived on the application of heat, he celebrated the mystic power of caloric after the following manner:

> Strange power of heat! thou yet dost show,
> Like winter earth, naked, or cloth'd with snow,
> But as quick'ning sun approaching near,
> The plants arise up by degrees,
> A sudden paint adorns the trees,
> And all kind nature's characters appear;
>
> So nothing yet in thee is seen,
> But when a genial heat warms thee within,
> A new-born wood of various lines there grows;
> Here buds an A, and there a B,
> Here sprouts a V, and there a T,
> And all the flourishing letters stand in rows.

The rationale of this famous experiment made on the ashes of the rose was attempted by Kircher. He supposed that the seminal virtue of every known substance, and even its substantial form, resided in its salt. This salt was concealed in the ashes of the rose. Heat put it in motion. The particles of the salt were quickly sublimed, and being moved about in the phial like a vortex, at length arranged themselves in the same general form they had possessed from nature. It was evident, then, from the result of this experiment, that there was a tendency in the particles of the salt to observe the same order of position which they had in the living plant. Thus, for instance, each saline corpuscle, which in its prior state had held a place in the stem of the rose-slip, sympathetically fixed itself in a corresponding position when sublimed in the chemist's vial. Other particles were subject to a similar law, and accordingly, by a disposing affinity, resumed their proper position, either in the stalk, the leaves, or the flowers; and thus, at length, the entire apparition of a plant was generated.

The next object of these philosophers was to apply their doctrine to the explanation of the popular belief in ghosts. As it was incontestably proved, that the substantial form of each body resided in a sort of volatile salt, it was perfectly evident in what manner superstitious notions must have arisen about ghosts haunting churchyards. When a dead body had been committed to the earth, the salts of it, during the heating process of fermentation, were exhaled. The saline particles then each resumed the same relative situation they had held in the living body, and thus a complete human form was induced, calculated to excite superstitious fear in the minds of all but Palingenesists.

It is evident from the foregoing account, that Palingenesy was nothing more than a chemical explanation of the discovery which Lucretius had made, with regard to the filmy substances that he had observed to arise from all bodies.

Yet, in order to prove that apparitions might be really explained on this principle, the *experimentum crucis* was still wanting. But this deficiency was soon supplied. Three alchymists had obtained a quantity of earth-mould from St Innocent's church, in Paris, supposing that this matter might contain the true philosopher's stone. They subjected it to a distillatory process. On a sudden they perceived in their vials forms of men produced, which immediately caused them to desist from their labours. This fact coming to the knowledge of the Institute of Paris, under the protection of Louis XIV., this learned body took up the business with much seriousness, and the result of their labours appears in the Miscellania Curiosa. Dr Ferrier, in a volume of the Manchester Philosophical Transactions, has been at the trouble of making an abstract of one of these French documents, which I prefer giving on account of its conciseness, rather than having recourse to the original dissertation.

" A malefactor was executed, of whose body a grave physician got possession for the purpose of dissection. After disposing of the other parts of the body, he ordered his assistant to pulverize part of the cranium, which was a remedy at that time admitted in dispensatories. The powder was left in a paper on the table of the museum, where the assistant slept. About midnight he was awakened by a noise in the room, which obliged him to rise immediately. The noise continued about the table, without any visible agent; and at length he traced it to the powder, in the midst of which he now beheld, to his unspeakable dismay, a small head with open eyes staring at him; presently two branches appeared, which formed into arms and hands; then the ribs became visible, which were soon clothed with muscles and integuments; next, the lower extremities sprouted out, and when they appeared perfect, the puppet (for his size was small) reared himself on his feet; instantly his clothes came upon him, and he appeared in the very cloak he wore at his execution. The affrighted spectator, who stood hitherto mumbling his prayers with great application, now thought of nothing but making his escape from the revived ruffian; but this was impossible, for the apparition planted himself in his way, and, after divers fierce looks and threatening gestures, opened the door and went out. No doubt the powder was missing next day."

But older analogous results were on record, indicating that the blood was the chief part of the human frame in which those saline particles resided, the arrangement of which gave rise to the popular notion of ghosts. Dr Webster, in his book on witchcraft, relates an experiment, given on the authority of Dr Flud, in which this very satisfactory conclusion was drawn.

" A certain chymical operator, by name La Pierre, near that place in Paris called Le Temple, received blood from the hands of a certain bishop to operate upon. Which he setting to work upon the Saturday, did continue it for a week with divers degrees of fire. But about midnight, the Friday following, this artificer, lying in a chamber next to his laboratory, betwixt sleeping and waking, heard a horrible noise, like unto the lowing of kine, or the roaring of a lion; and continuing quiet, after the ceasing of the sound in the laboratory, the moon being at the full, and, by shining, enlightening the chamber suddenly, betwixt himself and the window he saw a thick little cloud, condensed into an oval form, which, after, by little and little, did seem completely to put on the shape of a man, and making another and a sharp clamour, did suddenly vanish. And not only some noble persons in the next chambers, but also the host with his wife, lying in a lower room of the house, and also the neighbours dwelling in the opposite side of the street, did distinctly hear as well the bellowing as the voice; and some of them were awaked with the vehemency thereof. But the artificer said, that in this he found solace, because the bishop, of whom he had it, did admonish him, that if any of them from whom the blood was extracted should die, in the time of its putrefaction, his spirit was wont often to appear to the sight of the artificer, with pertubation. Also forthwith, upon Saturday following, he took the retort from the furnace, and broke it with the light stroak of a little key, and there, in the remaining blood, found the perfect representation of an human head, agreeable in face, eyes, nostrils, mouth, and hairs, that were somewhat thin, and of a golden colour."*

---

* Regarding this narrative, Webster adds,—" There were many ocular witnesses, as the noble person, Lord of Bourdalone, the chief secretary to the Duke of Guise; and he [Flud] had this relation from the Lord of Menanton, living in that house at the same time, from a certain doctor of physic, from the owner of the house, and many others."

CHAPTER IV.

THE OPINIONS ENTERTAINED THAT GHOSTS WERE EXTERNAL IDEAS, OR ASTRAL SPIRITS.

> "Most willing Spirits, that promise noble service."
> SHAKSPEARE.

The notions taught in the middle ages regarding the Soul was, that it pervaded the whole of the body, being, indeed, the active principle of assimilation, upon which "the attraction, the retention, the decoction, and the preparation" of the particles of food which were introduced into the body, ultimately depended. The proper seat of this principle, however, was the brain, a particular department of which formed its closet. This closet the Cartesians conceived to be situated in the pineal gland.

The five Senses were regarded by the early metaphysicians as nothing more than "*porters*" to the Soul; they brought to "her" the *forms of outward things*, but were not able themselves to discern them; such forms or *ideas* were then subjected to the various intellectual operations of the rational Soul or *mind*.

According to this view, ideas, which were originally considered as the actual forms of objects, were stored up by the Memory, and liable to be recalled. This doctrine was probably derived from Aristotle, who had some notion of impressions or images remaining after the impressing cause had ceased to act, and that these images, even during sleep, were recognised by the intellectual principle of man.

Such was the metaphysical view entertained for many centuries respecting ideas,—not that they were mere states of the immaterial mind, but that they were absolute forms or images presented to the Soul or Mind. It was, therefore, not a very difficult conjecture, after the memorable experiment of Palingenesy, that the apparition of the rose, which had been induced by its saline particles being sublimed, was truly the proper *idea* of the rose, or that the apparition, induced in a similar manner after an animal body had been decomposed, was the proper *idea* of the animal. These, then, were the *external ideas* of objects, or *astral spirits*, as they were also named, that were well calculated to solve many natural phenomena. For instance, when it was reported that a shower of frogs had taken place, philosophers contended that it was nothing more than a shower of *ideas*.

Dr Webster's explanation of *astral spirits* is as follows:—" If," says he, " the experiment be certainly true, that is averred by Borellus, Kircher, Gaffarel, and others (who might be ashamed to affirm it as their own trial, or as ocular witnesses, if not true), that the figures and colours of a plant may be perfectly represented, and seen in glasses, being by a little heat raised forth of the ashes. Then (if this be true) it is not only possible, but rational, that animals, as well as plants, have their ideas or figures existing after the gross body or parts be destroyed, and so these apparitions are but only those astral shapes and figures. But also there are shapes and apparitions of men, that must of necessity prove, that these corporeal souls, or astral spirits, do exist apart, and attend upon, or are near the blood or bodies."

It is evident that this notion of astral spirits was little different from the Lucretian view, that apparitions were films given off from all bodies. But Dr Webster and other philosophers pushed this doctrine still farther, so as to render it truly pneumatological. They even had in view the division which the ancients made of the substance of the body, when they conferred upon it more souls than one. The views of the Romans and Greeks were, that different souls might be possessed by every individual, as a rational soul derived from the gods, and a sentient one originating in the four elements; or that even three souls might subsist in one person; in which case different material tenements were allotted to these spiritual principles. For the first soul, a mortal or crustaceous body was provided; for the second soul, a divine, ethereal, and luciform organization; and for the third, an aerial, misty, or vaporous body. The soul which was attached to the crustaceous system hovered about it after death.

We shall now see how much Dr Webster and others were indebted to the ancients for the view that they took of three essential and distinct parts of man. "It is most evident," says this writer, "that there are not only three essential and distinct parts in man, as the gross body, consisting of earth and water, which at death returns to the earth again; the sensitive and corporeal soul or astral spirit, consisting of fire and air, that at death wandereth in the air, or near the body;

and the immortal and incorporeal soul, that immediately returns to God that gave it; but also, that after death they all three exist separately, the soul in immortality, and the body in the earth, though soon consuming; and the astral spirit, that wanders in the air, and, without doubt, doth make those strange apparitions, motions, and bleedings."

Mr Webster now illustrates his case by a very striking account of a spectral impression, in which the astral spirit of a murdered man is supposed to have retained all the cogitations impressed upon the mind at the hour of death, along with the faculties of concupiscibility and irascibility, by which it was compelled to seek for its revenge.

" About the year of our Lord 1623 or 24, one Fletcher of Rascal, a town in the North Riding of Yorkshire, near unto the forest of Gantress, a yeoman of good estate, did marry a young lusty woman from Thornton Brigs, who had been formerly kind with one Ralph Raynard, who kept an inn within half-a-mile from Rascal, in the high-road-way betwixt York and Thirske, his sister living with him. This Raynard continued in unlawful lust with the said Fletcher's wife, who, not content therewith, conspired the death of Fletcher, one Mark Dunn being made privy, and hired to assist in the murther. Which Raynard and Dunn accomplished upon the May-day, by drowning Fletcher, as they came all three together from a town called Huby; and acquainting the wife with the deed, she gave them a sack therein to convey the body, which they did, and buried it in Raynard's backside or croft, where an old oak-root had been stubbed up, and sowed mustard-seed upon the place, thereby to hide it. So they continued their wicked course of lust and drunkenness, and the neighbours did much wonder at Fletcher's absence; but his wife did excuse it, and said, that he was but gone aside for fear of some writs being served upon him. And so it continued until about the 7th day of July, when Raynard going to Topcliffe fair, and setting up his horse in the stable, the spirit of Fletcher, in his usual shape and habit, did appear unto him, and said,—' Oh, Ralph, repent, repent, for my revenge is at hand!' and ever after, until he was put in the gaol, it seemed to stand before him, whereby he became sad and restless; and his own sister, overhearing his confession and relation of it to another person, did, through fear of her own life, immediately reveal it to Sir William Sheffield, who lived in Rascal, and was a justice of peace. Whereupon they were all three apprehended and sent to the gaol at York, where they were all three condemned, and so executed accordingly, near to the place where Raynard lived, and where Fletcher was buried, the two men being hung up in irons, and the woman buried under the gallows. I have recited this story punctually as a thing that hath been very much fixed in my memory, being then but young; and as a certain truth, I being (with many more) an ear-witness of their confessions, and an eye-witness of their executions; and likewise saw Fletcher when he was taken up, where they had buried him in his cloaths, which were a green fustian doublet pinkt upon white, gray breeches, and his walking-boots, and brass spurrs without rowels."

We may now attend to Dr Webster's explanation of the foregoing case, agreeably to his notion of astral spirits:—" Some will say there was no extrinsic apparition to Raynard at all, but that all this did only arise from the guilt of his own conscience, which represented the shape of Fletcher in his fancy. But then, why was it precisely done at that time, and not at any others? it being far from the place of the murther, or the place where they had buried Fletcher, and nothing there that might bring it to his remembrance more than at another time; and if it had only arisen from within, and appeared so in his fancy, it had been more likely to have been moved when he was in, or near his croft, where the murthered body of Fletcher lay. But certain it is, that he affirmed that it was the shape and voice of Fletcher, as assuredly to his eyes and ears as ever he had seen or heard him in his life. And if it were granted that it was only intrinsic, yet that will not exclude the Divine Power, which doubtless at that time did labour to make him sensible of the cruel murther, and to remind him of the revenge approaching. And it could not be brought to pass either by the devil or Fletcher's soul, as we have proved before; and therefore, in reason, we conclude that either it was wrought by the Divine Power, to shew his detestation of murther, or that it was the astral or sydereal spirit of Fletcher seeking revenge for the murther." *

---

* Webster on Witchcraft, p. 297.

CHAPTER V.

THE OPINIONS ENTERTAINED THAT GHOSTS WERE ATTRIBUTABLE TO FANCY OR IMAGINATION.

"Horatio says, 'tis but our Phantasy."—HAMLET.

THE early metaphysicians conceived, that the five Senses that brought to the Soul apprehensions of touch, vision, hearing, smelling, and taste, were under the intermediate control of a personified moderator, named COMMON SENSE, by the means of whom all differences of objects were discerned. The Soul, through the medium of this ministering principle, who dwelt in the fore-part of the brain, not only learned the forms of the outward things brought to "her" by the Senses, but was enabled to make still farther distinctions, in which she was greatly superior to Common Sense. Common Sense knew nothing but differences; the Soul knew essences; Common Sense knew nothing but circumstances; the Soul knew substances; Common Sense recognised differences of sound; the Soul resolved concords.

A second ministering principle to the Soul was MEMORY, who kept a storehouse in the back-part of the brain, where all the species, ideas, or images of objects, which the external Senses had industriously collected, were treasured up.

A third ministering principle to the Soul was

Phantasy, (FANCY), or Imagination, whose seat was the middle cell of the brain. Phantasy retained objects brought by the Senses, examined more fully such species or ideas of objects as were perceived by Common Sense, arranged them, recalled the ideas which Memory had stored up, and compounded all things which were different in their kind, black and white, great and small. When Phantasy, "the handmaid of the Soul," as this principle was called, had finished her compounds, she committed them to the care of Memory, in whose storehouse much was remembered, much forgotten.

Such was the office of Phantasy, whose influence, when it began to be acknowledged, entirely changed the views which had been entertained regarding ghosts. "'Tis but our Phantasy," was the explanation given by Horatio of the ghost of Hamlet's father. It will be therefore interesting, to inquire in what manner Phantasy, (or, in more modern language, *Fancy*) was enabled to induce this illusion.

It was supposed, that while Common Sense and the five subordinate Senses were subject to laws of restraint, as in sleep, Fancy was always working day and night, as was evident from our dreams. But the labours of this industrious handmaid were always corrected by the overruling principle of the Soul. The Soul, by means of the faculty of *Wit*, looked into the result of Fancy's labours, and was then enabled to abstract shapes of things, to perceive the forms of individual objects, to anticipate, to compare, to know all universal essences or natures, as well as cause and effect. By the faculty of *Reason*, she moved from step to step, and in her progress rated objects accordingly. By the faculty of *Understanding*, she stood fixed on her ground, and apprehended the truth. By the faculty of *Opinion*, she lightly inclined to any one side of a question. By the faculty of *Judgment*, she could define any particular principle. By the faculty of *Wisdom*, she took possession of many truths. Now all this labour the Soul could not accomplish, unless Fancy, her handmaid, was obedient to the faculty of reason. But Fancy was not always to be thus controlled, the cause of which it will now be necessary to investigate.

It was next conceived, that the blood was subjected to great heat in the heart, where it was purified, and enabled to throw off delicate fumes named *Animal Spirits*. A set of nerves then formed the medium through which the Animal Spirits were conducted to the brain. They were there apprised by Fancy of the forms of all objects, and of their good or ill quality; upon which they returned to the heart, the seat of the affections, with a corresponding report of what was going on. If the report was good, it induced love, hope, or joy; if the contrary, hatred, fear, and grief. But, frequently, there was what Burton calls *læsa imaginatio*, or an ill Imagination or Fancy, which sometimes misconceiving the nature of sensible objects, would send off such a number of spirits to the heart, as to induce this organ to attract to itself more humours in order to " bend itself" to some false object of hope, or to avoid some unreasonable cause of fear. When this was the case, melancholic, sanguine, choleric, and other humours too tedious to be mentioned, were drawn into the heart—more animal spirits were concocted by heat, and these, ascending into the brain, perplexed Fancy by their number and diversity. She then became impatient of subordination, and no longer obeyed the faculty of Reason. Falling to work, in the most irregular manner, upon the ideas which Memory had stored up, she would produce the wildest compounds of sensible objects, such as we detect in the fictions of poets and painters, the chimeras of aerial castle-builders, and the *false shows* (as they were anciently named) of our waking visions.* " *Fracastorius*," says Burton, " referres all extasies to this force of imagination, such as lye whole dayes together in a trance: as that priest whom *Celsus* speaks of, that could separate himselfe from his senses when he list, and lye like a dead man, voide of life and sense. *Cardan* brags of himselfe, that he could doe as much, and that when hee list. Many times such men, when they come to themselves, tell strange things of heaven and hell, what visions they have seene. These apparitions reduce all those tales of witches progresses, dauncing, riding, transmutations, operations, &c. to the force of imagination and the divell's illusions."

Such was the popular view once entertained of the cause of apparitions. " It is all fancy or imagination!" is, indeed, the common explanation given of ghosts at

---

* This view has, in some little degree, pervaded Mr Locke's system. " The dreams of sleeping men," he remarks, " are all made up of the waking man's ideas, though, for the most part, oddly put together."

the present day, not only by the vulgar, but even by the physiologist and the metaphysician. But Dr Brown, in the view which he has taken of superstitious impressions, has very properly noticed more correct principles concerned with the production of spectral illusions; but still there is an unnecessary introduction of the word *fancy,* that, in this case, arbitrarily refers to some very curious laws, of which this able metaphysician has not given any explanation, but which he has considered in another part of his work, as meriting more attention than has hitherto been paid to the subject.

" What brighter colours the *fears of superstition* give to the dim objects perceived in twilight, the inhabitants of the village who have to pass the churchyard at any late hour, and the little students of ballad-lore, who have carried with them, from the nursery, many tales which they almost tremble to remember, know well. And in the second sight of this northern part of the island, there can be no doubt, that the objects which the seers conceive themselves to behold, are truly more vivid as conceptions, than, but for the superstition and the melancholy character of the natives, which harmonize with the objects of this foresight, they would have been; and that it is in consequence of this brightening effect of the emotion, as *concurring with the dim and shadowy objects* which the vapoury atmosphere of our lakes and valleys presents, that *Fancy, relatively to the individual, becomes a temporary reality.* The *gifted eye,* which has once believed itself favoured with such a view of the future, will, of course, ever after have a *quicker foresight,* and more frequent revelations; its own wilder emotion communicating still more vivid forms and colours to the objects which it dimly perceives."

After these very general observations on the opinions long entertained regarding the power of Fancy or Imagination, I shall now proceed to notice other remarkable views, which, at different times, have been taken of the influence of this personified principle of the mind.

Van Helmont supposed that the power of Fancy was not merely confined to the arrangement and compounding of forms brought into the brain through the medium of the Senses, but that this principle or faculty of the Soul was invested with the power of creating for herself ideas independently of the Senses. Thus, he conceived, that as every man has been a partaker of the image of the Deity, he has power to create, by the force of his Fancy or Imagination, certain ideas or entities of his own. Each conceived idea clothes itself in a species, or form, fabricated by Fancy, and becomes a seminal and operative entity subsisting in the midst of that vestment. Hence the influence of Fancy or Imagination upon the forms of offspring. " Ipsam speciem quam animus effigiat, fœtui inducit."

Another notion advocated by ancient metaphysicians was, that Fancy or Imagination could influence the Animal Spirits of others, so as to induce a corresponding influence on the heart, which was the seat of the affections. This opinion was maintained by Wierus, Paracelsus, Cardan, and others. " Why do witches and old women fascinate and bewitch children?" asks Burton; "but, as many think, the forcible Imagination of the one party moves and alters the spirits of the other." A very natural explanation is thus assigned for the effect of an evil eye.

In a much later period, however, Lavater conceived that the Imagination had a still more powerful influence, as it could operate on the minds of others much more directly than through the animal spirits. The Imagination of one individual could so act upon that of another individual, as to produce by this operation a vivid idea of the visible shape of the person from whom this influence had emanated. Thus, the Imagination of a sick or dying person, who deeply longs to behold some dear and absent friend, can so act upon the mind of the same friend as to produce an idea vivid enough to appear like a reality, and thus give rise to the notion of a phantasm. Nor is this operation of Fancy limited to space; it can act at any distance, and even pierce through stone walls. When a sailor is in a storm at sea, and about to perish, his powerful Imagination can so act upon the mind of any dear relative, whom he despairs of seeing again, as to produce on the mind of the same relative an idea of such intensity, as to form a proper spectre of the unfortunate mariner.

This theory was no doubt supposed to be well calculated to explain many coincidences of ghost-stories, and it is certain, that there are on record many ghost-stories, which are in every respect worthy of such an explanation.

CHAPTER VI.

THE OPINIONS WHICH ATTRIBUTE THE SUPPOSED INFLUENCE OF FANCY TO THE DIRECT OPERATIONS OF THE SOUL.

"Mens sine pondere ludit."—PETRONIUS.

THE opinion entertained in the middle ages respecting the Soul was, that it possessed an immaterial and immortal nature, and that it was endowed with such intellectual powers as wit, reason, understanding, opinion, judgment, and wisdom. No sooner, then, was this doctrine taught, than the attention of the learned became no less bent upon determining its connexion with the body, than in hazarding speculations regarding its occasional resumption of a human form after the body had mingled with its parent dust. It was owing, therefore, to this reason, that perfectly different views in time arose regarding the nature of apparitions.

The first supposed indication of the Soul's existence was the exercise of her faculties upon the innate ideas, or intuitive truths, which she had received for her natural dowry. Other objects about which she was occupied were the new apprehensions that were each moment conveyed to her through the medium of the five Senses. Upon the forms of things which Memory had stored up, she was employed in her private closet of the brain, where she determined the present and past, foresaw things to come, doubted and selected, traced effects and causes, defined, argued, divided compounds, contemplated virtuous and vicious objects, and reasoned upon general principles. But the result of her labours was not committed to Common Memory, but to another ministering principle named Intellectual Memory, where, in a separate storehouse, all acquired facts and general reasons were preserved, —these even remaining after death.

. The activity which the Soul was supposed to display upon ideas, even during sleep, gave rise to numerous learned speculations. " Dreams," says Mr Addison," look like the relaxations and amusements of the soul when she is disencumbered of her machine; her sports and recreations when she has laid her charge asleep. The soul is clogged and retarded in her operations, when she acts in conjunction with a companion that is so heavy and unwieldy in its motions. But in dreams," he adds, " she converses with numberless beings of her own creation, and is transported into ten thousand scenes of her own raising. She is herself the theatre, the actor, and the beholder." The same view has been made the subject of Dr Young's reveries. But Sir Thomas Brown had previously extended this notion much farther. " It is observed," he says, " that men sometimes, upon the hour of their departure, do speak and reason above themselves; for then the Soul, beginning to be freed from the ligaments of the body, begins to reason like herself, and to discourse in a strain above mortality."

Such was the idea which prevailed regarding the activity of the Soul, when unfettered by the dull and lethargic matter of which the body was composed. In comparing, then, the operations of the Soul or Mind with those attributed by other metaphysicians to her handmaid, Fancy or Imagination, it will be perfectly evident that they are in every respect the same. Indeed, the subordinate principle of Fancy had been only invented by pneumatologists, in order to give a superior character of excellence to the unaided operations of the Soul. If any thing went wrong with our thoughts,—if wild and ill-assorted perceptions,—if monsters, ghosts, and different chimeras arose, instead of regular and well-arranged ideas,—it was not the fault of the Soul, but of her wayward servant, *Fancy*. The different vapours sent from the heart, the seat of good or ill affections, could not injure the pure nature of the Soul, but might, very naturally, have an untoward effect upon her handmaid, Fancy. In short, there could not be *læsa anima*, but there might be *læsa imaginatio*. And when many metaphysicians were led to suppose that dreams were less attributable to Fancy than to the unaided activity of the Soul, they could not start this hypothesis without advancing arguments at the same time to shew, that such phenomena were rational, though far above all human comprehension; that they were truly worthy the pure character of the Soul, and of the divining faculty which, through this medium, she exercised. " In dreams," says Addison, " it is wonderful to remark with what sprightliness and alacrity the Soul exerts herself. The slow of speech make unpremeditated harangues, or converse readily in languages that they are but little acquainted with. The grave abound in pleasantries, the dull in repartees and points of wit."* But Sir Thomas Brown, to whom Addison refers for a similar opinion, had far exceeded this view. His words are these:—" Were my memory as faithful as my reason is fruitful, I would never study but in my dreams; and this time also would I choose for my devotions; but our grosser memories have then so little hold on our understandings, that they forget the story, and can only relate to our awakened souls a confused and broken tale of that that has passed." This is indeed a very curious view,—not ill calculated to explain the true origin of a few of the speculations entertained by the celebrated author himself of the *religio medici*. Nor can I help suspecting that some of the conjectures on the mind and its organs, which are inculcated at the present day, might have been no less studied in dreams,— that physiologists might have forgotten some connecting links of them when they awoke, and that, if there should be any imperfection in the doctrines which may have been derived from this source, it is owing to a part only of the vision having been remembered, so that, in the place of a well-arranged system, we are presented with what Sir Thomas Brown would style " a confused and broken tale."†

It thus appears, that the power assigned to the Soul, or to her handmaid, Fancy, was inconceivably great. With regard to Fancy in particular, I have shewn

---

* Spectator, No 487. † Ibid.

how it was at length argued, that this principle had not merely the power of compounding ideas or images from the less complicated forms that were either brought to her directly by the Senses, or that were recalled from the storehouse of Memory, but that she had even the independent power of creating to herself new ideas of her own; that metaphysicians did not even then place limits to their speculations, conceiving that the Fancy of one individual could so operate on the Soul of another, as to produce upon the mind that was passive a regular idea; and, if the action was very intense, a vivid phantasm. No investigation, therefore, could now remain, but to ascertain if Imagination or Fancy had not some influence upon external particles of matter, as well as upon the minds of others. It was accordingly debated in the schools, —if Imagination could not move external objects? Thus, the evil eye of a witch, which could cause haystacks to be burnt, cattle to be killed, or corn blighted, might, with greater reason, be assigned to the power of Fancy, when heightened in its virulence by pernicious vapours sent from the heart, the seat of the affections; and, on the same principle, might be explained the effect affirmed to have happened when a pretty woman was in a vapourish mood, the glance of whose eyes was said to have shivered a steel mirror.

The last speculation entertained was, that the effects attributed to Fancy might be performed by the Soul herself. In the days of Leibnitz, there were some notions entertained by this philosopher with regard to matter and mind, which gave rise to an opinion that Souls immediately after death passed into new and more attenuated bodies. But the puzzle was, how the resemblance could take place between the new body and the old one? The answer was, that there were certain harmonic movements which subsisted between the Soul and the particles of the new body; that the Soul, agreeably to the affections which she had received during life, could not only give a corresponding similitude to the material form of a ghost, as of a miser, but impel it to such harmonic movements as would naturally lead to the place where the defunct's strong box had been deposited. Hence the reason why that spot, above all others, should be haunted. But another objection to this theory was an awkward one. It was asked, How the Soul could so influence the harmonic movements of matter as not only to possess herself of a new material form, but of the very night-gown or morning-dress that the body, during life, might have worn? The objection has never been fairly answered.

CHAPTER VII.

THE NOTIONS ENTERTAINED THAT IDEAS, BY THEIR ACTION ON THE NERVES, GAVE RISE TO SPECTRAL IMPRESSIONS.

> " By repercussion beams engender fire;
> Shapes by reflection shapes beget;
> The voice itself when stopp'd does back retire,
> And a new voice is made by it."—COWLEY.

WHEN the Epicureans wished to explain the origin of dreams, they conceived that subtle images were either given off from other substances, or were spontaneously formed;—that these, after first penetrating the body, made corresponding impressions on the attenuated corpuscles of the material soul. This view differed from a later notion entertained regarding ideas in the following respect,—that ideas were material forms, not pervading the system from the exhalation of bodies, but regularly carried to the storehouse of Memory from unknown sources;—the transportation having been affected by means of the organs of Sense.

In connexion with this view it was conceived, that the nerves upon which sensations depended might not only be affected by external agents, but that they might be impressed by internal causes, when the consequence would be, that hallucinations would arise.

Rays of light, for instance, impressing the optic nerve from without, would cause the sensation of yellow, while corrupt humours, as those of jaundice, by impressing the nerves from within, would have the self-same effect. The next inference was, that, as an idea was really material, and might be treasured up by the memory, it could, in some unknown manner, find its way to the nerves, and impress them after the manner of internal causes influencing the mind. " I shall suppose," says a learned metaphysician, " that I have lost a parent whom I have loved—whom I have seen and spoken to an infinity of times. Having perceived him often, I have consequently preserved the material figure and perception of him in the brain. For it is very possible and reconcileable to appearances, that a material figure, like that of my deceased friend, may be preserved a long time in my brain, even after his death. By some intimate, yet unknown relation, therefore, which the figure may have to my body, it may touch the optic or acoustic nerves. In the very moment, then, that my nerves are affected in the same manner that they formerly were when I saw or listened to my living friend, I shall be necessarily induced to believe that I really see or hear him as if he were present."*

---

* Essay on Apparitions, attributed to M. Meyer, professor of the university of Halle, A. D. 1748.

CHAPTER VIII.

THE OPINIONS THAT SPECTRAL IMPRESSIONS WERE THE RESULT OF A FALSE JUDGMENT OF THE INTELLECT.

"For the effect of judgment is oft the cause of fear."
CYMBELINE.

AN opinion was entertained, late in the seventeenth century, that ghosts might arise from the reasoning faculty of the soul being unable to judge between realities and ideas. If the notion regarding ideas had been the same as that of Dr Brown, namely, that they were nothing more than states of the mind, this last view would not have been very unexceptionable. But still it was much blended with erroneous notions regarding the intellectual powers of the Soul, which I have no inclination at present to combat. Suffice it to say, that by a modified condition of the intellectual power, called by the name of *vitium subreptionis*, it was conceived, that " every thing of which a person had not a clear and distinct sensation, would not seem real; and every thing that resembled, in a certain mode, a certain idea or image, was precisely the same thing as that idea." But we have a much less distinct notion of this subtle metaphysical principle, than of the example which is given of it. " When the head," says a pneumatologist, is " filled with many stories which others have related to us of the ghosts of monks, nuns, &c., we find a resemblance between that which we may perceive and such tales. A man is influenced by the second judgment, and he takes what he has perceived for a true apparition. Imagination then heats him; intense and terrible images present themselves to his mind; the circulation of the blood is deranged, and he is affected with a frightful agitation. It is impossible to resist a fancy which, when it begins to wander, gives to simple ideas such a degree of force and clearness, that we take them for real sensations. A man may thus persuade himself that he has seen and heard things which have only existed in his own head."*

---

* This opinion is adverted to in M. Meyer's Treatise, to which I have in another place alluded.

CHAPTER IX.

THE DEVIL SUPPOSED TO BE A CAUSE OF GHOSTS.

> Movet phantasiam et ita obfirmat vanis conceptibus.
> AUSTIN. DE VIT. BEAT.

ALL metaphysical, all physiological, and all chemical opinions, having been, by various philosophers, considered as perfectly inadequate to the explanation of ghosts, it was asked, why the existence of them should not arise from the direct agency of the devil himself?

Some pneumatologists maintained that the devil was a slender and an incomprehensible spirit, who reigned in a thousand shapes, and, consequently, might assume, if such were his pleasure, the form of an angel. They taught that unclean spirits insinuating themselves in the body, and mingling in its humours, sported there with as much glee as if they had been inhaling the brightest region of the stars;— that they go in and out of the body as bees do in a hive;—and hence that melancholy persons are most subject to diabolical temptations. To this doctrine, taught by the learned clerkes of the 16th and 17th century, Hamlet evidently alludes, when he conceives that it might have been " a damned ghost" which he

REGARDING APPARITIONS. 49

had seen, or the result of some diabolical art operating through the medium of his *fantasie* or imagination —

> ——————"The spirit that I have seen
> May be a devil; and the devil hath power
> To assume a pleasing shape; yea, and, perhaps,
> Out of my weakness, and my melancholy,
> (As he is very potent with such spirits,)
> Abuses me to damn me."

Accordingly the regular plot of the drama turns upon the test to which the veracity of the apparition is submitted. The trial is satisfactory, and Hamlet declares that he will "take the ghost's word for a thousand pound."

Such were the views which never failed at one time to excite the suspicion of persons labouring under spectral impressions; and it is painful to contemplate them as they arose in the minds of many eminent individuals, among whom was Martin Luther. This astonishing man was evidently affected by some organic disease, owing to which, as well as to the extraordinary intellectual exertions to which his mind was stimulated during the progress of his wonderful work of reform, the usual state of his thought appears to have been at intervals materially disturbed. In the true spirit of the times, he contemplated his zealous labours as opposed to the works of the devil, and was particularly inclined to attribute the illusions under which he laboured to the machinations of evil spirits. One anecdote to this effect I find thus stated:—" Luther has related of himself, that being at prayer, contemplating how Christ hung on the cross and suffered for his sins, there appeared suddenly on the wall a bright shining vision, and therein appeared also a glorious form of our Saviour Christ, with his five wounds, steadfastly looking upon him, as if it had been Christ himself corporally. Now at the first sight he thought it had been some good revelation, yet presently recollected himself, and apprehending some juggling of the devil, (for Christ, as Luther says, appeareth unto us in his word, and in a meaner and more humble form, even as he was humbled on the cross for us,) therefore, said he, I spake to the vision in this manner: 'Away, thou unfounded devil, I know no other Christ than he that was crucified, and who, in his word, is pictured and preached to me;' whereupon the image vanished, which was the very devil himself."

The devil was also supposed to occasionally induce illusion by self-transformation, as the following curious story, to be found in Captain Bell's Table-talk of Luther, sufficiently shews :—

"A gentleman had a fine young wife, who died, and was also buried. Not long after, the gentleman and his servant lying together in one chamber, his dead wife, in the night-time, approached into the chamber, and leaned herself upon the gentleman's bed, like as if she had been desirous to speak with him. The servant (seeing the same two or three nights, one after another), asked his master whether he knew, that every night a woman in white apparel came into his bed? The gentleman said, 'No. I sleep soundly (said he), and see nothing.' When night approached, the gentleman, considering the same, laid waking in bed. Then the woman appeared unto him, and came hard to his bed-side. The gentleman demanded who she was? She answered, 'I am your wife.' He said, 'My wife is dead and buried.' She said, 'True, by reason of your swearing and sins I died; but if you would take me again, and would also abstain from swearing one particular oath, which commonly you use, then would I be your wife again.' He said, 'I am content to perform what you desire.' Whereupon his dead wife remained with him, ruled his house, laid with him, ate and drank with him, and had children together. Now it fell out, that on a time the gentleman had guests, and his wife, after supper, was to fetch out of his chest some banqueting-stuff; she staying somewhat long, her husband (forgetting himself), was moved thereby to swear his accustomed oath; whereupon the woman vanished that instant. Now seeing she returned not again, they went up unto the chamber to see what was become of her. There they found the gown which she wore, half lying within the chest, and half without; but she was never seen afterwards. '*This did the devil,*' (said Luther): 'he can transform himself into the shape of a man or woman.'"

King James conceived, that the wraiths or simulacra of the Scottish Highlands were attributable to the devil. The following dialogue appears in his Demonology:—

Phi. And what meane these kind of spirits, when they appeare in the shadow of a person newly dead, or to die, to his friends?

Epi. When they appeare upon that occasion, they are called wraithes in our language. Amongst the Gentiles the divell used that much, to make them believe that it was some good spirit that appeared to them then, either to forewarne them of the death of their friend, or else to discover unto them the will of the defunct, or what was the way of his slaughter; as it is written in the booke of the Histories prodigious.

But some metaphysicians were not content with maintaining that the phantasms of profane history were attributable to the devil; it was, indeed, a very favourite notion entertained by theologians, that the ghost of Samuel was nothing but an illusion caused by Satan to disturb the mind of Saul. Cowley, the poet, in his censure of those who blindly use their reason in divine matters, himself affords the best illustration of the false arguments against which his Philippic was directed :—

> " Sometimes their fancies they 'bove reason set,
> And fast, that they may dream of meat.
> Sometimes ill sp'rits their sickly souls delude,
> And bastard forms obtrude.
> So Endor's wretched sorceress, altho'
> She Saul through his disguise did know,
> Yet *when the devil comes up disguis'd*, she cries,
> Behold! the gods arise.

This ridiculous explanation of the text of Holy Writ arose from the notion, that magicians, through the means of the devil, often induced spectral illusions. A curious illustration of the prevalence of this belief, which extended even to modern days, is given in the Memoirs of the Duke of Berwick.

A French army encamped before Saragossa, in 1707, under the command of the Duke of Orleans :—

"The Count de la Puebla, to retain the people of Arragon in subjection as long as possible, and by that means to retard the progress of the Duke of Orleans, persuaded the inhabitants of Saragossa that the reports of the march of a fresh army from Navarre were false; and even that the camp which they saw was nothing real, but only a phantom produced by magic; in consequence of which the clergy made a procession on the ramparts, and from thence exorcised the pretended apparitions. It is astonishing that the people were so credulous as to entertain this fancy, from which they were not undeceived till the next day, when the Duke of Orleans' light horse, having pursued a guard of horse of Puebla's briskly to the very gates of the city, cut off several of their heads there. Then indeed the citizens were alarmed, and the magistrates appeared, to make their submission to his Royal Highness. I could not have believed what I have related, if I had not been assured of its truth at Saragossa by the principal people of the city." *

A similar notion of the devil's power to raise apparitions was even a superstition in the Highlands, which was supposed to account for some of the phenomena of second sight.—" A woman of Stornbay," says Martin, " had a maid who saw visions, and often fell into a swoon; her mistress was very much concerned about her, but could not find out any means to

---

* This extract from the " Memoires de Berwick" I quote from Dr Ferrier's translation of it, which is given in his excellent paper " on Popular Illusions." See Memoirs of the Philosophical Society of Manchester, vol. iii. p. 79.

prevent her seeing those things; at last she resolved to pour some of the water used in baptism on her maid's face, believing this would prevent her seeing any more sights of this kind. And accordingly she carried her maid with her next Lord's day, and both of them sat near the basin in which the water stood, and after baptism, before the minister had concluded the last prayer, she put her hand in the basin, took up as much water as she could, and threw it on the maid's face; at which strange action the minister and the congregation were equally surprised. After prayer, the minister inquired of the woman the meaning of such an unbecoming and distracted action; she told him, it was to prevent her maid's seeing visions; and it fell out accordingly, for from that time she never once more saw a vision of any kind. This account was given me by Mr Morison, minister of the place, before several of his parishioners, who knew the truth of it. I submit the matter of fact to the censure of the learned; but, for my own part, I think it to have been one of Satan's devices, to make credulous people have an esteem for holy water."*

There were again other views taken of Satan's influence. It was supposed that the devil was a great natural philosopher. " Summus opticus et physicus" [est,] says Hoffman, " propter diuturnam experientiam."† But no one so well as Dr Bekker, in his

---

* Martin's Description of the Western Isles of Scotland.
† " Di Diabole Potentia in Corpora."

Monde Enchanté, has shewn what the devil can do by dint of his knowledge of the laws of nature.

"I mean to speak of illusions, which Schottus, together with Delrio and Molina, declares to be of three sorts; those that are made by the change of the objects, those that are made by the change of the air, and those that happen by the change of the organs of the senses.

"*First*, Illusions are made by the change of the object, when one thing is substituted instead of another that has been suddenly and imperceptibly snatched away; or when an object is presented to the eyes, in such a state and manner as that it produces a false vision; or when any object made up of air, or of some other element, offers itself to the sight; or, *lastly*, when there appears any thing composed of different matters mingled together, and so skilfully prepared, that what existed before receives thereby another form and figure.

"*Second*, The change of the air is made by these ways, when the devil hinders, lest the object should pass through the air and hit our eyes; when he disposes the air that is betwixt the object and the eye in such a manner that the object appears in another figure than really it is; when he thickens the air to make the object appear greater than it is, and to hinder it from being seen in other places but the place he designs; when he moves the air in the place through which the object is to hit the eye, that the object, going through that part of the air, may also be moved, and that its figure may be presented to the eye otherwise than it is; and, *lastly*, when he mingles and confounds together several different figures, in order that in one only object there may appear many together.

"*Third,* The organs of the senses are changed; when they are either transferred from their places and altered; when their humours and active particles are corrupted and thickened; or when such a shining brightness passes before the eyes, that they are dazzled, so that it seems that a man raves waking."

Such was the hypothesis of learned demonologists. Satan was considered as deeply versed in all material and vital phenomena, and as inducing spectral impressions by the application of those laws which he so well comprehended.—Hence the compliment which Hoffman and others have paid to his great talents and learning. But as divers moral reasons prevent me from joining in this eulogium, I shall pay no farther tribute to so distinguished a character, than by presenting to the gentle reader as faithful a portrait of him as I have been able to procure. It is from an ancient grotesque sculpture of the 16th century, which still graces the oaken pannels of the ancient seat of the Prestwiches of Lancashire,—an unfortunate family, whose property fell a sacrifice to their steady perseverance in the cause of the royalists. A drawing of this curious design was very kindly undertaken for me by a friend, whose accurate and elegant sketches of the relics of past times have been frequently acknowledged by the antiquary. To "those gentle ones," therefore, that, in the language of our great bard, "will use the devil himself with courtesy," the subjoined sketch is respectfully submitted. A more philosophical devil was perhaps never depicted: he not only appears to be well versed in the abstruse metaphysics of the period in which he sat for his portrait, but seems to be in the very act of expounding them; and, since he has been regarded by very good authority as the efficient cause of all the phenomena in which we have been so seriously engaged, there cannot, surely, be any material impropriety in allowing him to grace the conclusion of the first part of these laborious lucubrations.

"Claudite jam rivos."

Ancient Sculpture at Holme-Hall, Lancashire. From a Drawing by Captain Jones, 29th Regiment.

PART II.

THE PARTICULAR MORBID AFFECTIONS WITH WHICH THE PRODUCTION OF PHANTASMS IS OFTEN CONNECTED.

PART II.

CHAPTER I.

THE PATHOLOGY OF SPECTRAL ILLUSIONS.

"I lost all connexion with external things; trains of vivid visible images rapidly passed through my mind."—*Sir Humphrey Davy on the Effects of the Nitrous Oxide.*

HAVING explained certain divers opinions, ancient as well as modern, which have been entertained on the subject of apparitions, I ought, in due course, to state the particular notion which I may be inclined myself to adopt in the course of the present dissertation. Simply, then, it is the view to which I briefly adverted in the first chapter of this work, when treating of Nicolai's illusions; namely, that *apparitions are nothing more than ideas, or the recollected images of the mind, which have been rendered as vivid as actual impressions.* This is a view, however, that by no means originates with myself; it has entered into the disquisitions of numerous metaphysical and pathological writers of the present day, among whom I might enumerate Hartly, Ferrier, Crichton, and Brown. Having stated, then, this hypothesis, my next object will be to give a general view of such causes as are principally instrumental in inducing those intense ideas which are currently recognised by the vulgar under the name of apparitions or phantasms. This should lead me to consider the case of Nicolai in a medical point of view. But before this can be done, it will be necessary to lay down a few general principles connected with this subject, which have hitherto met with little or no attention from physiologists. These arise from the explanation of certain states of the sanguineous system, in which a remarkable connexion between such states and an undue vividness of mental feelings appears to be established. It must be admitted, however, that such an inquiry is of extreme difficulty, and liable to innumerable sources of error, on which account a more than ordinary indulgence may be due to the attempt.

The essential view of the mind which I have adopted in preference to every other is that of the late much-lamented Professor of Moral Philosophy in the university of Edinburgh. Dr Brown, in considering the mind as simple and indivisible, conceives that every mental feeling is only the mind itself, existing in a certain state.

In endeavouring then to obtain a correct notion of certain vital properties of the human frame, and of the relation which the immaterial principle of the mind may bear to them, I shall commence with that important fluid, the blood, which, from the peculiarity of its properties, has induced physiologists to maintain its vitality. This inquiry, at the same time, may meet with some assistance from observations upon the effect of certain gases, which, when introduced into the lungs, exert an influence over the blood. The pulse, for instance, of persons inhaling the nitrous oxide, though it may vary in different individuals with regard to strength or velocity, never fails to be increased in fulness; which result would intimate, that the general volume of the circulating mass is, upon the application of a proper agent, susceptible of an increasing degree of expansion. On the other hand, in the earliest stage of the noxious influence of the febrile miasma, there is an evident diminution in the volume of the blood, as is indicated by a small contracted pulse, and an increasing constriction of the capillaries. Hence may be drawn the general conclusion, that the corpuscles of the vital fluid possess within themselves an inherent dilatibility and contractility, by the alternate force of which they are enabled to act upon the elastic coats of the vessels of the human body.

A more important observation, however, with regard to the very opposite effects of the gases alluded to yet remains to be stated. It would appear, that, with an increase of the volume of the circulating fluid, a general sense of pleasure is experienced. This fact is well illustrated in the delight expressed by the individuals, who, a number of years ago, submitted themselves to the experiments instituted with the view of ascertaining the effect of the nitrous oxide. The feelings which they experienced are described under such terms as " pleasurable thrillings extending from the chest to the extremities," or " sublime emotions." On the contrary, when there is an increasing contraction in the volume of the blood, indicated by a spastic disposition of the vessels sufficient to impede the general current of the circulating fluid, an opposite state of pain appears to be an invariable result. This fact is proved in the distressing feelings experienced during the earliest symptoms arising from the epidemic contagion of the febrile miasma.

It is on these principles, then, that I would attempt to explain the nature of the sanguineous influence or energy, as it is exercised during the course of circulation. In considering, also, the mind as simple and indivisible, as well as existing in certain states, its relation to the human frame appears to be singularly manifested by some general correspondence with the quality and degrees of these actions of the blood. We have seen, for instance, that with the peculiar influencing condition of the circulating fluid, a tendency either to pleasurable or painful feelings is in a remarkable degree connected. Proofs, therefore, may now be advanced, that with the varying force of this influence, the degree of intensity which takes place in the qualities of our mental states keeps a remarkable pace. Such evidence is afforded by a further reference to that singular compound, the nitrous oxide. When the effects of this gaseous inhalation were first tried, the general result was, that, in proportion as it influenced the circulation, sensations became more and more vivid. These were described under such terms as "An increased sensibility to touch,"—"A sense of tangible extension,"—"Visible impressions becoming more illuminated,"—"Luminous points arising to dazzle the vision"—"Hearing more acute, so that the smallest sound in the room was heard distinctly,"—"Feelings of such delight as almost to destroy consciousness." At the same time, grateful recollections of an uncommon intensity passed rapidly through the mind. One individual, in attempting to describe his feelings, could only compare them to those which he had experienced when witnessing an heroic scene upon the stage. Another person could only refer for a description of the state of his mind to the emotions raised within his breast, when, upon the occasion of the famous commemoration held at Westminster Abbey in honour of Handel, he heard seven hundred instruments playing at one time. As a further consequence, also, of this increased degree of pleasure, time never failed to appear longer than as measured by a watch.

These observations on the mental effects arising from a strong sanguineous influence, may be extended by directing our attention, in the next place, to the febrile miasma, the primary action of which forms a direct counterpart to the salubrious agency of the nitrous oxide. At Cadiz and Malaga, this pernicious gas has been found possessing its greatest degree of virulence; having been heightened in its effects by extraordinary heat and moisture, a stagnant atmosphere, crowded multitudes, and the decomposition of human effluvia. In this state it has been received into the circulation, when the effect of the blood, thus chemically altered, was to vivify mental impressions to no less a degree than if the nitrous oxide had been inhaled; at the same time, the quality of the feelings, thus rendered more intense, was of an opposite and painful kind. There was a general soreness which pervaded the whole system, of such an acuteness, that the contact of the internal air, or a new change of temperature, became insupportable. There was a distressing *leipyria,* or coldness of the surface of the body and of the extremities, while the interior parts felt as they were scorched with a fire. A great anxiety prevailed about the præcordia, while the images of the mind were rendered no less intense, being of such a painful description, and so increasing in their gloomy character, that they produced, as it was declared, an overwhelming dejection.

Having thus discovered in the nitrous oxide and in the febrile miasma two most important agents capable of affecting the quality of our mental feelings, we may lastly inquire into the effect which they can produce when their excitation is carried to an extreme height.

There are few of my readers, probably, who are not aware of the distinction which is always made between those states of the mind which are induced when causes impressing our organs of sense are present, and those which occur as revivals of prior mental states; the former being termed *sensations,* the latter *ideas,* or, more correctly, *renovated feelings.* Sensations and renovated feelings differ essentially in nothing but *degree.* Thus, the latter are *less intense, less vivid,* or *fainter,* than the former. This distinction is acknowledged by all metaphysicians. Dr Brown, for instance, remarks, that "there is a tendency in the mind to renovations of feeling less vivid, indeed, than the original affections of sense when external objects were present, but still so very similar to those primary states of the mind, as to seem almost copies of them in various degrees of vividness or faintness."

This metaphysical view being stated, I shall now once more advert to the action of the nitrous oxide on our mental feelings, from which we learn, that whenever sensations and ideas are simultaneously increased to a very great degree of vividness, the mind gradually becomes unconscious of all or most of its actual impressions, but more particularly of painful or disagreeable ones, while the recollected images of pleasurable thought, vivified to the height of sensations, appear, as it were, to take their place. "Whenever the operation of this gas," remarks Sir Humphry Davy, "was carried to its greatest height, the pleasurable thrilling gradually diminished, the sense of pressure was lost, impressions ceased to be perceived, vivid ideas passed rapidly through the mind." On another occasion, this great chemist describes his feelings after the following manner:—"Immediately after my return from a long journey, being fatigued, I respired nine quarts of nitrous oxide, having been precisely thirty-three days without breathing any. The feelings were different from those I had experienced on former experiments. After the first six or seven respirations, I gradually began to lose the perception of external things, and a vivid and intense recollection of some former experiments passed through my mind, so that I called out, What an amazing concatenation of ideas!" A third experiment by the same philosopher was perhaps attended with the most remarkable results. He was enclosed in an air-tight breathing box of the capacity of about nine cubic feet and a half, in which he allowed himself to be habituated to the excitement of the gas, which was then carried on gradually. After having, therefore, been in this place of confinement an hour and a quarter, during which time no less a quantity than 80 quarts were thrown in, he adds, " The moment after I came out of the box, I began to respire 20 quarts of unmingled nitrous oxide. A thrilling, extending from the chest to the extremities, was almost immediately produced. I felt a sense of tangible extension, highly pleasurable in every limb, my visible impressions were dazzling and apparently magnified. I heard distinctly every sound in the room, and was perfectly aware of my situation. By degrees, as the pleasurable sensation increased, I lost all connexion with external things; trains of vivid visible images rapidly passed through my mind, and were connected with words in such a manner, as to produce perceptions perfectly novel. I existed in a world of newly-connected and newly-modified ideas. When I was awakened from this semi-delirious trance by Dr Kinglake, who took the bag from my mouth, indignation and pride were the first feelings produced by the sight of the persons about me. My emotions were enthusiastic and sublime; and for a moment I walked round the room, perfectly regardless of what was said to me. As I recovered my former state of mind, I felt an inclination to communicate the discoveries I had made during the experiment. I endeavoured to recall the ideas,—they were feeble and indistinct. One recollection of terms, however, presented itself, and with the most intense belief and prophetic manner I exclaimed to Dr Kinglake, ' Nothing exists but thoughts, the universe is composed of impressions, ideas, pleasures, and pains.' "

Such is the interesting detail of a very important physiological experiment made by one of the most adventurous as well as profound philosophers of the present age. The visionary world to which he was introduced, consisting of nothing more than the highly vivid and embodied images of the mind, and the singular laws by which such phantasms (if they may be so called) are governed, form, in fact, the real object of the present dissertation.

A singular result, but varied by the opposite quality of pain, attends the incipient influence of the febrile miasma of Cadiz and Malaga. Sensation and ideas are, as under the action of the nitrous oxide, simultaneously vivified. The mind soon becomes insensible to actual impressions, these being succeeded by a new world of ideas, of the most frightful kind. Horrid spectral images arise, the forerunner of a suddenly diminished degree of excitement, of total insensibility, or of death.

Our inquiry will now perhaps be found not wholly devoid of interest. A pathological principle in this investigation has been established, that when sensations and ideas are, from some peculiar state of the sanguineous fluid, simultaneously rendered highly intense, the result is, that recollected images of thought, vivified to the height of actual impressions, constitute the states of the mind.

As it has now, I trust, been sufficiently shewn, that an adequate cause of spectral illusions may arise from an undue degree of vividness in the recollected images of the mind, I shall, in the next place, investigate those morbid states of the body, by which such an effect may be induced. That ideas are not unfrequently liable to be so excited as to equal in their intensity actual impressions, and thus to be mistaken for them, is a fact with which those who are in the habit of visiting the apartments of the sick cannot but be familiar. " From recalling images by an act of memory," remarks Dr Ferrier, " the transition is direct to beholding spectral objects which have been floating in the imagination;" and," adds this physician, on another occasion, " I have frequently, in the course of my professional practice, conversed with persons who imagined that they saw demons, and heard them speak; which species of delusion admits of many gradations and distinctions, exclusive of actual insanity." This observation every medical practitioner will confirm.

I may also remark, that, in pursuing the pathological inquiry in which we are engaged, our true course is at length rendered plain and direct. In judging from the operation of those peculiar gases, the nitrous oxide and febrile miasma, which, when inhaled, affect the composition of the blood, and, at the same time, exert a vivifying influence over the feelings of the

PRODUCTION OF SPECTRAL ILLUSIONS. 71

mind, it appears that our first proper object is to inquire, if there are not many morbid conditions of the body in which the blood, from its altered quality, may not produce the same consequences. In fact, the causes thus affecting the sanguineous system, may be considered as arising, in the first place, from hereditary or constitutional taints of the blood; 2dly, From the suppression of healthy or accustomed evacuations; 3dly, From adventitious matters directly admitted into the composition of this fluid; and, 4thly, From circumstances affecting the state of the circulating system through the medium of the nerves or brain. Lastly, I may be allowed to observe, that whenever such a vivifying influence can be proved to exist, no future difficulty will surely remain in accounting for the spectral illusions which must necessarily result, when ideas, from their high degree of excitement, are rendered as vivid as actual impressions.

CHAPTER II.

SPECTRAL ILLUSIONS RESULTING FROM THE HIGHLY-EXCITED STATES OF PARTICULAR TEMPERAMENTS.

> " But that I would not
> Affect you with more sadness, I could shew ye
> A place worth view,—
> Where people of all sorts, that have been visited
> With lunacies and follies, wait their cures.
> Here's fancies of a thousand stamps and fashions,
> Like flies in several shapes, buz round about ye,
> And twice as many gestures; some of pity,
> That it would make you melt to see their passions;
> And some as light again, that would content ye."
> BEAUMONT AND FLETCHER.

FROM the different mental dispositions observable in mankind, we are entitled to expect, that in each individual of the human race, there may be a constitutional tendency to some one prevailing state of feelings, either distinctly pleasurable or distinctly painful. In the temperament, for instance, named *sanguine*, the influence of the blood is indicated by an increasing dilatation of the sanguineous vessels, or by the greater tendency of the pulse to strength and fulness, while the general mental disposition is of a lively kind.* In the *melancholic* temperament, on the contrary, there appears to be an opposite quality of the circulating fluid, which, by its influence, induces a constricting disposition of the vessels, and a corresponding proneness to gloomy thoughts.† Pinel has referred the symptoms, named maniacal, to a very highly-excited state of these two temperaments; and this view leads to the rational doubt which may be entertained, that the cause of mania is less dependent upon the condition of the nervous system, than upon some particular or morbid quality of the circulating fluid.‡ " If the blood be imperfectly elaborated," remarks a modern writer, " or with a

---

* " Homines tali constitutione prediti," remarks Dr Gregory, " præter solitum sentientes et irritabiles observantur, et pulsus habent solito frequentiores, et sanguinis motum liberrimum, et secretiones et excretiones fere copiosas, raro obstructas, et animum plerumque lætum et hilarem, aliquando levem ; nam animi non secus ac corporis varietates a temperamento sæpe pendent."

† " Hoc temperamento prediti, animum habent gravem, sæpe tristem, meditabundum, haud facile commovendum, quo semel commotus est affectus tenacissimum, in negotiis indefessum in studiis acutissimum, in amore ferventissimum, fidelissimum, ad poesin sæpe aptum, in melancholiam et insaniam aliquando proclivem."—*Gregory's Conspectus Medicinæ Theor.* p. 229.

‡ " The form of the cranium," observes Dr Good, " its thickness, and other qualities,—the meninges, the substance of the brain, the ventricles, the pineal gland, the commissures, the cerebellum,—have all been analyzed in turn by the most dexterous and prying anatomists of England, France, Germany, and Italy, but with no satisfactory result.—*Good's Study of Medicine,* v. iii. p. 67.

disproportion of some of its constituent principles to the rest, the whole system partakes of the evil, and a diathesis or morbid habit is the certain consequence. And if it become once impregnated with a peculiar taint, it is wonderful to remark the tenacity with which it retains it, though often in a state of dormancy, or inactivity, for years, or even generations."* From this view, therefore, which the writer takes of the influence of the sanguineous fluid, he is led to entertain the opinion, that there is no other part of the system which we ought to regard as the predisposing cause of such corporeal disorders as gout, struma, or phthisis, and even of mental affections, as of madness. On this subject, also, I shall beg leave to add, that, as the cause of the sanguine and melancholic temperaments in their highly-excited states, can only be referable to some peculiar state of the blood, I must regard the symptoms of such states to be those which are described under the general name of *mania*. " The violence of maniacal paroxysms," says Pinel, " appears to be independent of the nature of the exciting cause, or to depend, at least, much more upon the consitution of the individual, or upon the different degrees of his physical and moral sensibility. Men of robust constitutions, of mature years, with black hair, and susceptible of strong and violent passions, appear to retain the same character when visited by this most distressing of human misfortunes. Their ordinary energy is augmented to outrageous fury. Violence, on the other hand, is seldom characteristic

---

* Good's Study of Medicine, v. 2, p. 34.

of the paroxysms of individuals of more moderate passions, with brown or auburn hair. Nothing is more common than to see men with light-coloured hair sink into soothing and pleasurable reveries; whereas it seldom or never happens that they become furious or unmanageable. Their pleasing dreams are, however, at length overtaken by, and lost amidst the gloom of an incurable fatuity."

From these remarks we are led to expect, that vivid feelings of a highly intense kind will be often found in those states which characterize mania. Pinel has accordingly declared, that, even during intervals of comparative calmness and reason, he has no where met, except in romances, with more fond husbands, more affectionate parents, more impassioned lovers, more pure and exalted patriots, than in an asylum for lunatics. Hence he argues, that persons of the greatest mental excitement, of the warmest passions, the most active imagination, the most acute sensibility, are chiefly prone to insanity.* When such, therefore, is the frequent mental condition of the maniacal patient, it will, in a theoretical point of view, be instructive once more to advert to the power of an agent, which is calculated above every other substance to illustrate the laws connected with the vividness of which our mental feelings are susceptible; and in tracing its operation, when the sensations and ideas which it influences are excited to an extreme degree of intensity, we may compare such a result with the state of mind

---

* " A melancholy reflection," says Pinel, " but such as is calculated to call forth our best and tenderest sympathies."

which subsists during the accession of the maniacal paroxysm. The institution of this comparison will, at the same time, give strength to the opinion, that there exists in mania a sanguineous and constitutional influence, analogous in its consequences to such as may be artificially produced by chemical agents affecting the composition of the blood. Thus I have before mentioned, that Sir Humphry Davy, in relating the particular feelings which he experienced during the excitement of the nitrous oxide, first noticed the increased acuteness of his sensations, which he described under such terms, as " a sense of tangible extension, or of visible impressions being rendered dazzling, and apparently magnified." In pointing out, also, the painful effect of the febrile miasma of Cadiz, it was observed, that the incipient indications of this influence were a general soreness over the body, or a sense of extreme cold or burning heat. It is curious then to remark, that by a similar increase of corporeal sensibility, though frequently represented under different forms, the earliest symptoms of an approaching maniacal paroxysm are frequently characterized. Pinel speaks of a patient whose vision was rendered so acutely sensible, that, in forming his judgment from the effects of the sun's light, he fancied that this luminary acted upon him at the distance of only four paces; he also described a motion which he experienced in his head as resembling that of gurgling or boiling. I likewise find it recorded of another lunatic, who, although he could usually take large quantities of snuff without sneezing, yet, upon the approach of a paroxysm, had his sense of smell rendered so intense,

PRODUCTION OF SPECTRAL ILLUSIONS.

that he became convulsed with the slightest aromatics. With respect to the state of mental ideas, when they are by the same cause and under similar circumstances affected, a proportionate degree of vividness is no less observable. Thus Sir Humphry Davy has observed of the commencing effect of the nitrous oxide, that vivid ideas of the most pleasing description rapidly passed through his mind, and that an intense recollection arose of some former experiments. It is remarkable also, that a patient cured by Dr Willis has, in the narrative of his own case, described a similar state of ideas as existing in mania. "I always," he relates, "expected with impatience the accession of the paroxysms, since I enjoyed during their presence a high degree of pleasure. They lasted ten or twelve hours. Every thing appeared easy to me. No obstacles presented themselves either in theory or practice. My memory acquired upon a sudden a singular degree of perfection. Long passages of Latin authors recurred to my mind. In general, I have great difficulty in finding rhythmical terminations; but then I could write in verse with as much facility as in prose." Such is the state of mind induced when the earlier stage of the interval of mental alienation is of a pleasurable kind: and, on the other hand, when it is of a painful description, symptoms are ushered in more resembling those which are induced by the febrile miasma; the mind being distracted with recollections of the most gloomy character.

It may be farther remarked, that the same analogy which I have traced continues to subsist in more advanced indications of mania. It has been shewn, for instance, that after the long-continued inhalation of the nitrous oxide, or in the more advanced state of the symptoms attending the baneful influence of the miasma of Cadiz, ideas, or the recollected images of the mind, acquire a degree of vividness equalling that of sensations. These are frequently no less the symptoms of mania after a paroxysm has attained its greatest height. Thus Pinel remarks, that a maniac conceived at different times that he had imaginary conferences with good and bad angels, and, according to the respective influences of their delusions, was mild or furious, inclined to acts of beneficence, or roused to deeds of ferocity. In an early period of history, when insane people, as was formerly the case in England, found no asylum, they were ever, in their desultory rambles, pursued by a vivid imagination with demons or furies. "We meet with such maniacs," says a critical writer on the Jewish customs, "in the synagogues, or places of religious worship—we meet with them in towns and cities, where they were allowed to ramble uncontrolled. Being thought to be inhabited by demons, they were esteemed sacred persons, and regarded with religious awe and reverence." Shakspeare has well shewn, in the character of Edgar, that such was likewise the state of madmen in this country. "Who gives any thing to poor Tom?" says the pretended demoniac, "whom the foul fiend hath led through fire and through flame, through pond and whirlpool, over bog and quagmire; that hath laid knives under his pillow, and halters in his pew; set ratsbane by his porridge; made him proud of heart, to ride on a bay trotting horse over four-inch'd bridges, to course his own shadow for a traitor." This is no incorrect illustration of the state of a frenzied imagination.

There is no writer, however, that has been more successful than Burton in elucidating from well-authenticated instances of spectral illusions, those highly-excited states of the sanguine and melancholic temperaments, which may be considered as maniacal. " Such as are commonly of a ruddy complexion and high-coloured," says this author, " are much inclined to laughter, witty and merry, conceited in discourse, pleasant, if they be not far gone, much given to music, dancing, and to be in women's company. They meditate wholly on such things, and think they see or hear plays, dancing, and such like sports, free from all fear and sorrow. Like him of Argus, that sat laughing all day long as if he had been at the theatre. Such another is mentioned by Aristotle, living at Abydos, a town of Asia Minor, that would sit, after the same fashion, as if he had been upon a stage, and sometimes act himself, sometimes clap his hands, and laugh as if he had been well pleased with the sight." The same writer remarks of another description of men, whose mental feelings have constitutionally a gloomy tendency,—" They are usually sad and solitary, and that continually and in excess; more than ordinary suspicious, more fearful, and have long, sore, and most corrupt imaginations; cold and black, bashful, and so solitary, that they will endure no company. They dream of graves, still and dead men, and think themselves bewitched or dead. If the symptoms be extreme, they think they hear hideous noises, see and talk with black men, and converse familiarly with devils, and such strange chimeras and visions, or that they are possessed by them, and that somebody talks to them, or within them." These illustrations of mania will be at present sufficient for my purpose. It would indeed fill a volume to treat of the various mental illusions which may be referred to the same cause:

> " See the strange working of dull melancholy !
> Whose drossy thoughts, drying the feeble brain,
> Corrupts the sense, deludes the intellect,
> And in the soul's fair table falsely graves
> Whole squadrons of phantastical chimeras,
> And thousand vain imaginations;
> Making some think their heads as big as horses,—
> Some that th' are dead,—some that th' are turn'd to wolves."
> OLD COMEDY OF LINGUA.

CHAPTER III.

SPECTRAL ILLUSIONS ARISING FROM THE HYSTERIC TEMPERAMENT.

> " O, how this mother swells up toward my heart!
> *Hysterica passio!* down, thou climbing sorrow,
> Thy element's below!"
>
> KING LEAR, *Act* 2, *Scene* 4.

WHEN the growth of the form is nearly completed, the circulating fluid necessary for the future support of the body is in superabundance, and unless corrected in the delicate system of the female, must, agreeably to the principles laid down, necessarily acquire a power of rendering unduly intense the feelings of the mind. Owing to this cause, then, arises what is named the hysteric temperament, which is so well described by Burton. "From hence," he remarks, "proceed a brutish kind of dotage, troublesome sleep, terrible dreams, a foolish kind of bashfulness in some, perverse conceits and opinions, dejection of mind, much discontent, and preposterous judgment. They are apt to loathe, dislike, disdain, to be weary of every object. Each thing almost is tedious to them. They pine away, are void of counsel, apt to weep, and tremble, timorous, fearful, sad, and out of all hopes of better fortunes. They take delight in doing nothing for the time, but love to be alone and solitary, though that does them more harm. And thus they are affected so long as this vapour lasteth; but by-and-by they are as pleasant and merry as ever they were in their lives; they sing, discourse, and laugh in any good company, upon all occasions. And so by fits it takes them now and then, except the malady be inveterate, and then it is more frequent, vehement, and continuate. Many of them cannot tell how to express themselves in words, how it holds them, what ails them. You cannot understand them, or well tell what to make of their sayings."

Such being the vivid mental feelings characteristic of the hysteric temperament, our present object is to search for some case in which they must have met with still greater excitement; we shall then be entitled to expect that effects will be produced not unlike those of certain gases, which exert an extraordinary influence on the blood. It fortunately happens that a recent example, which may suit our purpose, is very minutely detailed in the last volume of the Royal Society of Edinburgh, relative to a servant-girl, of the age of sixteen, who shewed general symptoms of plethora, obviously arising from the cause to which I have alluded.* The first symptom of her mental dis-

---

* Report on a communication from Dr Dyce of Aberdeen to the Royal Society of Edinburgh, " On Uterine Irritation, and its Effects on the Female Constitution;" by H. Dewar, M. D. F. R. S. Edinburgh. I am sorry to be under the necessity of differing in some respects from Dr Dewar, in the view which he has given of this case, as he has appeared to have referred all the symptoms of it to *Somnambulism*.

order was an unusual somnolency. This was succeeded by disturbed and talking dreams, in which she uttered wild incoherent expressions, or sang musical airs. Indications of somnambulism followed. She would fall asleep, imagine herself an episcopal clergyman, go through the ceremony of baptizing the children, and give an appropriate and *extempore* prayer. Or she would fancy herself living with her aunt, near London, and placing herself upon one of the kitchen-stools, ride upon it with a clattering noise, and take an imaginary journey to Epsom races. Such vivid dreams were soon afterwards alternated with *waking visions*. These illusions, or *wanderings*, as the girl herself named them, would suddenly come on while she was walking with her mistress's children, or was going to church,—while she was dressing herself,—while she was arranging the furniture of the house,—or while she was busily engaged in the duties of the pantry or of the dining-table. A paroxysm of this kind would sometimes last for an hour; and it differed from a dream in being characterized by fewer inconsistencies, by less glaring mistakes as to time and place, by its more frequent occurrence, and by occasionally giving way to a reproof or reprimand. "She answered," says the reporter of her case, "many questions distinctly, shewing at times scarcely any failure of her mental powers."

It may now be interesting to trace the progress of the symptoms which attended the paroxysms to which the girl became subject. About a quarter of an hour previous to each state of this kind she felt somewhat drowsy; a pain in the head, usually slight, but which, on one occasion, was very intense, succeeded; afterwards a cloudiness or mistiness came over her eyes;— a peculiar ringing noise stunned her ears, sometimes resembling the sound of carriage-wheels, and accompanied with a feeling of motion, as if she herself were seated in the vehicle. The state of all these sensations bore, in fact, some slight degree of resemblance to that which results from an incipient effect on the circulation after inhaling the nitrous oxide,—false yet vivid sensible impressions having been felt. Occasionally, however, the sensations of the girl were rendered still more highly acute; the eyelids appeared shut, though not entirely closed; the pupils were much contracted, and there was a great intolerance of light. She could not name objects when the light of the candle or fire shone fully upon them, but pointed them out correctly in the shade, or when they were dimly illuminated. She also recognised any of her acquaintance better by his shadow than by looking at his person. When the paroxysm fairly came on, which might be in any part of the day, the sensibility to external impressions gradually lessened; the eyes became half closed; the cornea was covered with a dimness or glaze, resembling that of a person in syncope; the pupils were dilated, and, although the iris was exposed to the direct rays of the sun, it shewed no perceptible contraction.* At the same time, in proportion as sensations were either diminishing in their degree of vividness, or were becoming, in a manner,

---

* The pulse, says Dr Dyce, was 70, and the extremities rather cold.

evanescent, ideas grew more intense. Thus, in one fit, as it is stated, " the girl performed, in the most correct manner, some of her accustomed duties relating to the pantry and the dinner-table. Dr Dyce went to see her; she gave him a wrong name, as formerly. Her mistress then desired her to stand straight up, look around, and tell where she was. She recovered instantly, but it was only for a little;—she very soon relapsed. When requested to read in an almanack held before her, she did not seem to see it, nor did she notice a stick which was held out to her. Being asked a second time to read, she repeated a portion of Scripture, and did not give a correct answer when asked where she was. Being desired to state what she felt, she put her hand to her forehead, and complained of her head, saying, she saw the mice running through the room. Mrs L—— mentioned that she had said the same thing on many former occasions, even when her eyes were shut; that she had also frequently imagined she was accompanied by a little black dog, which she could not get rid of. She did not, in general, express any particular uneasiness from such a cause; at times, however, she cried in consequence of it, and at other times laughed immoderately."

CHAPTER IV.

SPECTRAL ILLUSIONS OCCURRING FROM PLETHORA; FOR INSTANCE, FROM THE NEGLECT OF ACCUSTOMED PERIODICAL BLOOD-LETTING.

"Phlebotomy, many times neglected, may doe much harme to the body, when there is a manifest redundance of bad humors and melancholy blood; and when these humors heate and boyle, if this be not used in time, the parties affected, so inflamed, are in great danger to be mad; but if it be unadvisedly, unfortunately immoderately used, it doth as much harme by refrigerating the body, dulling the spirits, and consuming them."

BURTON's *Anatomy of Melancholy*, Part I. Sect. 2.

THE blood may, from nothing more than the excess in which it prevails throughout the system, prove a stimulant capable of inducing an undue vividness of thought. This curious fact appears to have formerly met with many satisfactory illustrations, when, in accordance with the humoral pathology once taught, periodical blood-letting was universally practised; and the *rationale* of such an effect must, from the principles laid down, be sufficiently evident. The comparative degree of vividness subsisting between sensations and ideas being regulated by the usual influencing condition of the circulating system, we may readily conceive, that whenever a wonted evacuation of the sanguineous fluid is stopped, the recollected images of the mind must be rendered liable to an undue degree of excitation. This is evident, from a remark occurring in Burton's Anatomy of Melancholy, where the mental effect resulting from a neglect of accustomed phlebotomy is, in the language of the humoral school of medicine, expressed under such metaphorical terms, as " an inflammation caused by hot and boiling humours."

That this view is far from hypothetical, the case of Nicolai, the Prussian bookseller, to which I have alluded in the first chapter, strikingly shews. This intelligent man had evidently certain trains of thought rendered unduly vivid from moral causes, the particular influence of which I shall consider hereafter; but a conspiring agent, much more excitable, was strictly of a pathological description, and resulted from a casual neglect of accustomed blood-letting. This very curious fact I shall give in another extract from Nicolai's case. " Several incidents," he observes, " connected with apparitions, seem to me of importance, though we might be apt to regard them in a secondary point of view; for we cannot determine of what consequence even a circumstance of the most trivial nature may be, if at any future period (in case more experiments of a like nature are ascertained) some suppositions or conclusions can be made respecting the origin of such phantoms, or respecting that law of association, according to which ideas are modified or follow one another.

" I was then, which is seldom the case, in a situation to make observations on myself. I took down, therefore, in a few words, what was most important, and related it immediately to several persons. My memory, which is extremely retentive, has, besides, treasured up the most minute circumstances; the more on that account, as this story has very often proved the subject of my impartial consideration, not only with regard to my own particular situation, but also in respect to its many psychological consequences. Its truth will, I hope, require no further assurance on my part, since a member of this academy (Mr Selle) is an unexceptionable witness of it, having, as my physician, received a daily account of all that happened to me.

" In the last ten months of the year 1790, I underwent several very severe trials, which greatly agitated me. From the month of September in particular, repeated shocks of misfortune had befallen me, which produced the deepest sorrow. It had been usual for me to lose blood by venesection twice a year. This was done once on the 9th of July, 1790, but towards the close of the year it was omitted. In 1783, I had been suddenly seized with a violent giddiness, which the physician imputed to an obstruction in the small muscles of the *abdomen*, proceeding from too intense an application to study, and my sedentary manner of life for many years. These complaints were removed by a three-years' medicinal course, and the rigid observance of a strict diet during that time. In the first stage of the malady the application of leeches had been particularly effective, and this remedy I had from that time regularly applied twice or thrice a year, whenever I felt congestion in the head. It was on the 1st of March, 1790, that the leeches had been last applied; the bleeding, therefore, and the clearing of the minuter blood-vessels by leeches, had, in 1790, been less frequently observed than usual. A circumstance too that could not tend to benefit my deplorable situation was, that from September I had been continually engaged in business which required the severest exertion, and which, from frequent interruptions, was rendered still more burthensome and distressing."

Nicolai then proceeded to give an account of the appearance of the first phantasm that presented itself before him, which was like the form of a deceased person; and he afterwards details the innumerable other spectral illusions with which he was haunted. This part of the narrative has been given in the first chapter of this dissertation. The most curious fact, however, still remains to be told; it is that interesting circumstance in the case which proves, that the detraction of blood in a system where the habitual evacuation of this vital fluid had been casually neglected, was sufficient, by a reduction of the sanguineous influence, to expel all the phantasms which had resulted from an undue vividness of ideas. "Though at this time," says Nicolai, "I enjoyed rather a good state of health both in body and mind, and had become so very familiar with these phantasms, that at last they did not excite the least disagreeable emotion, but, on the contrary, afforded me frequent subjects for amusement and mirth; yet as the disorder sensibly increased, and the figures appeared to me for whole days together, and even during the night, if I happened to awake, I had recourse to several medicines, and was at last again obliged to have recourse to the application of leeches.

"This was performed on the 20th of April, at eleven o'clock in the forenoon. I was alone with the surgeon; but during the operation, the room swarmed with human forms of every description, which crowded fast one on another; this continued till half-past four o'clock, exactly the time when the digestion commences. I then observed, that the figures began to move more slowly; soon afterwards the colours became gradually paler; every seven minutes they lost more and more of their intensity, without any alteration in the distinct figure of the apparitions. At about half-past six o'clock all the figures were entirely white, and moved very little; yet the forms appeared perfectly distinct; by degrees they became visibly less plain, without decreasing in number, as had often formerly been the case. The figures did not move off, neither did they vanish, which also had usually happened on other occasions. In this instance they dissolved immediately into air; of some even whole pieces remained for a length of time, which also by degrees were lost to the eye. At about eight o'clock there did not remain a vestige of any of them, and I have never since experienced any appearance of the same kind. Twice or thrice since that time I have felt a propensity, if I may be so allowed to express myself, or a sensation as if I saw something which in a moment again was gone. I was even surprised by this sensation whilst writing the present account, having, in order to render it more accurate, perused the papers of 1791, and recalled to my memory all the circumstances of that time. So little are we sometimes, even in the greatest composure of mind, masters of our imagination."

CHAPTER V.

THE SPECTRAL ILLUSIONS WHICH OCCASIONALLY OCCUR AS HECTIC SYMPTOMS.

" That sudden flow of spirits, bright and strong,
Which play'd in sprightly sallies round my heart;
Was it a gleam forewarning me from heav'n,
Of quick approaching fate? As tapers mount
Expiring into wide diffusive flame,
Give one broad glare, into the socket sink,
And sinking disappear. It must be so!—"

W. THOMPSON.

A VERY remarkable agent, observable in a number of diseases, and capable of imparting an undue degree of vividness to thought, is the cause of the fever usually named *Hectic*.

By most medical men, the proximate cause of hectic fever is considered to be absorbed pus; agreeably to which view, the affection is merely symptomatic of the numerous catalogue of diseases in which this substance, originating from abscesses or ulcers, enters into the circulation. By a few the cause is regarded as constitutional, and hence the opinion, that it is characterized by a peculiar temperament, the indications of which are a fair skin, blue eyes, yellow hair, lax fibre, and sanguine disposition; and that other fevers, as well as the diseased actions of various or-

gans of the body, may induce the true hectic state.*
On either notion, however, the cause of hectic fever
must be regarded as an agent very materially modi-
fying the quality of the sanguineous fluid; hence the
small, quick, and sharp pulse, the pyrectic indications
of cold and hot fits, with sweatings and other symptoms. Along with this influence exercised on the circulation, the mental feelings are highly vivified, while
the quality of them is of such an exhilarating character, as to cherish, amidst the most alarming indications, the fallacious prospect of returning health.
Whilst corporeal exhaustion gives token that the hectic victim is fast sinking to a premature grave, the
imagination, as if in cruel irony, is proportionally
rendered more and more lively. The wan and ema-
ciated student is buoyed up with blissful visions of
future scientific acquirements never to be realized:

>   " Fancy dreams
> Of sacred fountains, of o'ershadowing groves,
> Whose walks with god-like harmony resound:
> Fountains which Homer visits; happy groves
> Where Milton dwells. The intellectual power,
> On the mind's throne, suspends his graver cares
> And smiles."

In the still more advanced, yet moribund symptoms
of hectic fever, the vividness which ideas acquire,
becomes, in the highest degree, intense. Patients are
often deluded with the blissful visions which our great

---

* I much doubt the correctness of this latter view; it is advocated in Good's Study of Medicine, vol. ii. p. 165.

bard, with such exquisite feeling and taste, has dramatized in his pathetic representation of the dying moments of Catherine of Arragon:

     CATHERINE.
—— Saw you not, even now, a blessed troop
Invite me to a banquet; whose bright faces
Cast thousand beams upon me, like the sun?
They promised me eternal happiness;
And brought me garlands, Griffith, which I feel
I am not worthy yet to wear: I shall
Assuredly.
  * * * * *

     PATIENCE.
Do you note
How much her grace is alter'd on the sudden?
How long her face is drawn? How pale she looks,
And of an earthy cold? Mark her eyes.

     GRIFFITH.
She is going, wench; pray, pray.
     PATIENCE.
Heaven comfort her!

CHAPTER VI.

SPECTRAL ILLUSIONS FROM FEBRILE AND INFLAMMATORY AFFECTIONS.

> " External forms, forbidden, mount the winds,
> Retire to Chaos, or with night commix ;——
> Irregular and new ; as pain or ease
> The spirits teach to flow, and in the brain
> Direction diverse hold."
>
> <div style="text-align:right">THOMPSON's <i>Progress of Sickness.</i></div>

It has been sufficiently shewn, in treating of the general pathology of mental illusions, that the febrile miasma possesses a great power, through the medium of the circulation, of inducing an extreme vividness of ideas. This cause, variously operating under the modified forms which it acquires from different climates and soils, has frequently given rise to spectral impressions. Incidents of this kind, which more particularly occur during the delirium attending the typhoid state of fever, are indeed so common, that it is needless to dwell any longer upon this part of our inquiry.

Also in certain inflammatory states of the system, frequently, however, attended with an irritable state of the nerves, nothing is more common than for patients to see phantasms, or to hear imaginary sounds, while the dispelling of these illusions generally succeeds to a copious detraction of blood. A very curious

PRODUCTION OF SPECTRAL ILLUSIONS.

case of this kind is given in the 15th volume of Nicholson's Philosophical Journal, which shews every internal evidence of authenticity, although the narrator has not, like Nicolai, had the courage to affix to it his signature. " About twelve years ago, I had an attack of fever, arising from some deep-seated inflammation, which caused acute pain in the left side. It was occasioned by a cold caught at the breaking-up of the hard frost in the spring of 1795. The pulse was generally about 110 in the minute, and the illness, which lasted some weeks, was accompanied with disordered perception, through almost its whole duration. At the commencement of the fever, a slight defect of memory was perceived in forming the phrases for dictating a letter; but this did not last, and I found no difficulty afterwards in performing arithmetical and other processes by memory to as great an extent as my usual habits could have gone. The first night was attended with great anxiety, and the fatiguing and perpetual recurrence of the same dream. I supposed myself to be in the midst of an immense system of mechanical combination, all the parts of which were revolving with extreme rapidity and noise, and at the same time I was impressed with a conviction that the aim or purpose of this distracting operation was to cure my disorder. When the agitation was carried to a certain height, I suddenly awoke, and soon afterwards fell again into a doze, with repetition of the same dream. After many such repetitions it occurred to me, that if I could destroy the impression or conviction, there might be a probability that the delirious dream would change its form; and as the most likely method, I thought, that by connecting some simple visible object in my mind, with the notion of cure, that object might be made to occupy the situation of the rapidly moving objects in the dream. The consequence, in some measure, answered my expectation; for upon the next access, the recollection of the figure of a bottle, to which I had previously directed my mind, presented itself, the rotation ceased, and my subsequent dreams, though disturbed, were more various and less irritating.

"The medical treatment consisted in an external application of leeches to the side, venesection, and a saline mixture, which was taken internally.

"A second night was passed with much agitation in repeated dozing, with dreams, in which, except with regard to the strangeness and inconsistency of the objects that offered themselves, it was difficult to distinguish the time of sleep from that of wakefulness. None of that anxiety of mind remained which had added to the sufferings of the preceding night. When morning came, the state of the sensations had either undergone a change, or it was more easy, as Hartley remarks, for the real impressions of surrounding objects, to predominate over the phantasms of disease. Being perfectly awake, in full possession of memory, reason, and calmness, conversing with those around me, and seeing, without difficulty or impediment, every surrounding object, I was entertained and delighted with a succession of faces, over which I had no control, either as to their appearance, continuance, or removal.

"They appeared directly before me, one at a time, very suddenly, yet not so much so, but that a second

PRODUCTION OF SPECTRAL ILLUSIONS. 97

of time might be employed in the emergence of each, as if through a cloud or mist, to its perfect clearness. In this state each face continued five or six seconds, and then vanished, by becoming gradually fainter during about two seconds, till nothing was left but a dark opaque mist, in which almost immediately afterwards appeared another face. All these faces were in the highest degree interesting to me for beauty of form, and for the variety of expression they manifested of every great and amiable emotion of the human mind. Though their attention was invariably directed to me, and none of them seemed to speak, yet I seemed to read the very soul which gave animation to their lovely and intelligent countenances. Admiration and a sentiment of joy and affection when each face appeared, and regret upon its disappearance, kept my mind constantly rivetted to the visions before it; and this state was interrupted only when an intercourse with the persons in the room was proposed or urged."

The writer then gives certain other details relative to his case, which I shall notice in a more suitable part of this essay. He afterwards speaks of a temporary suspension of these visions, which he attributes to the effect of a medicine. "I do not remember," he adds, " how long these visions lasted, but think it was the next morning that they all vanished, at the very instant of taking a draught, composed of lemon-juice, saturated with potash, with a small addition of the pulvis Londinensis. I cannot think the effect was owing to any peculiar virtue of this medicine, (for it took place before the draught had actually entered the stomach,) but merely to the stimulus of the subacid cold fluid.

"How long the appearances were suspended I did not note, or have now forgotten. The fever continued with the same frequency of pulse, and pain in the side, attended with yawning and great increase of suffering while in the prone posture. Notwithstanding the saline antimonial medicine was continued, the figures returned; but they now consisted of books, or parchments, or papers containing printed matter. I do not know whether I read any of them, but am at present inclined to think they were either not distinctly legible, or did not remain a sufficient time before they vanished.

"It occurred to me, that all these delusions were of one sense only, namely, the sight; and, upon considering the recurrence of sounds, a few simple musical tones were afterwards heard, for one time only; soon after which, having dropped asleep, an animal seemed to jump upon my back, with the most shrill and piercing screams, which were too intolerable for the continuance of sleep. Diseased perceptions of the hearing did not again recur."

CHAPTER VII.

SPECTRAL ILLUSIONS ARISING FROM INFLAMMATION OF THE BRAIN.

" And often where no real ills affright,
Its visionary fiends, an endless train,
Assail with equal or superior might,
And through the throbbing heart, and dizzy brain,
And shivering nerves, shoot stings of more than mortal pain."
                                                        BEATTIE.

Our researches have hitherto been confined to the blood, which we have considered as giving rise, from its own independent chemical properties or bulk, to certain intense states of the mind. It is now of importance to inquire if similar effects may not be referred to nervous influence.

According to the very important physiological experiments of Dr Philip, it appears that the nervous system consists of parts endowed with the vital principle, yet capable of acting in concert with inanimate matter; and that in man, as well as in certain well-known animals, electricity is the agent thus capable of being collected by nervous organs, and of being universally diffused, for purposes intimately connected with the animal economy, throughout every part of the human system. The agency, therefore, of the nerves in contributing to produce numerous changes on the blood, and with them equally numerous states of the mind, must be very great; and it is for this reason, that throughout every part of the human body they accompany vessels in their course. One set of nerves takes a direction from the surface of the human body, or from its cavities; agreeably, also, to the impressions received from external matter, as well as to the differences of animal structure which occur in sensible organs, corresponding sensations and renovated feelings are excited. Hence, when we take into consideration the effect of certain gases on the blood in inducing definite qualities and degrees of vividness in our mental feelings, the conclusion is inevitable, that the nerves belonging to the sensitive organs of our frame cannot generate any mental affections without first producing those peculiar sanguineous effects which we have before described, and to which the immaterial principle of the mind seems, in some unknown manner, to be related. It may be also observed, that the mental feelings thus excited by the nervous influence on the circulation, bear a further relation to a set of nerves proceeding from small portions of the brain and spinal cord, which supply the muscles of voluntary motion; each distinct state of mind thus ultimately stimulating with a definite degree of force particular muscular fibres. But, besides the class of nerves concerned with voluntary motion, there is another and far more extensive description, which exercise, through the medium of the blood, an influence on the states of the mind. Nerves of this kind, consisting of a chain of ganglions, to which

PRODUCTION OF SPECTRAL ILLUSIONS. 101

communications from all parts of the brain and spinal marrow are sent, form the cause of the processes of secretion. The healthy exercise of these functions is attended with a temperature considerably raised above that of the surrounding medium, and hence arise the different mental states which result from salutary and morbid assimilations, or from the moderate, intense, or languishing circulation of the blood. It is then from these causes that various degrees of vividness may be imparted to our feelings.

This physiological view leads to the inference, that with respect to causes of irritation acting on the nervous system, they may either influence nerves connected with the transmission of sensations and ideas from external impressions, or they may influence those nerves which are concerned in the processes of secretion; in either case, however, the vividness of mental feelings cannot fail to be affected. On the other hand, by merely stimulating the nerves which are transmitted directly from the brain and spinal cord to the voluntary muscles, nothing more than irregular muscular actions can ensue. Causes of nervous irritation may also act in two ways; they may either directly influence the state of the blood, and with it the state of the mental feelings, or they may produce a similar effect, though far less in degree, by exerting a power over the elastic and involuntary muscular fibres of the heart, giving, by this means, either an increasing or diminishing resistance to the vital expansibility evinced in the volume of the circulating mass.

Dr Philip has mentioned, as a result of his experiments, that a chemical or mechanical agent very partially irritating the brain and nerves, is incapable of exciting the heart, but that it is influenced by all agents applied to any considerable portion of these organs, and that it feels the effect of such an influence as long as it is applied. Excitements of this kind are to be found in such inflammatory causes as sudden alternations of heat and cold, exposure to the rays of a vertical sun, the sudden suppression of accustomed evacuations, various kinds of poison, and inebriation. In certain forms of cerebral inflammation, the first symptoms evince an increasing intensity of all sensations. In the case of a lady, a patient of Dr Good, there was an intolerable acuteness of hearing and vision, insomuch that the slightest light and sound, even the humming of a fly, became insupportable. Ideas also were rendered more vivid. But as the inflammation increased, the acute sensibility to external impressions gradually diminished, while the recollected images of the mind assumed a most frightful reality. In an example which came under my own notice, ideas of vision were so intense, that although the patient closed his eyelids, he could not even then dispel the lively images of demons that haunted his bed. The sleep was moreover disturbed with the most horrible dreams.

A very curious case of spectral illusions is related by Dr Alderson of Hull, in which the irritation of the brain or its membranes seems to have resulted from an extended inflammation under the scalp.

"A few months ago," says this writer, "I visited Mr R., who was seized, in his passage from America, with a most excruciating headach. He obtained some temporary relief from the formation of matter under the scalp; swellings came on in the throat, and he had some difficulty of respiration when in bed. At this time, he complained to me that he had troublesome dreams, and that he seemed to dream whilst awake. In a short time after, he told me he had, for an hour or two, been convinced that he had seen his wife and family, when his right judgment told him that they were in America; and the impression was so strong a few nights afterwards, and the conversation he had with his son so very particular and important, that he could not help relating the whole to his friends in the morning, and requested to know if his wife and son were not actually arrived from America, and at that time in the house. I was sent for to hold consultation, and he evidently saw that they all took him to be insane. He therefore immediately turned to me, and asked me, whether the complaint he then had would bring on the imagination of spectres, and apparitions, and figures; for he had always hitherto been an unbeliever in ghosts, and in every thing else; he felt, and his friends likewise acknowledged, that he was perfectly sane, and strong in mind as ever he was in his life. Having satisfied him with the nature and extent of his complaint, and that it would soon vanish with his bodily sufferings, he and his friends were made easy in their minds; but the phantoms became at length more troublesome, so that he could not bear to go into his bed-room, where every picture brought with it the association, and conjured up the spirits of the departed, or introduced a train of unpleasant companions. He remained after this in a low room, and was for a time free from intruders; but in a bright brass lock he again saw his transatlantic friends, and never afterwards could he look to it but he saw them; and when I have been with him, and have purposely taken up a book, I have seen him hold conversation in his mind's eye with them; and I have momentarily known him consider me as hearing and seeing them too—I say momentarily, for he is a man of strong parts, and perfectly convinced of the nature of the complaint; for whenever I spoke, and he turned from the lock, he could converse on religion, physic, and politics, as well as ever. He then changed his house; the matter again formed under the scalp, and he is now in a state of convalescence, and totally free from such visitations."*

The effect induced on the brain by intoxication from ardent spirits, which have a strong tendency to inflame this organ, is attended with very remarkable effects. These have been lately described as symptoms of *delirium tremens*.† Many cases, indeed, are recorded, which shew the liability of the patient to long-continued spectral impressions. " I was called," says Dr Armstrong, " to visit Mr B. J., a short spare man, in the ——— year of his age; who, I was told, was so very ungovernable, that his friends had provided a strait-waistcoat for him, and only waited my approbation to put it on. I found him in a state of extreme perturbation, impressed with the idea that

---

* Edinburgh Medical and Surgical Journal, vol. vi. p. 291.

† An excellent thesis on this subject was written in the year 1821, by Dr Begbie of Edinburgh,

two men were lurking in the adjoining room, who were determined to murder him, and who had repeatedly, in the course of the morning, fired pistols at him with that intention. In order to escape from the supposed assassins, he had just made an attempt to leap through the chamber-window, and had only been prevented from so doing by the interference of some relations, with whom he had been struggling very hard. I endeavoured to pacify him, by assuring him that no one should do him an injury, and at last prevailed upon him to sit down. Occasionally, however, he looked at me suspiciously; and, upon the least noise being made below stairs, started and stared wildly round the room. His breathing was rather hurried. He occasionally sighed deeply, and at intervals he was attacked with a dry hollow-sounding cough, which appeared to shake his whole frame. His face was pale, and his countenance full of anxiety. To all my questions his answers were confused, and not at all to the purpose; he hesitated almost at every syllable, and mistook the pronunciation of many words. On inquiry, I learnt that he had latterly been in a state of intoxication, more especially in the preceding week, and on Saturday the 14th of November; since which time he had taken less stimulus than usual, with the intention of becoming temperate. The following particulars were likewise related to me. On Sunday, the 15th of November, he complained of being very languid, took little food, and only drank about two glasses of wine, a small quantity of ale, and half a glass of gin. Towards the evening he grew rather feverish, and passed an uneasy and sleepless night. He remained nearly in the same state during the ensuing Monday, till late in the afternoon, when he was seized with a violent hollow clanging cough, which made him perspire profusely, and was very troublesome through the night, which he passed, as before, without sleep. On Tuesday morning he had a severe fit of coughing, after which he became exceedingly fretful and irritable, the slightest contradiction throwing him into an excessive passion. In the latter part of the day he refused both wine and food, asserting that he was confident some wicked people were watching an opportunity to poison him; and, when preparing to go to bed in the evening, suddenly started, as if somebody was about to lay hands upon him. He soon afterwards, however, went to bed, but obtained no rest whatever. From this period the distraction of mind increased, and he was in constant alarm about the safety of his person. At an early hour the next evening, he desired to go to bed; but, hearing a noise made by a servant beneath his chamber, he leapt up in great agitation, declaring that two men had just entered the house with the design of murdering him. Being somewhat calmed by the kindness of his friends, he went to bed again, and begged them to be watchful in the night. He did not seem at all disposed to sleep, but talked at intervals about his life being in imminent danger from fire-arms and poison, and kept constantly gathering the bed-clothes about him till daylight, when he rose, much agitated with the fear of assassination, and has since continued restless and alarmed."

Dr Armstrong, after detailing several other symptoms, mentions the result of a visit paid him three days afterwards. "He has taken his wine, food, and medicine, whenever presented to him; but has had no sleep in the night, though he remained very quiet till about six o'clock this morning, when, one of the people who sat up with him refusing to let him go down stairs, he burst into a violent passion, attempted to break open the door of his chamber, and insisted that he was not in his own house, but detained by force in some other. His wife, on hearing the noise, came into the room, and told him he might go down stairs, or anywhere he thought proper, and endeavoured, in a good-humoured way, to convince him that he was really at home; and at length succeeded, by shewing him the different apartments of the house. Shortly afterwards he requested a cup of coffee, which he appeared to relish; and then went to bed again, and fell into a sound tranquil sleep, from which he has not yet awakened. Not wishing to disturb the patient, I left the house without seeing him; but, on calling again about two o'clock in the afternoon, found that he had just risen, collected and rational upon every subject, but had no very distinct recollection of any thing that had passed during his illness."*

A case, even still more curious, is related by Dr Alderson.† "I was called upon," he observes, "some time ago, to visit Mr ———, who, at that time, kept a dram-shop. Having at different times attended, and thence knowing him very well, I was struck with

---

* Edinburgh Medical and Surgical Journal, vol. ix. p. 146.
† Ibid. vol. vi. p. 288.

something singular upon my first entrance. He went up stairs with me, but evidently hesitated occasionally as he went. When he got into his chamber, he expressed some apprehension lest I should consider him as insane, and send him to the asylum at York, whither I had not long before sent one of his pot-companions. Whence all these apprehensions?—What is the matter with you?—Why do you look so full of terror? He then sat down, and gave me a history of his complaint.

" About a week or ten days before, after drawing some liquor in his cellar for a girl, he desired her to take away the oysters which lay upon the floor, and which he supposed she had dropped;—the girl, thinking him drunk, laughed at him, and went out of the room.

" He endeavoured to take them up himself, and to his great astonishment could find none. He was then going out of the cellar, when at the door he saw a soldier, whose looks he did not like, attempting to enter the room in which he then was. He desired to know what he wanted there; and upon receiving no answer, but, as he thought, a menacing look, he sprung forward to seize the intruder, and to his no small surprise found it a phantom. The cold sweat hung upon his brow—he trembled in every limb. It was the dusk of the evening as he passed along the passage—the phantom flitted before his eyes—he attempted to follow it, resolutely determined to satisfy himself; but as it vanished, there appeared others, and some of them at a distance, and he exhausted himself by fruitless attempts to lay hold of them. He hastened to his family, with marks of terror and confusion; for, though a man of the most undaunted resolution, he confessed to me that he never had before felt what it was to be completely terrified. During the whole of that night, he was constantly tormented with a variety of spectres, sometimes of people who had been long dead, and other times of friends who were living; and harassed himself with continually getting out of bed, to ascertain whether the people he saw were real or not. Nor could he always distinguish who were and who were not real customers, as they came into the rooms in the daytime, so that his conduct became the subject of observation; and though it was for a time attributed to private drinking, it was at last suspected to arise from some other cause; and when I was sent for, the family were under the full conviction that he was insane, although they confessed, that, in every thing else, except the foolish notion of seeing apparitions, he was perfectly rational and steady; and during the whole of the time that he was relating his case to me, and his mind was fully occupied, he felt the most gratifying relief, for in all that time he had not seen one apparition; and he was elated with pleasure indeed, when I told him I should not send him to York, for his was a complaint I could cure at home. But whilst I was writing a prescription, and had suffered him to be at rest, I saw him suddenly get up, and go with a hurried step to the door. What did you do that for?— he looked ashamed and mortified:—he had been so well whilst in conversation with me, that he could not believe that the soldier whom he saw enter the room was a phantom, and he got up to convince himself.

"I need not here detail particularly the medical treatment adopted; but it may be as well just to state the circumstances which probably led to the complaint, and the principle of cure. Some time previously he had had a quarrel with a drunken soldier, who attempted, against his inclination, to enter his house at an unseasonable hour, and in the struggle to turn him out, the soldier drew his bayonet, and, having struck him across the temples, divided the temporal artery; in consequence of which he bled a very large quantity before a surgeon arrived, as there was no one who knew that, in such a case, simple compression with the finger, upon the spouting artery, would stop the effusion of blood. He had scarcely recovered from the effects of this loss of blood, when he undertook to accompany a friend in his walking-match against time, in which he went forty-two miles in nine hours. Elated with success, he spent the whole of the following day in drinking, but found himself, a short time afterwards, so much out of health, that he came to the resolution of abstaining altogether from liquor. It was in the course of the week following that abstinence from his usual habits, that he had the disease. It kept increasing for several days till I saw him, allowing him no time for rest. Never was he able to get rid of these shadows by night when in bed, nor by day when in motion; though he sometimes walked miles with that view, and at others got into a variety of company. He told me he suffered even bodily pain, from the severe lashing of a waggoner with his whip, who came every night to a particular corner of his bed, but who always disappeared when he jumped out of bed to retort, which he did several nights successively. The whole of this complaint was effectually removed by bleeding with leeches, and active purgatives. After the first employment of these means, he saw no more phantoms in the daytime; and after the second, only once saw his milkman in his bed-room, between sleeping and waking. He has remained perfectly rational and well ever since, and can go out in the dark as well as ever, having received a perfect conviction of the nature of ghosts."

CHAPTER VIII.

SPECTRAL ILLUSIONS ARISING FROM A HIGHLY-EXCITED STATE OF NERVOUS IRRITABILITY ACTING GENERALLY ON THE SYSTEM.

> " This bodiless creation Ecstacy
> Is very cunning in."—HAMLET.

THE examples brought forward in the last chapter have, I trust, sufficiently illustrated the delusions liable to occur from an extremely morbid state of the nervous system. We had previously seen, that although an undue vividness of ideas directly results from certain changes induced in the circulating fluid, such changes might not only be traced to an inherent quality of the blood, arising from constitutional affections, or to the suppression of customary and natural evacuations, but that they might also ensue from adventitious agents of a chemical nature introduced into the system. In extending these researches, we further added to such causes of spectral impressions the influence of the nervous system, which nothing appeared more forcibly calculated to illustrate than inflammatory states of the brain or its membranes. Such extreme cases, therefore, of nervous irritability, which take their rise from manifest derangements of organic structure, give us the best reason to expect

PRODUCTION OF SPECTRAL ILLUSIONS. 113

that consequences no less singular in their nature may result from causes of a latent kind, where a highly-excited state of the nervous influence, not often to be detected by actual examination, either generally or partially affects the circulating system.

Agreeably to the view which I have given of nervous fibres, they may be described as of three kinds. Fibres of the first description take their course from the external organs of sense, or from sensitive cavities; and, in transmitting their influence to the sanguineous system, thereby induce corresponding sensations and renovated feelings. Fibres of the second kind are connected through a system of ganglions with the brain and spinal cord; their action on the blood being for the processes of secretion and assimilation, while, at the same time, they are capable of rendering the affections of the mind more or less vivid. Nervous fibres of a third class have no antecedent connexion with our mental states, but, in inducing muscular motion, obey the stimulus of the will. According to this notion, therefore, the particular mental excitability about to be described, arises from the influence of fibres of the first and second kind, and hence spectral illusions may occur, although the motific nerves should not be unduly excited; which not unfrequently happens when phantoms disturb the imagination of persons, who, from the regularity with which muscular motions at the same time obey the will, are supposed to be in perfect health. In the second place, spectral illusions may occur when there is an equally intense excitement of the motific nerves. In such a case, the particular affection is induced,

H

which in Dr Good's Nosology bears the name of *Carus Ecstasis*. This writer has conceived, that in the diffusion of the motific influence, an excess of supply is equally felt by the extenor and flexor muscles. Hence the muscles are thrown into a rigid and permanent spasm, which gives to the body so erect a position, and so lofty and unalterable a demeanour, that the unhappy visionary, from this imposing air of inspiration, has not unfrequently both deluded himself and others with the notion, that his dreams were supernatural visitations. In the third place, the voluntary motific nerves may be *irregularly* incited; or, in other words, the balance of action subsisting between the flexor and extensor muscles may be so disturbed, that the frame will appear to be variously convulsed or incurvated. I believe this to be one of the varieties of Ecstasis which nosologists have, perhaps rather loosely, referred to Epilepsy; but, as all the causes of the latter affection are by no means decidedly pointed out, it would, for the present, be a prudent step not to disturb the appellation.* In many instances of epilepsy, there has been such a flow of spirits as to indicate, that a very powerful nervous influence was generally diffused throughout the human frame, while, as har-

---

* Dr Wilson Phillip has shewn from experiments, that the nerves connected with voluntary muscles are more powerfully incited by mechanical than chemical causes of irritation. Thus we see the reason why Exostosis, or why foreign substances affecting the nervous system, should occasionally operate as causes of the convulsions of epilepsy; and why convulsions in general should be regarded as merely incidental to spectral illusions.

bingers of the paroxysm, there has not only been the well-known *aura epileptica*, but also a wild display of phantasms. A woman, whose case is related by Portius, was always warned of an approaching fit by the appearance of her own image in a mirror; and Sauvage mentions, that even during the paroxysm dreadful spectres have been seen. It is likewise a curious fact, that in such forms of the disease, real objects have occasionally seemed magnified to an extraordinary degree, while, among coloured substances, a green hue has predominated. Another form of Ecstasis is that which occasionally occurs as a symptom in *catalepsy*, where the influence of those nerves which are connected with voluntary muscles is so diminished, that the limbs are unable to resist external force, but yield to it with readiness, and retain any position in which they may be placed. I shall, lastly, observe, that a general state of nervous irritability not unfrequently exercises its influence on the system, in concurrence with a highly-excited condition of the sanguine or melancholic temperament. An increase of action here takes place in that extensive system of nerves, upon which the processess of assimilation depend. This effect is pointed out by the peculiar symptoms, which arise in the organs more immediately connected with digestion. " From the centre of the epigastric region," says Pinel, " are propagated, as it were by a species of irradiation, the accession of insanity, when all the abdominal system even appears to enter into the sad confederacy. The patient complains of a sense of tightness in the region of the stomach, want of appetite, obstinate constipation, and a sensation of heat in the bowels, which obtains a temporary relief from copious draughts of cooling liquids."—" This reaction of the epigastric region upon the functions of the understanding is so far from oppressing and obscuring them, that it appears even to augment their vivacity and strength. The imagination is exalted to the highest pitch of development and fecundity. Thoughts the most brilliant and ingenious, comparisons the most apt and luminous, give to the maniac an air of supernatural enthusiasm and inspiration. The recollection of the past appears to unroll with great rapidity, and what had long been not thought of and forgotten, is then presented to the mind in glowing and animated colours."—In another place the same eloquent writer adds, "Dreams of ecstacy, and visions of heavenly pleasure, are the ordinary preludes to paroxysms of maniacal devotion: as those of unfortunate love are preceded by similar interruptions of sound and healthful sleep. The beloved object appears under the form of an exquisite beauty, with every other advantage, greatly exaggerated by the magic power of fancy. But the too happy dreamer, after an interval of more or less continuance of reason and calmness, awakes once more the noisy, the disconsolate, and the furious maniac."*

---

* Pinel's Treatise on Insanity; translation by D. D. Davis, M.D. pages 17 and 28.

CHAPTER IX.

THE SPECTRAL ILLUSIONS OF HYPOCHONDRIACKS.

"There is nothing so vaine, absurd, ridiculous, extravagant, impossible, incredible, so monstrous a chymera, so prodigious and strange, such as painters and poets durst not attempt, which they will not really feare, faine suspect and imagine unto themselves."
BURTON'S ANATOMY OF MELANCHOLY.

NOT unfrequently a partial and irregular state of nervous irritability acts in concurrence with highly-excited conditions of certain temperaments. This gives rise, in very sanguine or melancholic constitutions, to the symptoms of hypochondrism. The irregular action of those nerves, upon which the production of external impressions and the renovated feelings of the mind depends, is indicated by false afflictions communicated to the organs of sense, particularly to those of touch. Hence the imaginary diseases of which hypochondriacks suppose they are the subject, as well as the ideal transformation of the texture of their bodies into such substances as glass, lead, or feathers. At the same time, the irregular action of other nerves, concerned in the processes of assimilation, is productive of the usual morbid state which takes place of the digestive organs. Burton has summed up the extravagancies of hypochondriacks in a few words: " Humorous are they beyond all measure, they faigne many absurdities voide of reason; one supposes himself to be a dog, cock, beare, horse, glasse, butter, &c. He is a giant, a dwarfe, as strong as an hundred men, a lord, duke, prince, &c. And if he be told he hath a stinking breath, a great nose, that he is sick, or inclined to such or such a disease, he beleeves it eftsoones, and by force of imagination will worke it out." It is useless to dwell much longer upon this disease, as no spectral impressions occur in it, which have not been described in the chapter that treated of the illusions of mania or melancholia. I might perhaps mention, that the quality of such phantasies not unfrequently harmonizes with any false conceit that may prevail. This circumstance is not unaptly described in the old comedy of Lingua:—

> " Lately I came from fine Phantaste's house.—
> No sooner had I parted out of doors,
> But up I held my hands before my face,
> To shield mine eyes from the light's piercing beams;
> When I protest I saw the sun as clear,
> Through these my palms, as through a perspective:
> No marvel; for when I beheld my fingers,
> I saw my fingers were transform'd to glass,
> Opening my breast, my breast was like a window,
> Through which I plainly did perceive my heart:
> In whose two conclaves I discern'd my thoughts
> Confus'dly lodged in great multitudes."

CHAPTER X.

CERTAIN LESS FREQUENT MORBID SOURCES OF SPECTRAL ILLUSIONS.

"Of various forms unnumber'd spectres more."
DRYDEN's VIRGIL.

HAVING shewn, from various authentic medical cases, the liability of spectral illusions to arise from many morbid affections which are of very frequent occurrence, it is by no means necessary to my present object, that this part of the investigation should proceed to a much greater extent.—I first stated, that certain gases, when inhaled, alter the composition of the blood, rendering, at the same time, more vivid some particular quality of our mental feelings. Might not then other aeriform substances be found, which would have nearly the same effect? An eminent medical practitioner, from whose ingenious essay on apparitions I have freely quoted, insinuates the probability, that necromancers, in imposing upon any object of their art, may occasionally avail themselves of some gaseous matters, which, when inhaled,

—————— " by magic sleights
Shall raise such artificial sprights,
As by the strength of their illusion
Shall draw him on to his confusion."

"The celebrated conjurer or master-mason," remarks Dr Alderson of Hull, "whom we had here some years ago, told me, that he could give me a recipe for a preparation of antimony, sulphur, &c. which, when burnt in a confined room, would so affect the person shut up in it, that he would fancy he saw spectres and apparitions." Notwithstanding, however, the liberal offer made to this gentleman, the existence of such a fumigation stands in great need of confirmation.—But, besides the inhalation of gases, there are several poisons, particularly of the narcotic kind, such as opium, henbane, the conium maculatum, bella-donna, &c. which, when introduced into the system by the organs of digestion, have the effect of inducing delirium, and occasionally spectral illusions. In the violent mental excitement of hydrophobia it has been recorded, that the phantasm of the dog which inflicted the fatal wound has sometimes haunted the bed of the wretched patient.

In the constitutional affection of gout, where an altered quality of the circulating fluid is evinced by its tendency to a morbid secretion of calcareous matter, similar states of mind, particularly in the recedent form of the disease, have been experienced. An excitement of gouty inflammation, instead of attacking the hands or feet, has, from some occasional cause, been transferred to the brain, in which case, violent acute sensations have ensued, and these again have been followed by the most vivid yet painful ideas. To such symptoms spectral illusions have sometimes supervened, as the following case, related by Dr Alderson, sufficiently well illustrates:—

"I was soon after called," says this writer, " to visit Mrs B., a fine old lady about 80 years of age, whom I have frequently visited in fits of the gout. At a period when, from her general feelings, she rather expected the gout, she was seized with an unusual deafness, and great distension in the organs of digestion. From this time she was visited by several of her friends, whom she had not invited, and whom she at first so far considered as actually present, that she told them she was very sorry that she could not hear them speak, nor keep up conversation with them: she would therefore order the card-table, and rang the bell for that purpose. Upon the entrance of the servant, the whole party disappeared—she could not help expressing her surprise to her maid that they should all go away so abruptly; but she could scarcely believe her when she told her that there had been nobody in the room. She was so ashamed, that she suffered, for many days and nights together, the intrusion of a variety of phantoms, and had some of her finest feelings wrought upon by the exhibition of friends long lost, and who only came to cheat her fancy, and revive sensations that time had almost obliterated. She determined, however, for a long time, not to complain, and contented herself with merely ringing her bell, finding she could always get rid of the phantoms by the entrance of her maid, whenever they became distressing. It was not till some time after that she could bring herself to relate her distresses to me. She was all this time convinced of her own rationality, and so were those friends who really visited her; for they never could find any one circumstance in her conduct and conversation to lead them to suspect her in the smallest degree deranged, though unwell. This complaint was entirely removed by cataplasms to the feet, and gentle purgatives; and terminated, a short time afterwards, in a regular slight fit of the gout. She has remained ever since, now somewhat more than a year, in the perfect enjoyment of her health and faculties."*

The first object of this dissertation has at length been completed. It is manifest, that with numerous morbid affections of the body, arising from variously excited states of the circulating system, or of the nervous influence, the production in the mind of spectral illusions is necessarily connected. Of such affections, Scot, in his Discovery of Witchcraft, has well remarked, that "though they appeare in the mind of man, yet are they bred in the bodie, and proceed from this humor, which is the very dregs of blood, nourishing and feeding these places, from whence proceed fears, cogitations, superstitions, fastings, labours, and such like. This maketh sufferance of torments, and (as some saie) foresight of things to come."

---

* Edinburgh Medical and Surgical Journal, vol. vi. p. 291.

PART III.

PROOFS THAT THE OBJECTS OF SPECTRAL ILLUSIONS ARE FREQUENTLY SUGGESTED BY THE FANTASTIC IMAGERY OF SUPERSTITIOUS BELIEF.

PART III.

CHAPTER I.

EXPLANATION OF THE MODE IN WHICH THE IDEAS WHICH ARE SUGGESTED BY VARIOUS POPULAR SUPERSTITIONS BECOME RECALLED IN A HIGHLY VIVIFIED STATE, SO AS TO CONSTITUTE THE IMAGERY OF SPECTRAL ILLUSIONS.

"Each molehill-thought swells to a huge Olympus."—DRYDEN.

IN this department of our investigation an attempt will be made to show, that in well-authenticated ghost-stories of a supposed supernatural character, ideas, which are rendered so unduly intense as to induce spectral illusions, may be traced to such fantastical objects of prior belief, as are incorporated in the various systems of superstition, which for ages have possessed the minds of the vulgar. But before this object can be satisfactorily accomplished, it will be necessary to take a brief review of the progress of our research. By this means we shall be better prepared to notice an important law of the mind, by which past sensations may be recalled in various states of faintness or intensity.

This inquiry has hitherto proceeded upon the general view, that an undue sanguineous action imparts a disproportionate degree of vividness to our ideas. Nicolai, indeed, in the narrative read by him to the Royal Society of Berlin, from an attentive consideration of the phenomena which attended his illusions, could not refrain from expressing the same suspicion, namely, that they had some inexplicable connexion with the state of the circulating system. His words are these: " The natural vivacity of imagination renders it less wonderful, that after a violent commotion of the mind, a number of phantasms should appear for several weeks in succession. Their leaving me on the application of leeches, shews clearly that some anomaly in the circulation of the blood was connected with their appearance; though it may perhaps be too hasty a conclusion to seek for the cause in that alone. It seems, likewise, remarkable, that the beginning of the apparitions, after the disturbance in my mind was settled, as well as the alteration which took place, when they finally left me, happened exactly at the time when digestion commenced. And it is no less remarkable, that the apparitions, before they entirely ceased, lost their intensity of colours; and that they did not vanish or change as formerly, but seemed gradually to dissolve into air."*

From the doctrine inculcated in this dissertation,

---

* Nicholson's Journal, vol. vi. p. 176.

the conjecture of Nicolai will not, perhaps, appear to be devoid of foundation. In the view which I took of the opposite effects of the nitrous oxide and febrile miasma, it was shewn, that the highly-vivid state of pleasurable feelings which the former was capable of exciting, corresponded to a dilating action of the blood exerted on the vascular system, the indication of which was an increasing diastole of the heart and fulness of the pulse; while the opposite effects of the latter agent were connected with an undue influence of the systole of the heart, with a hard pulse, and a constricting tendency of the capillaries.

Next, with regard to the action of morbific causes upon our various mental states, it was remarked, that we always distinguish between those feelings which are induced, when causes impressing our organs of sense are present, and those which occur as revivals of prior mental states; the former being termed *sensations*, the latter *ideas*, or, more correctly, renovated feelings.

When past feelings, therefore, are renovated, they are always in a less vivid state than actual impressions; and, in a healthy condition of the system, a definite degree of intensity may be supposed to subsist between sensations and ideas, the latter being *proportionally* less intense, less vivid, or fainter than the former. But, from the influence of disease, these ideas may be renovated in a state of vividness so great, as to nearly or altogether equal in intensity actual impressions. An ample proof of this fact is afforded in the case of Nicolai, whose imagination was liable to be rendered unduly vivid by the plethoric habit of body under which he laboured. "I must observe," he says, "that my imagination possesses in general a great facility in picturing. I have, for example, sketched in my mind a number of plans for novels and plays, though I have committed very few of them to paper, because I was less solicitous to execute than to invent. I have generally arranged these outlines when, in a cheerful state of mind, I have taken a solitary walk, or when, travelling, I have sat in my carriage, and could only find employment in myself and my imagination. Constantly, and even now, do the different persons whom I imagine in the foundation of such a plot, present themselves to me in the most lively and distinct manner; their figure, their features, their manner, their dress, and their complexion, are all visible to my fancy. As long as I meditate on a fixed plan, and afterwards carry it into effect,—even when I am interrupted, and when I must begin it again at different times, all the acting persons continue present in the very same form in which my imagination at first produced them."*

I shall now endeavour to discover the exact order in which a morbific cause acts upon ideas, when, by

---

* Those droll philosophers, the Phrenologists, account for all this by supposing that Nicolai possessed the ORGAN OF WONDER.

GLOUCESTER.
That would be ten days' *wonder* at the least.

CLARENCE.
That's a day longer than a *wonder* lasts.
3d *Part of King Henry VI. Act* 3, *Scene* 2.

rendering them as vivid as actual impressions, it gives rise to spectral illusions.

The law by which ideas are renovated, is usually explained by metaphysicians under the name of *association*. Thus, it is a law, that whenever any sensation of a definite nature and quality is repeated, it will be immediately followed by a renewal of the feelings with which it was before associated, their repetition taking place agreeably to their prior order. The number of fainter feelings which may thus return is indefinite, and only meets with interruption from some new sensation, and along with it some new train of renovated feelings or ideas. It may, therefore, be shown, from a narrative inserted in the 15th volume of Nicholson's Philosophical Journal (from which I have before made a large quotation), that when a morbific cause so operates upon ideas, as to render them as vivid as actual impressions, the effect is produced in the order of their natural association. " I had a visit," says the writer, " from Dr C⸺, to whom, among other remarks" [relative to his illusions], " I observed, that I then enjoyed the satisfaction of having cultivated my moral habits, and particularly in having always endeavoured to avoid being the slave of fear.—' I think,' said I, ' that this is the breaking up of the system, and that it is now in progress to speedy destruction. In this state, when the senses have become confused, and no longer tell me the truth, they still present me with pleasing fictions, and my sufferings are mitigated by that calmness which allows me to find amusement in what are probably the concluding scenes of life.'—I give these self-congratulations without scruple, more particularly because they led to an observation of fact which deserves notice. When the doctor left me, my relaxed attention returned to the phantasms, and, some time afterwards, instead of a pleasing face, a visage of extreme rage appeared, which presented a gun at me, and made me start; but it remained the usual time, and then gradually faded away.—This immediately shewed me the probability of some connexion between my thoughts and these images; for I ascribed the angry phantasm to the general reflection I had formed in conversation with Dr C———.* I recollected some disquisitions of Locke, in his Treatise on the Conduct of the Mind, where he endeavours to account for the appearance of faces to persons of nervous habits. It seemed to me, as if faces, in all their modifications, being so associated with our recollections of the affections of passions, would be most likely to offer themselves in delirium; but I now thought it probable, that other objects could be seen if previously meditated upon. With this motive it was that I reflected upon landscapes and scenes of architectural grandeur, while the faces were flashing before me; and after a certain considerable interval of time, of which I can form no precise judgment, a rural scene of hills, valleys,

---

* To what part of the writer's remark to Dr C——— does this supposed connexion refer? Does he allude to the reflection, in which he mentions having avoided being the slave of *fear* ? In this case I must suppose he means, that the idea of a man threatening his life then arose in his mind; which idea afterwards returning, became, by the vivifying operation of a morbific cause, converted into a genuine phantasm.

and fields, appeared before me, which was succeeded by another and another in ceaseless succession; the manner and times of their respective appearance, duration, and vanishing, being not sensibly different from those of the faces. All the scenes were calm and still, without any strong lights or glare, and delightfully calculated to inspire notions of retirement, of tranquillity, and happy meditation."—The same writer adds in another place,—" the figures returned, but now they consisted either of books, or parchments, or papers, containing printed matter. I do not know whether I read any of them, but am at present inclined to think they were not either distinctly legible, or did not remain a sufficient time before they vanished. I was now so well aware of the connexion of thought with their appearances, that, by fixing my mind on the consideration of manuscript instead of printed type, the papers appeared, after a time, only with manuscript-writing; and afterwards, by the same process, instead of being erect, they were all inverted, or appeared upside down."

This case decidedly shews, that a morbific cause vivifies ideas in a natural order of association.

After this satisfactory illustration of the order in which ideas are vivified by morbific causes, the extent of this action ought next to be investigated.

1st, A morbific cause of phantasms may exert a transient influence upon thought; or, after vivifying certain ideas to the height of actual impressions, a long interval may occur before there is a recurrence of the illusion. Nicolai's first spectral impression was of this kind; its subject was that of a deceased person, which, after haunting him for a few moments, did not return until several hours had expired.

2dly, A morbific cause of spectral illusions may, *with very little intermission,* influence ideas as they occur in their natural order of association. Thus, in a case recorded in the Pschyology of Bonnet, a gentleman labouring under some morbid affection of the brain, saw, while awake, various figures of animals, of human beings, of chariots, or of buildings, all in motion, which would successively approach towards him, recede, and disappear. But, at the same time, numerous sensations and ideas, unaffected in their degree of vividness, must have constantly interrupted this succession of spectral impressions, otherwise the judgment could not, as the narrative decidedly states, have remained entire.

3dly, A morbific cause of the same kind may, in its vivifying action, extend to some definite quality of sensations and ideas, whether that quality be pleasurable or painful. To the indications of this general action I have very frequently alluded, particularly in my description of the effects on the mind of the nitrous oxide and febrile miasma.

These remarks on the mode in which ideas may be renovated in a highly-intense state, will enable us, whenever we would wish to explain such popular narratives on the subject of ghosts or demonology as may be considered authentic, to apply with more success those pathological principles relative to spectral illusions which I have endeavoured to establish. For, in adverting to the subject of those waking visions detailed in the first chapter of this work, which Nicolai the Prussian bookseller experienced, it is evident that his intense imagination was impressed with no appearance which was of itself supernatural. The objects of his *second sight* (to use the well-known term of the Scottish Highlanders), were all of the most familiar kind,—men and women in their natural form and aspect, horses, dogs, or birds. Not of this earthly nature, however, were the illusions of superstitious ages, which constantly teemed either with angels or demons. In reference, then, to the view which I have taken, that spectral illusions ought to be regarded as nothing more than recollected images of the mind, which have been rendered by disease as intense as actual impressions, and which have been recalled in this vivid state by the well-known law of association, the figures of many phantasms may be indiscriminately referred to the delineations of those enthusiastic declaimers, historians, or poets, who have boldly attempted to supply from their own wild phantasy, the forms which they have supposed to have been imperfectly described in sacred records. From the imagination of ecclesiastical writers; from the stone or carved images of saints and angels, which have adorned the walls of religious edifices; or from emblematical pictures or portraits, which might have otherwise met with a popular diffusion, the sensible forms assumed by apparitions of this kind have been derived. By a high-wrought embellishment, they have been as determinately fixed in the mind as any familiar object which may be found in nature. No wonder then, that when, from some morbid state of the system, the superstitious have been rendered liable to spectral impressions, the figures of saints, angels, ghosts, or demons, should, above all other shapes, have formed the subject of their waking visions.

The late Dr Ferrier took some pains to trace to their real source the spectral figures which have been attributed to demoniacal visits. Thus, in his observations on the work of Remy, the commissioner in Lorraine for the trial of witches, he makes the following remark:—" My edition of this book was printed by Vincenti, at Lyons, in 1595. It is entitled *Dæmonolatreia*. The trials appear to have begun in 1583. Mr Remy seems to have felt great anxiety to ascertain the exact features and dress of the demons, with whom many persons supposed themselves to be familiar. Yet nothing transpired in his examinations, which varied from the usual figures exhibited by the gross sculptures and paintings of the middle age. They are said to be black-faced, with sunk but fiery eyes, their mouths wide, and smelling of sulphur, their hands hairy, with claws, their feet horny and cloven." There is, also, in another part of Dr Ferrier's work, the following account given of a case which passed under his own personal observation:— " I had occasion," he observes, " to see a young married woman, whose first indication of illness was a spectral delusion. She told me, that her apartment appeared suddenly to be filled with devils, and that her terror impelled her to quit the house with great precipitation. When she was brought back, she saw the whole staircase filled by diabolical forms, and was in agonies of fear for several days. After this first impression wore off, she heard a voice tempting her to self-destruction, and prohibiting her from all exercises of piety. Such was the account given by her when she was sensible of the delusion, yet unable to resist the horror of the impression. When she was nearly recovered, I had the curiosity to question her, as I have interrogated others, respecting the forms of the demons with which she had been claimed; but I never could obtain any other account, than that they were very small, very much deformed, and had horns and claws, like the imps of our terrific modern romances." To this illustration of the general origin of the figures of demoniacal illusions, I might observe, that in the case of a patient suffering under *delirium tremens*, which came under my notice, the devils who flitted around his bed, were described to me as exactly like the forms that he had recently seen exhibited on the stage in the popular drama of Don Giovanni.

Dr Ferrier of Manchester was among the first to shew the importance of explaining the causes, which have given rise to the illusive creations of the mind. " I conceive," says this acute and ingenious writer, " that the unaffected accounts of spectral visions should engage the attention of the philosopher as well as the physician. Instead of regarding these stories with the horror of the vulgar, or the disdain of the sceptic, we should examine them accurately, and should ascertain their exact relation to the state of the brain and of the external senses."* It must be

---

* Ferrier's Theory of Apparitions, p. 139.

confessed, however, that, in narratives of this kind, the circumstances most interesting to the pathologist, either from having been considered as unnecessary or inconvenient to the purposes or views of superstition, appear in most instances to have been altogether suppressed. The field of inquiry is, therefore, in this particular department of our dissertation, rather limited; and hence the necessity of pointing out beforehand the various morbific causes of spectral impressions, by which the true nature of phantasms may admit of a readier explanation, than by having recourse for such a purpose to the extravagancies of a supernatural agency. Yet still a few scattered glimpses of truth break through the mysterious stories which excite the attention of the learned and the vulgar, and, by the light which such rays afford, I shall avail myself, however feebly it may gleam through the obscure and gloomy regions of demonology.

The object, then, to be held in view in this department of our inquiry, is simply this:—While an attempt will be made to apply the medical cases which have been adduced towards the explanation of many supposed visitations of good and evil spirits, it will be always necessary to demonstrate in what manner the subject of the illusions thus induced has corresponded with the fanciful imagery which owes its origin to various preconceived superstitions. In connexion, likewise, with the illustrations which I shall adduce of the morbid origin of many supernatural visitants recorded in popular narratives, it may not be uninstructive to glance at the opinions entertained through a number of ages, relative to their nature, functions, and proper business, upon our globe. By this means, a conclusion may be ultimately drawn fatal to the existence of that world of spirits, which Superstition has depicted from no other source than its own wild, fallacious, and morbid phantasy.

A question, however, may now be started by some few individuals, if this inquiry can with propriety be conducted on the general preconceived supposition, that every well-attested instance, where a communication with apparitions of various kinds is supposed to have been held, ought to be regarded in no other light than as a pathological case? To any such objection I would reply, that there is only one line of demarcation, beyond which researches of this kind cannot meet with any application. This is to be found in the pages of sacred history. Concerning the manner in which the Deity, for signal purposes, has formerly chosen to hold an immediate communion with the human race, it would be irrelevant to offer any observations. At the same time, it may be necessary to observe, that as we are not warranted, for many reasons, which may be defended on scriptural grounds, to suppose that any direct converse with good or evil spirits, connected with either the Jewish or the Christian dispensation, has extended beyond the Apostolic age, there will be no hesitation on my part to proceed on the hypothesis, that all the subsequent visitations of this nature which have been recorded, deserve a medical rather than a theological investigation.

CHAPTER II.

REMARKS ON THE APPARITIONS OF GOOD SPIRITS, RECORDED IN POPULAR NARRATIVES.

> ——————" Spirits, when they please,
> Can either sex assume, or both ; so soft
> And uncompounded is their essence pure,
> Not ty'd or manacled with joint or limb,
> Nor founded on the brittle strength of bones,
> Like cumbrous flesh ; but in what shape they chuse,
> Dilated or condens'd, bright or obscure,
> Can execute their airy purposes."—MILTON.

THE present chapter will be devoted to the consideration of benignant spirits, and the apparitions to which they have given rise.

From the evidence of the Holy Scriptures, we are authorised to infer nothing more respecting those spiritual beings named angels, but that they are ministers whom the Deity has employed to execute his special commissions. And happy would it have been, if the early Christians and Jews had been contented with this simple information, without framing a system on the subject, which, as a learned divine of the church of England has remarked, savours more of some heathen mythology than of Christianity.* The Egyp-

---

* Wilson's Archæological Dictionary, article *Angels*. The same doctrine has likewise met with a successful exposure from Bishop Horsley.

tians, for instance, believed in the constant attendance of three angels upon every individual. The Romans supposed, that such genii, as they named them, were messengers between the gods and the human race; conceiving, therefore, with the Pythagoreans, that two were sufficient for any single individual, one was supposed to be of a good and the other of an evil quality. "These," as Sheridan has remarked in his notes to Persius, " were private monitors, who, by their insinuations, disposed each man to good or evil actions; they were not only reporters of his crimes in this life, but registers of them against his trials in the next." The Jews founded their belief in good and evil spirits, partly from the evidence of the Scriptures, and partly from the notions of the Pagans. Some of their angels were created out of the elements of fire, and others out of the wind. Whenever they issued from their allotted place, they forfeited their immortality. They instructed mankind in wisdom and knowledge. Every thing in the world was under their government. Even to the various herbs of the field, supposed at that time to be twenty-one thousand in number, presiding angels were affixed. Other good spirits had their respective dominion over plants, trees, rain, hail, thunder, lightning, fire, fishes, reptiles, animals, men, cities, empires, and nations.* Such a notion, unfortunately for the Christian world, very early accompanied the spreading of the Gospel. And, indeed, during a very long period afterwards, evident traces might be discovered of the prevalence of the same

---

* Stehelins' Traditions of the Jews, vol. ii. p. 71.

popular opinion which is mentioned by Symmachus, namely, " that the Divine Being had distributed to cities various guardians, and that as souls were communicated to infants at their birth, so particular genii were assigned to particular societies of men."

When the church of Papal Rome prevailed throughout Christendom, this belief was so far modified, that the functions of ministering angels were assigned to the spirits of departed saints, who at length became so numerous, as to very materially obstruct the ordinary current of human affairs. Hence the very just declamation against so overwhelming an interference from the pen of the dauntless Reginald Scot, who compares it to that of heathen deities; this writer not making the distinction at the time, that the saints of the Roman calendar were the proper successors of the tutelar angels of the Jewish talmud. " Surelie," says he, in a strain of most bitter irony, " there were in the Popish church, more of these antichristian gods in number, more in common, more private, more publicke, more for lewd purposes, and more for no purpose, than among all the heathen, either heretofore or at this present time; for I dare undertake, that for everie heathen idol I might pronounce twentie out of the Popish church. For there were proper idols of every nation, as St George on horseback for England, St Andrew for Burgundie and Scotland, St Michael for France, St James for Spain, St Patrike for Ireland, St Davie for Wales, St Peter for Rome and some part of Italie. Had not every citie in all the Pope's dominions his severall patrone: as Paule for London, Denis for Paris, Ambrose for Millen, Louen for Gaunt, Romball for Mackline, St Marks Lion for Venice, the three Magician Kings for Cullen, and so of other? Yea, had they not for everie small towne and everie village and parish (the names whereof I am not at liberty to repeat) a several idol; as St Sepulchre, for one; St Bride for another; St All Hallowes, All Saints, and our Ladie for all at once? Had they not hee idols and shee idols, some for men, some for women, some for beasts, and some for fowles? And doo you not thinke that St Martine might be opposed to Bacchus? If St Martine be too weake, we have St Urbane, St Clement, and manie other to assist him. Was Venus and Meretrix an advocate for whores among the Gentiles? Behold, there were in the Romish church to encounter them, St Aphra, St Aphrodite, and St Maudline. Was there such a traitor among the heathen idols as St Thomas Becket? or such a whore as St Bridget? I warrant you, St Hugh was as good a huntesman as Anubis. Was Vulcane the protector of the heathen smithes? Yea forsooth, and St Euloge was patron for ours. Our painters had Luke, our weavers had Steven, our millers had Arnold, our tailors had Goodman, our souters had Crispine, our potters had St Gore with a devil on his shoulders and a pot in his hand. Was there a better horseleech among the gods of the Gentiles than St Loy? or a better sow-gelder than St Anthonie? or a better tooth-drawer than St Apolline? I believe that Apollo Parnopeius was no better a rat-catcher than St Gertrude, who hath the Pope's patent and commendation therefore. The Thebans had not a better shepherd than St Wendeline, nor a better gissard to keep their sheep than Gallus. But for physicke and surgerie our idols exceeded them all. For St John and St Valentine excelled at the falling evil, St Roch was good at the plague, St Petromill at the ague. As for St Margaret, she passed Lucina for a midwife, and yet was but a maide; in which respect St Marpurge is joined with her in commission. For madmen, and such as are possessed with devills, St Romane was excellent. For botches and biles Cosmus and Damean; St Clare for the eies; St Apolline for teeth; St Job for the pox; and for sore brests St Agathe was as good as Ruminus."—This is the expostulation of honest Reginald Scot, who, in the true spirit of the reforming age in which he lived, comes to the conclusion, " that all these antichristian gods, otherwise called popish devils, are as rank devils" as the Dii gentium spoken of in the Psalms, or as the Dii montium, the Dii terrarum, the Dii populorum, the Dii terræ, the Dii filiorum, or the Dii alienii, cited in other places of the Scripture.

I have quoted thus freely from Scot's denunciation of the Romish saints, because it is an evidence of the ascendency over the mind, which these successors to the guardian angels of still earlier sects of Christians must have excited, while it no less satisfactorily accounts for the peculiar character imparted to the spectral illusions of Popish times.

When the tenets of Rome were succeeded by those of the reformed church, the influence of tutelar saints began to decline. Still it was found very inconvenient to the peculiar doctrines taught in the sixteenth and seventeenth centuries, that there should not be some hypothesis to account for human actions, which philosophy could not explain. Thus, the learned author of the Religio Medici has summed up, after the following manner, the views of the learned on the subject:—" Therefore for spirits," he remarks, " I am so far from denying their existence, that I could easily believe, that not only whole countries, but particular persons, have their tutelary and guardian angels. It is not a new opinion of the Church of Rome, but an old one of Pythagoras and Plato. There is no heresie in it, and if not manifestly defined in Scripture, yet it is an opinion of a good and wholesome use in the course and actions of man's life, and would serve as an hypothesis to solve many doubts, whereof common philosophy affordeth no solution." It is evidently for this reason, so well explained by Sir Thomas Brown, that the hierarchy of angels soon became a leading feature in the pneumatology of the schools; poets even vying with grave metaphysicians, in rendering every compensation to these ministering spirits for the neglect into which they had fallen, when their benignant offices had been usurped by the saints of the Romish church:—

> How oft do they their silver bowers leave,
> To come to succour us, that succour want?
> How oft do they with golden pinions cleave
> The flitting skies, like flying pursuivant,
> Against foul fiends to aid us militant?
> They for us fight, they watch and duly ward,
> And their bright squadrons round about us plant,
> And all for love, and nothing for reward:
> O why should heavenly God to man have such regard?
>
> SPENSER.

A doctrine, thus sanctioned by the most eminent men of the age, again made its way among the vulgar, and in the course of time gave rise to the grossest superstitions. Thus, in a popular work, entitled, " Curiosities, or the Cabinet of Nature, by Robert Basset," published in the year 1637, when a question is asked, *" Wherefore is it that the childe cryes when the absent nurse's brests doe pricke and ake?"* the answer is as follows :—" By that the nurse is hastened home to the infant to supply the defect; and the reason is, that either at that very instant that the infant hath finished his concoction, the breasts are replenished, and, for want of drawing, the milke pains the breast, as it is seen likewise in milch cattell: or rather, *the good genius of the infant* seems by that means to solicite or trouble the nurse in the infant's behalfe: which reason seemeth the more firm and probable, because sometimes sooner, sometimes later, the child cryeth; neither is the state of nurse and infant alwayes the same." While this quotation illustrates the popular use that was made of the doctrine of guardian angels, an extract, which I shall give from another author will prove, that the superstition at length very properly incurred the censure of divines. Thus, in Newton's " Trial of a Man's own selfe," the author cautions the Christian against the trusting " to the helpe, protection, and furtherance of angels, either good or bad, for the avoiding of any evill, or obtaining of any good ;" and he considers this belief as derived from " that paultring mawmetrie and heathenish worshipping of that domesticall god, or familiar angell, which was thought to be appropried to everie particular person." A later writer, who has noticed the doctrine of guardian angels, is the learned and pious Nelson. He believes in their common ministry about the persons of good men, and that they are present in all public assemblies of God's worship; but he very properly cautions his readers against worshipping them, since they are nothing more than ministers to mankind. This doctrine, if it does not meet with a complete sanction from Scripture, is at least so divested of all the serious objections which can be urged against it on the score of idolatry, that none surely but the merest cavillers would venture to engage in the unwelcome task of its refutation.*

It may be now interesting to ascertain the opinions entertained on the general form and character of those angelic beings which have imparted a peculiar character to the numerous spectral illusions, that have in different periods of the Christian era been recorded. During the ascendency of popish saints, the belief in an hierarchy of angels had rather languished than expired; and when, in an early period of the Reformation, the doctrine began to be revived, the corporeal shape, or material habitation, attributed to such spirits, was checked by the authoritative voice of the metaphysicians. "Now for that immaterial world," says Sir Thomas Brown, "methinks we need not wander

---

* I may remark that, regarding the general history of the superstitions connected with tutelar saints, there is an interesting article on the subject in Ellis' edition of Brand's Popular Antiquities, 4to, vol. i. p. 281, to which I have been occasionally indebted.

so far as the first moveable; for, even in this material fabrick, the spirits walk as freely exempt from the affection of time, place, and motion, as beyond the extremest circumference; do but extract from the corpulency of bodies, or resolve things beyond their first matter, and you discover the habitation of angels." Such a doctrine would of necessity be very puzzling to the poets, whose descriptions always include material images; no alternative, therefore, remained for them but to revive the opinion that angels were capable of subsisting either with or without any sensible forms. Of this view, so strongly inculcated in the seventeenth century, particularly by Milton, it is an interesting circumstance, that the author of the sublime tragedy of Manfred has recently availed himself.

MANFRED.

I would behold ye face to face. I hear
Your voices, sweet and melancholy sounds,
As music on the waters; and I see
The steady aspect of a clear large star;
But nothing more. Approach me as ye are,
Or one, or all, in your accustom'd forms.

SPIRIT.

We have no forms beyond the elements,
Of which we are the mind and principle:
But choose a form—in that we will appear.

Cowley, the most metaphysical poet of his time, was more anxious than any other descriptive writer, to render his spirits as little revolting as possible to the pneumatology of the schools; he, therefore, with becoming taste, fashioned the bodies and clothes of his angels with all the attenuated materials which he could discover, such as air, clouds, dew, solar rays, meteors, vapours, and rainbows :—

> Then, Gabriel, (no bless'd sp'rit more kind or fair)
> Bodies and clothes himself with thicken'd air;
> All like a comely youth in life's fresh bloom,
> Rare workmanship, and wrought by heav'nly loom!
> He took for skin a cloud more soft and bright,
> Than e'er the mid-day sun pierced thro' with light;
> Upon his cheeks a lively blush he spread,
> Wash'd from the morning beauty's deepest red;
> An harmless flaming meteor shone for hair,
> And fell adown his shoulders with loose care:
> He cuts out a silk mantle from the skies,
> Where the most sprightly azure pleased the eyes;
> This he with starry vapours spangles all,
> Took in their prime ere they grow ripe, and fall;
> Of a new rainbow, ere it fret or fade,
> The choicest piece took out, a scarf is made;
> Small streaming clouds he does for wings display,
> Nor virtuous lovers' sighs more soft than they;
> These he gilds o'er with the sun's richest rays,
> Caught gliding o'er pure streams on which he plays.
>   Cowley's *Davideis*, Book 2d.

The reason of my dwelling thus fully upon the source whence the guardian spirits of popular belief have derived their peculiar character, will now, I trust, be sufficiently obvious. An interpretation has been attempted of a certain quality of apparitions, which with weak minds has long served to confirm the incessant operation of tutelary genii.

I shall next attempt to illustrate, from a few well-authenticated apparitions of good spirits, those predisposing causes that have been intimately connected with the production of all such illusions. But I must here repeat the caution, that pathological cases of this kind are, from various causes, difficult to be obtained; the real state of the *seer's* health being but too frequently deemed unworthy of note, and in some instances purposely withheld.

It may then, in the first place, be observed, that highly-excited states of the sanguineous or melancholic temperaments, conspiring with great nervous irritability, have, more than any other causes, given rise not only to the particular apparitions of which I am about to treat, but to those of every other quality. With what truth has Pinel remarked, that " the history of insanity claims alliance with all the errors and delusions of ignorant credulity ; with those of witchcraft, demoniacal possession, oracles, and divination. As such," adds this excellent writer, " these are subjects by no means unworthy the consideration of a medical philosopher ; and especially of him whose peculiar office it is to administer health and consolation to minds distressed and diseased. Information, from whatever source, merits acceptance, but occasionally it must be sought where ordinary inquirers are either unable or too indolent to look for it." *

The life of Saint Teresa is a very instructive instance of the effects of Melancholia. " Her frame," says Mr Townsend, who, in his Tour through Spain,

---

* Pinel on Insanity. Trans. by Dr Davis, p. 45.

has given an abstract of her life, " was naturally de-
" licate, her imagination lively, and her mind incapable of being fixed by trivial objects, turned with
avidity to those which religion offered, the moment
they were presented to her view. But unfortunately
meeting with the writings of St Jerom, she became
enamoured of the monastic life, and, quitting the line
for which nature designed her, she renounced the
most endearing ties, and bound herself by the irre-
vocable vow. Deep melancholy then seized on her,
and increased to such a degree, that for many days
she lay both motionless and senseless, like one who is
in a trance. Her tender frame thus shaken, prepared
her for ecstacies and visions, such as it might appear
invidious to repeat, were they not related by herself
and by her greatest admirers. She tells us that, in
the fervour of her devotion, she not only became insensible to every thing around her, but that her body
was often lifted up from the earth, although she endeavoured to resist the motion; and Bishop Yepez
relates in particular, that when she was going to receive the Eucharist at Avila, she was raised in a rap-
ture higher than the grate, through which, as is usual
in nunneries, it was presented to her." The writer
then makes us acquainted with several particulars of
the visions which she experienced, as, for instance,
that she often heard the voice of God when she was
recovered from a trance,—that she frequently saw St
Peter and St Paul standing on her left hand, and
that, " once when she held the cross which was at
the end of her beads, our Lord took it from her, and
when he restored it, she saw it composed of four large

gems incomparably more precious than diamonds. These had his five wounds engraved upon them after a most curious manner; and he told her that she should always see that same appearance. And so she did; for from that time she no longer saw the matter of which the cross was made, but only these precious stones, although no one saw them but herself." Mr Townsend's general conclusion on this interesting case is too important to be omitted. "It is curious," he remarks, " yet most humiliating, to see a person of this description, amiable and respectable as St Teresa, deceived, and, with the best intentions, deceiving others. In this instance, we can readily account for the delusion, from the delicacy and weakness of her frame, the strength of a disturbed imagination, and the prevalence of superstition. But when we see men of the finest understandings, in perfect health, of different and distant nations, in all ages, treading upon the same enchanted ground, we can only wonder; for who can give any rational account of the aberrations of our reason?" This is, indeed, an excellent observation; I must, however, dispute the propriety of one remark, in which the writer supposes that the objects of such illusions may be in perfect health. On the contrary, I believe that no apparitions of profane history were ever seen under any such circumstances, but that they have universally arisen from morbific causes.

Another interesting narrative of nearly the same kind is to be found in Dr Crichton's "Enquiry into the Nature and Origin of Mental Derangement." This author has translated, from the Psychological

Magazine of Germany, a very curious account, drawn up by a lady of good credit, relative to the celestial sights which she had witnessed. This female, who in other respects possessed considerable intelligence, had such a belief in the reality of her visions, that she commences her account with an acknowledgment to the Lord of Lords, for the singular and gracious condescension with which she has been favoured. The able physician, however, to whose learned dissertation I am indebted for this case, has satisfactorily proved from certain confessions of the lady, that an *aura epileptica*, with other equally well-known symptoms, were felt during the prevalence of these illusions. As I have, therefore, on a former occasion, endeavoured to shew, that a general state of nervous irritability, not unfrequently heightened in its effect by a strongly-excited sanguineous or melancholic temperament, is a predisposing cause of spectral impressions, I must consider, that the following example affords an ample elucidation of such an affection, which may occur either with or without the adventitious symptoms of convulsion.

The illusions which this lady experienced first came on in the fourth year of her age, while she was sitting with her little doll upon her knees; and for the greater convenience of dressing and undressing it, resting her feet upon a large folio Bible. " I had scarcely taken my place," she observes, " above a minute, when I heard a voice at my ear say, ' Put the book where you found it;' but as I did not see any person, I did not do so. The voice, however, repeated the mandate, that I should do it immediately;

and, at the same time, I thought somebody took hold
of my face. I instantly obeyed with fear and trembling; but not being able to lift the book upon the
table, I called the servant-maid to come quickly and
assist me. When she came and saw that I was alone
and terrified, she scolded me, as nobody was there."
It may be remarked of this part of the account, that
the voice which the narrator heard can only be
regarded as a renovated feeling of the mind, resulting
from some prior remonstrances that she might have
incurred from her protectors, whenever she treated
with unbecoming irreverence the holy volume;—
while the impression of a person taking hold of her
face, may be referred to some morbid sensation of
touch, incidental to many nervous affections, which
would easily associate itself with the imaginary rebuke of her mysterious monitor, so as to impart to
the whole of the illusion a certain degree of connexion
and consistency. The *patient* (for such I shall call
her) next describes the extreme diligence and the peculiar delight with which, as she grew up in years,
she read twice over, from the beginning to the end,
the pages of the Scriptures; and she likewise dwells
upon her constant endeavour to render the Bible
more intelligible, by often hearing sermons and reading religious books. It is certainly of importance to
know the subject of her incessant and anxious studies,
as it is well calculated to explain the nature of her
visions, which, as we might expect, were generally of
a religious description.

We are, in the next place, told by the same lady,
that, after she had reached her seventh year, she saw,

when playing, a clear flame which seemed to enter through the chamber-door, while in the middle of it was a long bright light about the size of a child of six years old. The phantasm remained stationary for half an hour near the stove of the room, and then went out again by the room-door; the white light first, and the flame following it. After this vision, we hear of no other until the lady is married, when, unfortunately, her husband made her life so bitter to her that she could think only of death. Hence must have necessarily arisen the combining influence of strong mental emotions, which could not but act as powerful exciting agents upon a frame, the mental feelings of which, from constitutional causes, were of the most intense kind. Spectral illusions would of course become very frequent. Thus, on one occasion, when she had received some ill treatment from her husband, she made a resolution to desist from prayer, thinking the Lord had forsaken her; but, upon farther consideration, she repented of this purpose, and, after returning thanks to Heaven, went to bed. She awakened towards the morning, and then, to her astonishment, found that it was broad daylight, and that at her bed-side was seated a heavenly figure in the shape of a man about sixty years of age, dressed in a bluish robe, with bright hair, and a countenance shining like the clearest red and white crystal. He looked at her with tenderness, saying nothing more than '*Proceed, proceed, proceed.*' These words were unintelligible to her, until they were solved by another phantasm, young and beautiful as an angel, who appeared on the opposite side of the bed, and more explicitly added, '*Proceed in prayer, proceed in faith, proceed in trials.*' After this incident, a strange light appeared, when she immediately felt herself pulled by the hairs of her head, and pinched and tormented in various ways. The cause of this affliction she soon discovered to be the devil himself, who made his *debût* in the usual hideous form under which he is personated, until at length the angel interfered and pushed away the foul fiend with his elbow. "Afterwards," as the lady added, "the light came again, and both persons looked mournfully at it. The young one then said, 'Lord, this is sufficient;' and he uttered these words three times. Whilst he repeated them, I looked at him, and beheld two large white wings on his shoulder, and therefore I knew him to be an angel of God. The light immediately disappeared, the two figures vanished, and the day was suddenly converted into night. My heart was again restored to its right place, the pain ceased, and I arose." *

A few remarks may next be made on the blessed spirits with which dying persons are said to have occasionally held converse. "Oh!" said a female, as I find it recorded in Turner's History of remarkable Providences, "if you saw such a glorious sight as I

---

* On two occasions it is stated in the narrative, that the lady was favoured with a sight of our Saviour. Another vision is likewise related of a very remarkable kind. But it is probable, from the account which she gives, that these illusions took place in her sleeping dreams. The ecstacy now described is not liable to this objection, as it occurred during an epileptic fit.

now see, you would rejoice with me. For I see a vision of the joys of heaven, and of the glory that I shall go into, and I see infinite millions of angels attendant upon me, and watching to carry my soul into the kingdom of heaven." Respecting such a narrative as this, I shall merely repeat the observation which I made, that it is by no means uncommon in a far-advanced and moribund state of hectic symptoms, and, indeed, in the last stage of many other corporeal affections, that the patient should see apparitions, which may also be of a cheering description. The frequency of this incident being kept in view, an explanation is readily afforded of the numerous communications which pious individuals on their deathbed are supposed to have held with benignant spirits. That all such alleged visitants, as they stand recorded in profane history, are illusory, I must decidedly maintain; and, since the devoutest of Christians only partakes with humanity in general, by being occasionally liable, from such causes, to spectral impressions, no regret ought to arise, that the angels which he has seen are the mere phantasies of his diseased imagination. It is rather consolatory to think, that, on such occasions, the quality of his waking visions has accidentally harmonized so well with the prospect of those heavenly blessings, which are promised as the reward of a well-spent life.

The foregoing observations lead me, in the next place, to notice the angelic spirits which have not unfrequently visited persons of dissipated habits, particularly those who have laboured under such mental affections as supervene to habits of inebriety. Every medical man is aware of the phantasies resulting from *delirium tremens,* of which I have already adduced some very curious examples. I entertain, therefore, little doubt, but that in this state of mind, drunkards have not unfrequently enjoyed a friendly intercourse with imaginary spirits of a benignant quality. " Some, through weaknesses of body," says Reginald Scot, " have such imperfect imaginations. Drunken men also sometimes suppose they see trees walk, according to that which Solomon saith to the drunkards, ' thine eyes shall see strange visions and marvellous appearances.'" Of the angels who have condescended to hold an intercourse with mortals of this description, the case of Major Wilkie, as related by Baxter, in his Certainty of the World of Spirits, as well as by other writers, affords a memorable example. This gentleman was a Scottish engineer, who was employed in the civil wars which took place between the parliament and the unfortunate Charles. He is described as a scholar of no mean attainments, but as a great drinker, and possessing a very heated brain, which did not, however, impair his reasoning powers. He lived for some time in Coventry, at which place he affirmed, that he was constantly surrounded by both good and bad spirits, the former of whom were evidently the most friendly to him, as they endowed him with a spirit of prophecy. Thus he maintained, that the phenomena of thunder and lightning were nothing more than the wars of spirits, by means of which, and a vision that he enjoyed at Paris, he predicted the issue of the war with the parliament, and the near approach of the millennium. He was constantly attended, like some ancient Roman, with two genii, one of a benignant, and the other of an evil character; but the influence of the former prevailed, as, from this source of intelligence, he was enabled to expound the Scriptures in a way perfectly different from that of ordinary commentators. For instance, he amused his followers with a learned disquisition on the devil's contention about the body of Moses; nor did he fail to notice other equally important texts of the Scriptures. It is added, that this gentleman afterwards became distracted, and, unfortunately, died from want.—There is also another ghost-story of nearly a similar purport, which is recorded by three or four writers of the seventeenth century. In Turner's History of remarkable Providences it is thus related:—" A gentleman, formerly seeming pious, of late years hath fallen into the sin of drunkenness; and when he has been drunk, and slept himself sober, something knocks at his bed-head, as if one knocked on a wainscot; when they remove the bed, it follows him; besides loud noises in other parts where he is, that all the house heareth. It poseth me to think what kind of spirit this is, that hath such a care of this man's soul (which makes me hope he will recover). Do good spirits dwell so near us? or are they sent on such messages? or is it his guardian angel? or is it the soul of some dead friend that suffereth, and yet retaining love to him, as Dives did to his brethren, would have him saved? God keepeth yet such things from us in the dark."

The last case which I shall give on this subject, is that of John Beaumont, the author of a "Treatise on Spirits, Apparitions," &c. which was published in the year 1705. He is well described by Dr Ferrier, as "a man of a hypochondriacal disposition, with a considerable degree of reading, but with a strong bias to credulity." Labouring under this corporeal affection, he saw hundreds of imaginary men and women about him, though, as he adds, he never saw any in the night-time, unless by fire or candle-light, or in the moonshine. " I had two spirits," he says, " who constantly attended me, night and day, for above three months together, who called each other by their names; and several spirits would call at my chamber-door, and ask whether such spirits lived there, calling them by their names, and they would answer they did. As for the other spirits that attended me, I heard none of their names mentioned, only I asked one spirit, which came for some nights together, and rung a little bell in my ear, what his name was, who answered *Ariel*. The two spirits that constantly attended myself appeared both in women's habit, they being of a brown complexion, about three feet in stature; they had both black loose net-work gowns, tied with a black sash about the middle, and within the net-work appeared a gown of a golden colour, with somewhat of a light striking through it. Their heads were not drest in top-knots, but they had white linen caps on, with lace on them about three fingers' breadth, and over it they had a black loose net-work hood."

These are the few well-authenticated instances which I shall now offer on the present subject of our inquiry, although they might have been easily multiplied even to an enormous extent.

CHAPTER III.

GENERAL REMARKS ON THE APPARITIONS CONNECTED WITH DEMONOLOGY.

> " 'Tis said thou holdest converse with the things
> Which are forbidden to the search of man;
> That with the dwellers of the dark abodes,
> The many evil and unheavenly spirits
> Which walk the valley of the shade of death,
> Thou communest."   TRAGEDY OF MANFRED.

OUR next object is to investigate the general origin of that quality of apparitions, the vivid mental images of which have been derived from systems of demonology. It will therefore be worth while to preface this inquiry with a very brief historical sketch of the superstitions connected with this subject of popular belief.

The name of demon was given by the Greeks and Romans to certain spirits or genii, who appeared to men either to do them service or injury. The Platonists made a distinction between their gods, or *Dii Majorum Gentium,*—their demons, or those beings which were not dissimilar in their general character to the good and evil angels of Christian belief,—and their heroes. The Jews and early Christians restricted the appellation of demons to beings of a malignant nature, or to devils; and it is to the early opinions entertained by this people, that the outlines of later systems of demonology may be traced.

"The tradition of the Jews concerning evil spirits or devils," says a learned writer on the subject, "are various; some of them are founded upon Scripture; some borrowed from the notions of the pagans; some are fables of their own invention; and some are allegories." It would be a disagreeable task to recount the peculiar notions of this people on the origin of their demons; suffice it to say, that they were considered either as the distinct progeny of Adam or of Eve, which had resulted from an improper intercourse with supernatural beings, or of Cain. As this doctrine was naturally very revolting to some few of the early Christians, they maintained that demons were the souls of departed human beings, who were still allowed to interfere in the affairs of the earth, either to assist their friends or to persecute their enemies. This doctrine, however, did not ultimately prevail.

It would be very difficult for any one at the present day, considering our little familiarity with the writings of ancient pneumatologists, to attempt giving, in a condensed form, the various opinions entertained in an early period of the Christian era, and during the middle ages, on the nature of the demons of popular belief. Such an undertaking was, however, attempted two centuries and a half ago by Reginald Scot, and his chapter on the subject is so comprehensive, and at the same time so concise, as to render an abridgment of it unnecessary. "I, for my own part," says this writer, "do also thinke this argument about the nature and substance of divels and spirits to be difficult, as I am persuaded that no one author hath in anie certaine or perfect sort hitherto written thereof. In which respect I can neither allow the ungodly and prophane sects and doctrines of the Sadduces and Peripateticks, who denie that there are any divels or spirits at all; nor the fond and superstitious treatises of Plato, Proclus, Plotinus, Porphyrie; nor yet the vaine and absurd opinions of Psellus, Nider, Sprenger, Cumanus, Bodin, Michael, Andræas, Janus Matthæus, Laurentius, Ananias, Iamblicus, &c.; who, with manie others, write so ridiculouslie in these matters, as if they were babes fraied with bugges; some affirming that the soules of the dead become spirits, the good to be angels, the bad to be divels; some that spirits or divels are onelie in this life; some, that they are men; some, that they are women; some, that divels are of such gender that they list themselves; some, that they had no beginning, nor shall have ending, as the Manicheis mainteine; some, that they are mortall and die, as Plutarch affirmeth of Pan; some, that they have no bodies at all, but receive bodies according to their phantasies and imaginations; some, that their bodies are given unto them; some, that they make themselves. Some saie they are wind; some, that they are the breath of living creatures; some, that one of them began another; some, that they were created of the least part of the masse whereof the earth was made; and some, that they are substances betweene God and man, and that some of them are terrestrial, some celestial, some waterie, some airie, some fierie, some starrie, and some of each and every part of the elements, and that they know our thoughts, and carrie our good works and praiers to God, and returne his benefits back unto us, and that they are to be worshipped; wherein they meete and agree jumpe with the papists."—" Againe, some saie, that they are meane between terrestrial and celestial bodies, communicating part of each nature; and that although they be eternall, yet they are moved with affections; and as there are birds in the aire, fishes in the water, and wormes in the earth, so in the fourth element, which is the fier, is the habitation of spirits and divels."—" Some saie they are onelie imaginations in the mind of man. Tertullian saith they are birds, and flie faster than any fowle in the aire. Some saie that divels are not, but when they are sent; and therefore are called evil angels. Some thinke that the divel sendeth his angels abrode, and he himself maketh his continuall abode in hell, his mansion-place."

It was not, however, until a much later period of Christianity, that more decided doctrines relative to the origin and nature of demons were established. These tenets involved certain very knotty points relative to the fall of those angels, who, for disobedience, had forfeited their high abode in heaven. The Gnostics, of early Christian times, in imitation of a classification of the different orders of spirits by Plato, had attempted a similar arrangement with respect to an hierarchy of angels, the gradation of which stood as follows:—The first and highest order was named seraphim; the second cherubim; the third was the order of thrones; the fourth, of dominions; the fifth, of virtues; the sixth, of powers; the seventh, of principalities; the eighth, of archangels; the ninth, and lowest, of angels. This fable was, in a pointed manner, censured by the apostles; yet still, strange to say, it almost outlived the pneumatologists of the middle ages. These schoolmen, in reference to the account that Lucifer rebelled against heaven, and that Michael, the archangel, warred against him, long agitated the momentous question, What orders of angels fell on this occasion? At length, it became the prevailing opinion that Lucifer was of the order of seraphim. It was also proved, after infinite research, that Agares, Belial, and Barbatos, each of them deposed angels of great rank, had been of the order of virtues; that Bileth, Focalor, and Phœnix, had been of the order of thrones; that Gaap had been of the order of powers; and that Purson had been both of the order of virtues and of thrones, and Murmur, of thrones and of angels. The pretensions of many other noble devils were likewise canvassed, and, in an equally satisfactory manner, determined. Afterwards, it became an object of inquiry to learn, How many fallen angels had been engaged in the contest? This was a question of vital importance, which gave rise to the most laborious research, and to a variety of discordant opinions. It was next agitated, Where the battle was fought? in the inferior heaven, in the highest region of the air, in the firmament, or in paradise? how long it lasted? whether during one second, or moment of time (*punctum temporis*), two, three, or four seconds? These were queries of very difficult solution; but the notion which ultimately prevailed was, that the engagement was concluded in exactly three seconds from the date of its commencement; and that while Lucifer, with a number of his followers, fell into hell, the rest were left in the air to tempt man. A still newer question arose out of all these investigations, Whether more angels fell with Lucifer, or remained in heaven with Michael? Learned clerks, however, were inclined to think, that the rebel chief had been beaten by a superior force, and that, consequently, devils of darkness were fewer in number than angels of light.

These discussions, which, during a number of successive centuries, interested the whole of Christendom, too frequently exercised the talents of the most erudite characters in Europe. The last object of demonologists was to collect, in some degree of order, Lucifer's routed forces, and to re-organize them under a decided form of subordination, or government. Hence, extensive districts were given to certain chiefs that fought under this general. There was Zimimar, " the lordly monarch of the north," as Shakspeare styles him,* who had his distinct province of devils; there was Gorson, the King of the South; Amaymon, the King of the East; and Goap, the Prince of the West. These sovereigns had many noble spirits subordinate to them, whose various ranks were settled with all the preciseness of heraldic distinction; there

---

* This king is invoked in the First Part of Shakspeare's Play of Henry the Sixth, after the following manner:—
 " You speedy helpers that are substitutes
 Under the lordly monarch of the north—
 Appear!"

were Devil Dukes, Devil Marquises, Devil Counts, Devil Earls, Devil Knights, Devil Presidents, and Devil Prelates. The armed force under Lucifer seems to have comprised nearly twenty-four hundred legions, of which each demon of rank commanded a certain number.* Thus, Beleth, whom Scot has described as " a great king and terrible, riding on a pale horse, before whom go trumpets and all melodious music," commanded eighty-five legions; Agares, the first duke under the power of the East, commanded thirty-one legions; Leraie, a great marquis, thirty legions; Morax, a great earl and a president, thirty-six legions; Furcas, a knight, twenty legions; and, after the same manner, the forces of the other devil chieftains were enumerated.†

Such were once the notions entertained regarding the history, nature, and ranks of devils. My next object will be to shew, that, with respect to their strange and hideous forms, the apparitions connected with the popular belief on this subject, were derived from the descriptive writings of such demonologists, as either maintained that demons possessed a decided corporeal form, and were mortal, or that, like Milton's spirits, they could assume any sex, and take any shape they chose.

When, in the middle ages, conjuration was regularly practised in Europe, devils of rank were supposed to appear under decided forms, by which they

---

* To estimate the force of Lucifer, multiply 6666, the number of devils of which a legion consists, by 2400.

† See Scot's Discovery of Witchcraft, book 15. chap. 2; and his discourse of devils and spirits in the same book.

were as well recognized, as the head of any ancient family would be by his crest and armorial bearings. Along with their names and characters, were registered such shapes as they were accustomed to adopt. A devil would appear, either like an angel seated in a fiery chariot; or riding on an infernal dragon, and carrying in his right hand a viper; or assuming a lion's head, a goose's feet, and a hare's tail; or putting on a raven's head, and mounted on a strong wolf. Other forms made use of by demons were those of a fierce warrior, or of an old man riding upon a crocodile with a hawk in his hand. A human figure would arise having the wings of a griffin; or sporting three heads, two of them being like those of a toad and of a cat; or defended with huge teeth and horns, and armed with a sword; or displaying a dog's teeth, and a large raven's head; or mounted upon a pale horse, and exhibiting a serpent's tail; or gloriously crowned, and riding upon a dromedary; or presenting the face of a lion; or bestriding a bear, and grasping a viper. There were also such shapes as those of an archer, or of a Zenophilus. A demoniacal king would ride upon a pale horse; or would assume a leopard's face and griffin's wings; or put on the three heads of a bull, of a man, and a ram, with a serpent's tail, and the feet of a goose; and, in this attire, sit on a dragon, and bear in his hand a lance and a flag; or, instead of being thus employed, goad the flanks of a furious bear, and carry in his fist a hawk. Other forms were those of a goodly knight; or of one who bore lance, ensigns, and even sceptre; or of a soldier, either riding on a black horse, and surrounded with a flame of fire;

or wearing on his head a duke's crown, and mounted on a crocodile; or assuming a lion's face, and, with fiery eyes, spurring on a gigantic charger; or, with the same frightful aspect, appearing in all the pomp of family distinction, on a pale horse; or clad from head to foot in crimson raiment, wearing on his bold front a crown, and sallying forth on a red steed. Some infernal duke would appear in his proper character, quietly seated on a griffin; another spirit of a similar rank would display the three heads of a serpent, a man, and a cat; he would also bestride a viper, and carry in his hand a firebrand; another, of the same stamp, would appear like a duchess, encircled with a fiery zone, and mounted on a camel; a fourth, would wear the aspect of a boy, and amuse himself on the back of a two-headed dragon. A few spirits, however, would be content with the simple garbs of a horse, a leopard, a lion, an unicorn, a night-raven, a stork, a peacock, or a dromedary; the latter animal speaking fluently the Egyptian language. Others would assume the more complex forms of a lion or of a dog, with a griffin's wings attached to each of their shoulders; or of a bull equally well-gifted; or of the same animal, distinguished by the singular appendage of a man's face; or of a crow clothed with human flesh; or of a hart with a fiery tail. To certain other noble devils were assigned such shapes as those of a dragon with three heads, one of these being human; of a wolf with a serpent's tail, breathing forth flames of fire; of a she-wolf, exhibiting the same caudal appendage, together with a griffin's wings, and ejecting from her mouth hideous matter. A lion would appear, either with the head of a branded thief, or astride upon a black horse, and playing with a viper, or adorned with the tail of a snake, and grasping in his paws two hissing serpents.

These were the varied shapes assumed by devils of rank; it would, therefore, betray too much of an aristocratical spirit, to omit noticing the forms which the lower orders of such beings displayed. In an ancient Latin poem, describing the lamentable vision of a devoted hermit, and supposed to have been written by St Bernard in the year 1238,* those spirits, who had no more important business upon earth than to carry away condemned souls, were described as blacker than pitch: as having teeth like lions, nails on their fingers like those of the wild-boar, on their forehead horns, through the extremities of which poison was emitted, having wide ears flowing with corruption, and discharging serpents from their nostrils. The devout writer of these verses has even accompanied them with drawings, in which the addition of the cloven feet is not omitted. But this appendage, as Sir Thomas Brown has learnedly proved, is a mistake, which has arisen from the devil frequently appearing to the Jews in the shape of a rough and hairy goat, this animal being the emblem of sin-offerings.†

---

* A translation of this very curious work was printed for private distribution by William Yates, Esq. of Manchester, for a copy of which I have been indebted to this gentleman.

† Sir Thomas Brown, who thinks that this view may be confirmed by expositions of Holy Scripture, remarks, that " whereas it is said, thou shalt not offer unto devils; (the original word is

It is worthy of farther remark, that the form of the demons described by St Bernard, differs little from that which is no less carefully pourtrayed by Reginald Scot 350 years later, and, perhaps, by the demonologists of the present day. "In our childhood," says he, "our mother's maids have so terrified us with an ouglie divell having hornes on his head, fier in his mouth, and a taile in his breech, eies like a bason, fangs like a dog, clawes like a beare, a skin like a niger, and a voice roring like a lion,—whereby we start and are afraid when we heare one cry *bough*."

It is still a curious matter for speculation, worth while noticing—Why, after the decay of the regular systems of demonology taught in the middle ages, we should still attach the same hideous form to the devil? The learned Mede has remarked, "that the devil could not appear in human shape while man was in his integrity; because he was a spirit fallen from his first glorious perfection; and, therefore, must appear in such shape which might argue his imperfection and abasement, which was the shape of a beast; otherwise, no reason can be given, why he should not rather have appeared to Eve in the shape of a woman than of a serpent. But since the fall of man, the case is altered; now we know he can take upon him the shape of man. He appears, it seems, in the shape of man's imperfection, either for age or de-

---

Seghuirim), that is, rough and hairy goats, because in that shape the devil most often appeared, as is expounded by the Rabins; as Tremellius hath also explained; and as the word Ascimah, the God of Emath, is by some conceived."

formity, as like an old man (for so the witches say); and perhaps it is not altogether false, which is vulgarly affirmed, that the devil, appearing in human shape, has always a deformity of some uncouth member or other, as though he could not yet take upon him human shape entirely, for that man himself is not entirely and utterly fallen as he is." Grose also, but with infinitely less seriousness than the truly pious writer whom I have just quoted, has confirmed this view, by saying, that " although the devil can partly transform himself into a variety of shapes, he cannot change his cloven feet, which will always mark him under every appearance."

But enough of such fancies, originating with those, who, says Scot, " are so carnally-minded, that a spirit is no sooner spoken of, but immediatelie they thinke of a black man with cloven feet, a pair of hornes, a taile, clawes, and eies as broad as a bason. But surelie the devil were not so wise in his generation as I take him to be, if he would terrifie men with such uglie shapes, though he could do it at his pleasure."*

Absurd as all these descriptions truly are, relative

---

* There are some courageous individuals, however, to whom the censure of Scot cannot apply. Baxter has recorded a case relative to one Mr White of Dorchester, Assessor to the Westminster Assembly at Lambeth, who, being honoured with a visit one night from the arch-fiend, treated him with a cool contempt, to which his satanic majesty has not often been accustomed. " The devil, in a light night, stood by his bedside; the Assessor looked awhile whether he would say or do any thing, and then said, ' If thou hast nothing to do, I have; and so turned himself to sleep.' "

to the external forms of demons, I have not noticed them without due deliberation. During the middle ages, the hideous figures, which divers degrees of demons were supposed to assume, found very prominent places among the grotesque sculptures and carvings of religious buildings, and even disfigured the wainscots of the domestic halls of our ancestors. No wonder then, that, even at the present day, they should continue to make an impression upon weak intellects, or upon the vulgar. When fear has impressed their forms deeply on the minds of the superstitious, and when, from morbific causes, ideas have become as vivid as sensations, apparitions of hideous demons have haunted the maniacal visionary, or have disturbed the pillows of the languishing or of the dying.

With the view of illustrating other accounts of apparitions, I must still advert to the doctrines of demonology which were once taught. Although the leading tenets of this occult science may be traced to the Jews and early Christians, yet they were matured by our early communication with the Moors of Spain, who were the chief philosophers of the dark ages, and between whom and the natives of France and Italy a great communication subsisted. Toledo, Seville, and Salamanca, became the great schools of magic. At the latter city, prelections on the black art were, from a consistent regard to the solemnity of the subject, delivered within the walls of a vast and gloomy cavern. The schoolmen taught, that all knowledge and power might be obtained from the assistance of the fallen angels. They were skilled in the abstract sciences, in the knowledge of precious stones, in alchymy, in the various languages of mankind and of the lower animals, in the belles lettres, in moral philosophy, pneumatology, divinity, magic, history, and prophecy. They could control the winds, the waters, and the influence of the stars; they could raise earthquakes, induce diseases, or cure them, accomplish all vast mechanical undertakings, and release souls out of purgatory. They could influence the passions of the mind—procure the reconciliation of friends or foes—engender mutual discord—induce mania and melancholy—or direct the force and objects of the sexual affections.

Such was the object of demonology, as taught by its most orthodox professors. Yet other systems of it were devised, which had their origin in causes attending the propagation of Christianity. For it must have been a work of much time to eradicate the universal belief, that the Pagan deities, who had become so numerous as to fill every part of the universe, were fabulous beings. Even many learned men were induced to side with the popular opinion on the subject, and did nothing more than endeavour to reconcile it with their acknowledged systems of demonology. They taught that such heathen objects of reverence were fallen angels in league with the prince of darkness, who, until the appearance of our Saviour, had been allowed to range on the earth uncontrolled, and to involve the world in spiritual darkness and delusion. According to the various ranks which these spirits held in the vast kingdom of Lucifer, they were suffered, in their degraded state, to take up their abode in the air, in mountains, in springs, or in seas.

But, although the various attributes ascribed to the Greek and Roman deities were, by the early teachers of Christianity, considered in the more humble light of demoniacal delusions, yet for many centuries they possessed great influence over the minds of the vulgar. In the reign of Hadrian, Evreux in Normandy was not converted to the Christian faith, until the devil, who had caused the obstinacy of the inhabitants, was finally expelled from the Temple of Diana. To this goddess, during the persecution of Diocletian, oblations were rendered by the inhabitants of London. In the 5th century, the worship of her existed at Turin, and incurred the rebuke of Saint Maximus. From the 9th to the 15th century, several denunciations took place of the women, who in France and Germany travelled over immense spaces of the earth, acknowledging Diana as their mistress and conductor. In rebuilding Saint Paul's cathedral in London, remains of several of the animals used in her sacrifices were found; for slight traces of this description of reverence subsisted so late as the reign of Edward the First, and of Mary. Apollo, also, in an early period of Christianity, had some influence at Thorney, now Westminster. About the 11th century, Venus formed the subject of a monstrous apparition, which could only have been credited from the influence which she was still supposed to possess. A young man had thoughtlessly put his ring around the marble finger of her image. This was construed by the Cyprian goddess as a plighted token of marriage; she accordingly paid a visit to her bridegroom's bed at night, nor could he get rid of his bedfellow until the spells of an exorcist had been invoked for his relief. In the year 1536, just before the volcanic eruption of Mount Etna, a Spanish merchant, while travelling in Sicily, saw the apparition of Vulcan attended with twenty of his Cyclops, as they were escaping from the effects which the overheating of his furnace foreboded.*

To the superstitions of Greece and Rome we are also indebted for those subordinate evil spirits named *genii*, who, for many centuries, were the subject of numerous spectral illusions. A phantasm of this kind appeared to Brutus in his tent, prophesying that he should be again seen at Philippi. Cornelius Sylla had the first intimation of the sudden febrile attack with which he was seized, from an apparition who addressed him by his name; concluding, therefore, that his death was at hand, he prepared himself for the event, which took place the following evening. The poet Cassius Severus, a short time before he was slain by order of Augustus, saw, during the night, a human form of a gigantic size,—his skin black, his beard squalid, and his hair dishevelled. The phantasm was, perhaps, not unlike the evil genius of Lord Byron's Manfred:—

> " I see a dusk and awful figure rise
> Like an infernal god from out the earth;
> His face wrapt in a mantle, and his form
> Robed as with angry clouds; he stands between
> Thyself and me—but I do fear him not."

---

* See an interesting dissertation on this subject in Douce's Illustrations of Shakspeare, vol. i. p. 382. It is also noticed in the Border Minstrelsy, vol. ii. p. 197.

The emperor Julian was struck with a spectre clad in rags, yet bearing in his hands a horn of plenty, which was covered with a linen cloth. Thus emblematically attired, the spirit walked mournfully past the hangings of the apostate's tent.*

We may now advert to the superstitious narratives of the middle ages, which are replete with the notices of similar marvellous apparitions. When Bruno, the Archbishop of Wirtzburg, a short period before his sudden death, was sailing with Henry III., he descried a terrific spectre standing upon a rock which overhung the foaming waters, by whom he was hailed in the following words:—" Ho! Bishop, I am thy evil genius. Go whither thou choosest, thou art and shalt be mine. I am not now sent for thee, but soon thou wilt see me again." To a spirit commissioned upon a similar errand, the prophetic voice may be probably referred, which was said to have been heard by John Cameron, the Bishop of Glasgow, immediately before his decease. He was summoned by it, says Spottiswoode, " to appear before the tribunal of Christ, there to atone for his violence and oppressions."

But it is curious, that a superstition nearly similar has been perpetuated in the Highlands of Scotland even to the present day. " There is a species of spirits," says Sir Walter Scott, in his Border Minstrelsy, " to whom, in the Highlands, is ascribed the guar-

---

* Dio of Syracuse was visited by one of the furies in person, whose appearance the soothsayers regarded as indicative of the death which occurred of his son, as well as of his own dissolution.

dianship or superintendence of a particular clan, or family of distinction. Thus the family of Gurlinbeg was haunted by a spirit called Garlin Bodachar; that of the Baron of Kinchardin by Lamhdearg or Red Hand, a spectre, one of whose hands is as red as blood; that of Tullochgorm by May Moulach, a female figure, whose left hand and arm were covered with hair, who is also mentioned as a familiar attendant upon the clan Grant."—I need scarcely remind my readers of the truly sublime manner in which this superstition is made the subject of a striking incident in the popular romance of Waverley.

I shall not pursue the subject of Genii much farther. The notion of every man being attended by an evil genius was abandoned much earlier than the far more agreeable part of the same doctrine, which taught, that, as an antidote to this influence, each individual was also accompanied by a benignant spirit. " The ministration of angels," says a writer in the Athenian oracle, " is certain, but the manner *how* is the knot to be untied. 'Twas generally believed by the antient philosophers, that not only kingdoms had their tutelary guardians, but that every person had his particular genius, or good angel, to protect and admonish him by dreams, visions, &c. We read that Origen, Hierome, Plato, and Empedocles in Plutarch, were also of this opinion; and the Jews themselves, as appears by that instance of Peter's deliverance out of prison. They believed it could not be Peter, but his angel. But for the particular attendance of bad angels, we believe it not; and we must deny it, till it finds better proof than conjectures."

Such were the objects of superstitious reverence derived from the Pantheon of Greece and Rome, the whole synod of which was supposed to consist of demons, who were still actively bestirring themselves to delude mankind. But, in the west of Europe, a host of other demons, far more formidable, were brought into play, who had their origin in Celtic, Teutonic, and even Eastern fables; and as their existence, as well as influence, was not only by the early Christians, but even by the reformers, boldly asserted, it was long before the rites to which they had been accustomed were totally eradicated. Thus, in Orkney, for instance, it was customary, even during the last century, for lovers to meet within the pale of a large circle of stones, which had been dedicated to the chief of the ancient Scandinavian deities. Through a hole in one of the pillars, the hands of contracting parties were joined, and the faith they plighted was named the promise of Odin, to violate which was infamous. But the influence of the *Dii Majores* of the Edda was slight and transient, in comparison with that of the duergar or dwarfs, who figure away in the same mythology, and whose origin is thus recited. Odin and his brothers killed the Giant Ymor, from whose wound ran so much blood, that all the families of the earth were drowned, except one that saved himself on board a bark. These gods then made of the giant's bones, of his flesh, and his blood, the earth, the water, and the heavens. But in the body of the monster, several worms had, in the course of putrefaction, been engendered, which, by order of the gods, partook of both human shape and reason. These little beings possessed the most delicate figures, and always dwelt in subterraneous caverns or clefts of rocks. They were remarkable for their riches, their activity, and their malevolence.* This is the origin of our modern fairies, who, at the present day, are described as a people of small stature, gaily dressed in habiliments of green.† They possess material shapes, with the means, however, of making themselves invisible. They multiply their species; they have a relish for the same kind of food that affords a sustenance to the human race, and when, for some festal occasion they would regale themselves with good beef or mutton, they employ elf-arrows to bring down their victims. At the same time, they delude the shepherds with the substitution of some vile substance, or illusory image, possessing the same form as that of the animal which they have taken away. These sprites are much addicted to music, and when they make their excursions, a most exquisite band of music never fails to accompany them in their course. They are addicted to the abstraction

---

* Sir Walter Scott has supposed that this mythological account of the duergar bears a remote allusion to real history, having an ultimate reference to the oppressed Fins, who, before the arrival of invaders, under the conduct of Odin, were the prior possessors of Scandinavia. The followers of this hero saw a people, who knew how to work the mines of the country better than they did; and, therefore, from a superstitious regard, transformed them into spirits of an unfavourable character, dwelling in the interior of rocks, and surrounded with immense riches.—*Border Minstrelsy*, vol. ii. p. 179.

† It is said that, in Orkney, they were often seen clad in complete armour.—*Brand's Description of Orkney*, 8vo, *Edinburgh*, 1701, *p.* 63.

of the human species, in whose place they leave substitutes for living beings, named *changelings*, the unearthly origin of whom is known by their mortal imbecility, or some wasting disease. When a limb is affected with paralysis, a suspicion often arises that it has been either touched by these sprites, or that, instead of the sound member, an insensible mass of matter has been substituted in its place.

In England, the opinions originally entertained relative to the duergar or dwarfs, have sustained considerable modifications, from the same attributes being assigned to them as to the Persian *peris*, an imaginary race of intelligences, whose offices of benevolence were opposed to the spiteful interference of evil spirits. Whence this confusion in the proper Teutonic mythology has originated is doubtful; conjectures have been advanced, that it may be traced to the intercourse which the crusaders had with the Saracens, and that from Palestine was imported the corrupted name, derived from the Peris, of *fairies*;—for under such a title the Duergar of the Edda are now generally recognised. The malevolent character of the dwarfs being thus sunk in the opposite qualities of the Peris, the fairies' Blessing became, in England, proverbial: " Grant that the sweet fairies may nightly put money in your shoes, and sweep your house clean." In more general terms, the wish denoted, " Peace be to this house"*

---

* In Germany, probably for similar reasons, the dwarfs have acquired the name of *elves*—a word, observes Mr Douce, derived from the Teutonic *helfen*, which etymologists have translated *juvare*.

Fairies, for many centuries, have been the objects of spectral impressions. In the case of a poor woman of Scotland, Alison Pearson, who suffered for witchcraft in the year 1586, they probably resulted from some plethoric state of the system, which was followed by paralysis. Yet, for these illusive images, to which the popular superstitions of the times had given rise, the poor creature was indicted for holding a communication with demons, under which light fairies were then considered, and burnt at a stake. During her illness, she was not unfrequently impressed with sleeping and waking visions, in which she held an intercourse with the queen of Elfland and the *good neighbours*. Occasionally, these capricious spirits would condescend to afford her bodily relief; at other times, they would add to the severity of her pains. In such trances or dreams, she would observe her cousin, Mr William Sympsoune of Stirling, who had been conveyed away to the hills by the fairies, from whom she received a salve that would cure every disease, and of which the Archbishop of Saint Andrews himself deigned to reap the benefit. It is said in the indictment against her, that " being in Grange Muir with some other folke, she, being sick, lay downe; and, when alone, there came a man to her clad in green, who said to her, if she would be faithful, he would do her good; but she, being feared, cried out; but naebodie came to her, so she said, if he cam in God's name, and for the gude of her saul, it was well; but he gaed away; he appeared another tyme like a lustie man, and many men and women with him;—at seeing him she signed herself, and prayed and past with them, and saw them making merrie with pypes, and gude cheir and wine:—She was carried with them, and when she telled any of these things, she was sairlie tormented by them; and the first time she gaid with them, she gat a sair straike frae one of them, which took all the poustie [power] of her side frae her, and left an ill-far'd mark on her side.

"She saw the gude neighbours make their sawes [salves] with panns and fyres, and they gathered the herbs before the sun was up, and they cam verie fearful sometimes to her, and flaide [scared] her very sair, which made her cry, and threatened they would use her worse than before; and at last they tuck away the power of her haile syde frae her, which made her lye many weeks. Sometimes they would come and sitt by her, and promise that she should never want if she would be faithful; but if she would speak and tell of them, they should murther her. Mr William Sympsoune is with them who healed her, and telt her all things;—he is a young man, not six years older than herself, and he will appear to her before the court comes;—he told her he was taken away by them; and he bidd her sign herself that she be not taken away, for the teind of them are tane to hell everie yeare."*

Another apparition of a similar kind may be found in the pamphlet which was published A. D. 1696, under the patronage and recommendation of Dr Fowler, Bishop of Gloucester, relative to Ann Jefferies, " who

---

* Minstrelsy of the Scottish Border, vol. ii. page 215.

was fed for six months by a small sort of airy people, called fairies." There is every reason to suppose, that this female was either affected with hysteria, or with that highly-excited state of nervous irritability, which, as I have shewn, gives rise to ecstatic illusions. The account of her first fit is the only one which relates to the present subject. In the year 1695, says her historian, " she then being nineteen years of age, and one day knitting in an arbour in the garden, there came over the hedge to her (as she affirmed) six persons, of a small stature, all cloathed in green, which she called *fairies:* upon which she was so frighted, that she fell into a kind of convulsive fit: but when we found her in this condition, we brought her into the house, and put her to bed, and took great care of her. As soon as she recovered out of the fit, she cries out, ' They are just gone out of the window; they are just gone out of the window. Do you not see them?' And thus, in the height of her sickness, she would often cry out, and that with eagerness; which expressions we attributed to her distemper, supposing her light-headed." This narrative of the girl seemed highly interesting to her superstitious neighbours, and she was induced to relate far more wonderful stories, upon which not the least dependence can be placed, as the sympathy she excited eventually induced her to become a rank impostor.*

---

* Before dismissing the subject of fairies, I shall slightly advert to the strange blending which took place of Grecian and Teutonic fables. " We find," says Sir Walter Scott, " the elves, occasionally arrayed in the costume of Greece and Rome, and the

But besides fairies, or elves, which formed the subject of many spectral illusions, a domestic spirit deserves to be mentioned, who was once held in no small degree of reverence. In most northern countries of Europe, there were few families that were without a shrewd and knavish sprite, who, in return for the attention or neglect which he experienced, was known to

> "——————— Sometimes labour in the quern,
> And bootless make the breathless housewife churn ;
> And sometimes make the drink to bear no barm."

Mr Douce, in his Illustrations of Shakspeare, has shewn, that the Samogitæ, a people formerly inhabiting the shores of the Baltic, who remained idolatrous so late as the 15th century, had a deity named Putscet, whom they invoked to live with them, by placing in the barn, every night, a table covered with bread, butter, cheese, and ale. If these were taken away, good fortune was to be expected ; but, if they were left, nothing but bad luck. This spirit is the same as the goblin-groom, Puck, or Robin Goodfellow of the English, whose face and hands were either of a russet or green colour, who was attired in a suit of leather, and armed with a flail. For a much lesser fee than was originally given him, he would assist in threshing, churning, grinding malt or mustard, and sweep-

---

fairy queen and her attendants, transformed into Diana and her nymphs, and invested with their attributes and appropriate insignia." Mercury was also named by Harsenet in the year 1602, the Prince of the Fairies.

ing the house at midnight.* A similar tall "lubbar-fiend," habited in a brown garb, was known in Scotland. Upon the condition of a little wort being laid by for him, or the occasional sprinkling, upon a sacrificial stone, of a small quantity of milk, he would ensure the success of many domestic operations. According to Olaus Magnus, the northern nations regarded domestic spirits of this description as the souls of men who had given themselves up during life to illicit pleasures, and were doomed, as a punishment, to wander about the earth, for a certain time, in the peculiar shape which they assumed, and to be bound to mortals in a sort of servitude. It is natural, therefore, to expect, that these familiar spirits would be the subject of many apparitions, of which a few relations are given in Martin's Account of the Second Sight in Scotland. "A spirit," says this writer, "called Browny, was frequently seen in all the most considerable families in the isles and north of Scotland, in the shape of a tall man; but within these twenty or thirty years he is seen but rarely."

It is useless to pursue this subject much farther. In the course of a few centuries, the realms of superstition were, in the west of Europe, increased to an almost immeasurable extent. The consequence was,

---

* "He would chafe exceedingly," says Scot, "if the maid or good-wife of the house, having compassion of his nakedness, laid anie clothes for him, beesides his messe of white bread and milke, which was his standing fee. For in that case he saith, What have we here? Hemton hamten, here will I never more tread nor stampen."

that the air, the rocks, the seas, the rivers, nay every lake, pool, brook, or spring, became so filled with spirits, both good and evil, that of each province it might be said, in the words of the Roman satirist, " Nostra regio tam plena est numinibus, ut facilius possis deum quam hominem invenire." Hence the modification which took place of systems of demonology, so as to admit of the classification of all descriptions of devils, whether they had been derived from Grecian, Roman, Teutonic, Celtic, or Eastern systems of mythology. " Our schoolmen, and other divines," says Burton, in his Anatomy of Melancholy, " make nine kinds of bad divels, as Dionysius hath of angels. In the *first rank* are those false gods of the Gentiles, which were adored heretofor in several idols, and gave oracles at Delphos and elsewhere, whose prince is Belzebub. The *second rank* is of liars and equivocaters, as Apollo, Pythius, and the like. The *third* are those vessels of anger, inventers of all mischief, as that of Theutus in Plato. Esay calls them vessels of fury; their prince is Belial. The *fourth* are malicious, revengeful divels, and their prince is Asmodeus. The *fifth* kind are coseners, such as belong to magicians and witches; their prince is Satan. The *sixth* are those aerial divels that corrupt the air, and cause plagues, thunders, fires, &c. spoken of in the Apocalyps and Paule; the Ephesians name them the princes of the aire: Meresin is their prince. The *seventh* is a destroyer, captaine of the furies, causing wars, tumults, combustions, uproares, mentioned in the Apocalyps, and called Abaddon. The *eighth* is that accusing or calumniating divel, whom the Greeks call Διάβολος, that drives us to despaire. The *ninthe* are those tempters in several kindes, and their prince is Mammon."

But this arrangement was not comprehensive enough; for, as Burton adds, " no place was void, but all full of spirits, devils, or other inhabitants, not so much as an haire-breadth was empty in heaven, earth, or waters, above or under the earth,—the earth was not so full of flies in summer as it was at all times of invisible devils." Pneumatologists, therefore, made two grand distinctions of demons; there were celestial demons, who inhabited the regions higher than the moon; while those of an inferior rank, as the Manes or Lemures, were either nearer to the earth, or grovelled on the ground. Psellus, however, " a great observer of the nature of devils," seems to have thought, that such a classification destroyed all distinction between good and evil spirits; he therefore denied that the latter ever ascended the regions above the moon, and contending for this principle, founded a system of demonology, which had for its basis the natural history and habitations of all demons. He named his first class *fiery devils*. They wandered in the region near the moon, but were restrained from entering into that luminary; they displayed their powers in blazing stars, in firedrakes, in counterfeit suns and moons, and in the *cuerpo santo*, or meteoric lights, which, in vessels at sea, flit from mast to mast, and forebode foul weather. It was supposed that these demons occasionally resided in the furnaces of Hecla, Etna, or Vesuvius.—The second class consisted of *aerial devils*. They inhabited the atmosphere, causing tempests, thunder, and lightning; rending asunder oaks, firing steeples and houses, smiting men and beasts, showering down, from the skies, stones,* wool, and even frogs; counterfeiting in the clouds the battles of armies, raising whirlwinds, fires, and corrupting the air, so as to induce plagues.—The third class were *terrestrial devils;* such as lares, genii, fauns, satyrs, wood-nymphs, foliots, Robin Goodfellows, or trulli. —The fourth class were *aqueous devils;* as the various descriptions of water-nymphs, of mermen, or of merwomen.—The fifth were *subterranean devils,* better known by the name of dæmones metallici, metal men, *Getuli* or *Cobali.* They preserved treasure in the earth, and prevented it from being suddenly revealed; they were also the cause of horrible earthquakes.— Psellus's sixth class of devils were named *lucifugi.* They delighted in darkness; they entered into the bowels of men, and tormented those whom they possessed with phrenzy and the fallen sickness. By this power they were distinguished from earthy and aerial devils, who could only enter into the human mind, which they either deceived or provoked with unlawful affections.

Nor were speculations wanting with regard to the common nature of these demons. Psellus conceived that their bodies did not consist merely of one ele-

---

* Psellus speaks with great contempt of this petty instance of malevolence to the human race. " Stones are thrown down from the air," he remarks, " which do no harm, the devils having little strength, and being mere scarecrows." So much for the origin of meteoric stones.

ment, although he was far from denying that this might not have been the case before the fall of Lucifer. It was his opinion, that devils possessed corporeal frames capable of sensation; that they could both feel and be felt; that they could injure and be hurt; that they lamented when they were beaten, and that if stuck into the fire, they even left behind them ashes,—a fact which was demonstrated in a very satisfactory experiment made by some philosopher upon the borders of Italy;—that they were nourished with food peculiar to themselves, not receiving the aliment through the gullet, but absorbing it from the exterior surface of their bodies, after the manner of a spunge; that they did not hurt cattle from malevolence, but from mere love of the natural and temperate heat and moisture of these animals; that they disliked the heat of the sun, because it dried too fast; and, lastly, that they attained a great age. Thus, Cardan had a fiend bound to him twenty-eight years, who was forty-two years old, and yet considered very young. He was informed, from this very authentic source of intelligence, that devils lived from two to three hundred years, and that their souls died with their bodies. This very philosophical statement was, nevertheless, combated by other observers. " Manie," says Scot, " affirmed that spirits were of aier, because they have been cut in sunder and closed presentlie againe, and also because they vanished awaie so suddenlie."

But a truce to these absurdities, of which I begin to suspect that my readers may be no less wearied than myself. Still the inquiry was necessary for my purpose, as I trust it will now be apparent, that most of the fantastical images, which have long formed the subject of the spectral illusions of superstition, have kept pace, either with Pagan systems of mythology, with Christian systems of demonology, or with the no less superstitious views entertained, relative to the hierarchy of benignant genii. Yet, in the impressive language of Lord Byron,

>————————————"What are they?
> Creations of the mind? The mind can make
> Substance, and people planets of its own,
> With beings brighter than have been, and give
> A breath to forms which can outlive all flesh."

CHAPTER IV.

GENERAL REMARKS ON THE APPARITIONS OF DEPARTED SPIRITS.

" Ghosts fly on clouds and ride on winds," said Connal's voice of wisdom. " They rest together in their caves, and talk of mortal men."—*Poem of Fingal.*

It is the most reasonable of expectations, that the various morbific causes, which are capable of imparting to the recollected images of the mind the vividness of actual impressions, should have for their subject the forms of deceased as well as of living individuals. In the narrative, for instance, of Nicolai, given in the first chapter of this work, the following remarkable passage occurs :—" There appeared many other phantasms, sometimes representing acquaintances. Those whom I knew were composed both of living and deceased persons, though the number of the latter was comparatively small." This instance of spectres produced by disease, illustrates also the alleged paleness of ghosts, or the misty and cloudy appearance which they assume. For the same writer remarks of certain of the phantasms which he saw, that they appeared to him in their natural size, and as distinct as if alive; though the colours seemed *somewhat paler* than in real nature." It is evident, that this impression must have resulted from the spectral idea of colour not quite equalling in intensity the vividness of an immediate sensation; indeed, Nicolai has related of certain other forms, that " soon afterwards their colour began to fade, and at seven o'clock they were entirely white." The mode in which ghosts are said to disappear, is also well displayed in the same case. The phantoms beheld by this philosopher would suddenly withdraw or vanish. On other occasions, they would grow by degrees more obscure;—they would dissolve in the air; nay, sometimes, fragments of them would continue visible a considerable time:

MACBETH.
" The earth hath bubbles, as the water has,
And these are of them :—Whither are they vanish'd ?—

BANQUO.
Into the air; and what seem'd corporal
As breath into the wind."

From another writer, I have quoted an account of spectral forms nearly similar. " They appeared before me," it is said, " one at a time, very suddenly, yet not so much so, but that a second of time might be employed in the emergence of each, as if through a cloud or mist, to its perfect clearness. In this state each form continued five or six seconds, and then vanished, by becoming gradually fainter during about two seconds, till nothing was left but a dark and pale mist, in which, almost immediately afterwards, appeared another face. All these faces were, in the highest degree, interesting to me, for beauty of form, and the variety of expression they manifested of every great and amiable emotion of the human mind." How well do these circumstances incidental to morbid illusions agree with the description of a Highland bard. " Who comes from the place of the dead,—that form with the robe of snow ; white arms and dark-brown hair ? It is the daughter of the chief of the people ; she that lately fell ! Come let us view thee, O maid ! thou that hast been the delight of heroes ! The blast drives the phantom away ; white, without form, it ascends the hill."*

It must be confessed, that the popular belief of departed spirits occasionally holding a communication with the human race, is replete with matter of curious speculation. Some Christian divines, with every just reason, acknowledge no authentic source whence the impression of a future state could ever have been communicated to man, but from the Jewish prophets or from our Saviour himself. Yet it is certain, that a belief in an existence after death has, from time immemorial, prevailed in countries, to which the knowledge of the gospel never could have extended, as among certain tribes of America. Can then this notion have been intuitively suggested ? Or is it an extravagant supposition, that the belief might have often arisen not only from dreams, but from those spectral illusions, to which men in every age, from the occasional influence of morbific causes, must have been subject ? And what would be the natural self-persuasion, if a savage saw before him the apparition of a departed friend or acquaintance, endowed with the semblance of life, with motion, and with signs of mental intelli-

---

* See Note to *Croma*, in Macpherson's Ossian, vol. ii.

gence, perhaps even holding converse with him? Assuredly, the conviction would scarcely fail to arise of an existence after death. The pages of history attest this fact:

> " If ancestry can be in aught believ'd,
> Descending spirits have convers'd with man,
> And told him secrets of the world unknown."

But if this opinion of a life hereafter had ever among heathen nations such an origin, it must necessarily be imbued with the grossest absurdities incidental to so fallacious a source of intelligence. Yet still the mind has clung to such extravagancies with avidity; " for," as Sir Thomas Brown has remarked, " it is the heaviest stone that melancholy can throw at a man, to tell him he is at the end of his nature; or that there is no future state to come, unto which this seems progressively and otherwise made in vain." It has remained, therefore, for the light of revelation alone, to impart to this belief the consistency and confirmation of divine truth, and to connect it with a rational system of rewards and punishments.

From the foregoing remarks, we need not be surprised, that a conviction of the occasional appearance of ghosts or departed spirits, should, from the remotest antiquity, have been a popular creed, not confined to any distinct tribe or race of people; and when it is considered that such illusions are nothing more than recollected images of the mind presented in a highly-excited state, it is natural to expect that the imaginary beings of another world would appear to put on the same corporeal forms, and adopt the same manners, as those to which they had been accustomed in an earthly state of existence. Dr Barclay, in speaking of the simulacra of the Romans, has very properly remarked, that " the dress and its fashions were represented as well as the body, while, in all the poetical regions of the dead, chariots, and various species of armour, were honoured likewise with their separate simulacra; so that these regions, as appears from the Odyssey, Æneid, and Edda, were just the simulacra of the manners, opinions, customs, and fashions, that characterized the times and countries in which their poetical historians flourished."*

The religious effect of this belief has been by no one more ably demonstrated than by the learned Farmer. He has satisfactorily shewn that the worship of the heathen nations corresponded to their notions of human ghosts, and was founded upon it.† Dreams also have deeply entered into the tenets of many religions, —such phenomena having been ever regarded as prophetic indications communicated to mankind by supernatural influence. Aristotle wrote on divination by dreams, as well as Zeno, Cleanthes, Chrysippus, and other ancient philosophers.

But it is certain that the popular belief relative to ghosts did not always recommend itself to the more refined opinions of philosophic sects. " For ghosts were thought," says Dr Farmer, " to come from their subterraneous habitations, or from their graves, to partake of the entertainment provided for them.

---

* Barclay on Life and Organization, page 14.
† See Note 3.

Blood, in particular, was an acceptable libation to ghosts, and more particularly to the ghosts of heroes."* It was, therefore, to correct the loose opinions entertained regarding the nature of the gods, and the souls of the dead, that Pneumatology put forth its pretensions as a distinct science. Consequently, in examining the stories of apparitions recorded by the Greeks and Romans, it will be found, that they vary in their character according to the different doctrines which were urged by the learned on this subject, and which, in course of time, began to prevail among the vulgar. For it was by various sects supposed, either that the soul was corporeal, being formed from warm air, or from water, or from fire, or from corporeal vapours; or, on the other hand, that the soul was immortal,—that it was a harmony of heat, cold, moisture, and dryness,—that it was part of one universal soul, or that different souls might be possessed by one individual.† Thus it was an opinion, that, after the dissolution of the body, every man was possessed of three different kinds of ghosts, which were distinguished by the names of Manes, Anima, and Umbra. These were disposed of after the following manner: the Manes descended into the infernal regions, the

---

* Farmer on Worship of Human Spirits, page 434.

† For a summary of the opinions entertained by the ancients on this subject, see Dr Barclay's Inquiry into the Opinions, Ancient and Modern, concerning Life and Organization, section 2d and 3d. A more valuable present to philosophy has seldom been rendered, than by this successful exposure of ancient and modern errors concerning matter and mind.

Anima ascended to the skies, and the Umbra hovered about the tomb, as being unwilling to quit its connexion with the body. Dido, for instance, when about to die, threatens to haunt Æneas with her *umbra;* at the same time, she expects that the tidings of his punishment will rejoin her *manes* below.*

Lucretius conceived, that the various apparitions of deceased friends were subtle images which constantly rose from the surfaces of all bodies, which made an impression on our organs of sense, and which communicated this notion to the soul. This opinion, strange as it is, entered more or less into many systems on the same subject, which were taught by the schoolmen of the middle ages, although the obligation due to Lucretius has not been generally acknowledged.†

---

* For the notion of this threefold soul, see the verses attributed to Ovid:—

"Bis duo sunt homini: MANES, CARO, SPIRITUS, UMBRA:
Quatuor ista loci bis duo suscipiunt,
Terra tegit CARNEM, tumulum circumvolat UMBRA,
Orcus habet MANES, SPIRITUS astra petit."

† We detect a similar view in the reveries of the sympathetic philosophers of the eighteenth century, and in the doctrine of the transmission of spirits, which was taught by Lavater. Yet older philosophers (Psellus for instance) were so heretical, as to believe that demons were material. Paracelsus, who conceived that the elements were inhabited by four kinds of demons, viz. spirits, nymphs, pigmies, and salamanders, also argued their materiality, but thought they possessed *caro non-adamica.* Cudworth maintained the materiality of angels. But, as I have no leisure at present to enter into a view of these very learned disquisitions, I must re-

But it is unnecessary to allude any more to opinions of this kind, chiefly pneumatological, which were entertained by the Greeks and the Romans relative to ghosts. It is sufficient to say, that the notion of souls revisiting the globe after death has been a popular creed, not confined to the vulgar, but supported by modern no less than by ancient philosophers.

---

sign the discussion to other hands; and, for this purpose, shall take the liberty of introducing the gentle reader to a set of very modest and unassuming pneumatologists, who, in the opinions they advance on this same puzzling subject of spirits, only repeat the doctrines which they have heard from authority that none may question. When the Gardener, in Addison's sprightly comedy of the Drummer, inquires " how the spirit gets into the house when all the gates are shut," the following dialogue occurs :—

Butler. Why, look ye, Peter, your spirit will creep you into an augre-hole. He'll whisk you through a key-hole, without so much as justling against one of the wards.

Coachman. I verily believe I saw him last night in the Town-close.

Gardener. How did he appear?

Coachman. Like a white horse.

Butler. Pho, Robin, I tell you he has never appeared yet, but in the shape of the sound of a drum.

Coachman. This almost makes one afraid of one's own shadow. As I was walking from the stable t'other night without my lantern, I fell across a beam, and I thought I had stumbled over a spirit.

Butler. Thou might'st as well have stumbled over a straw. Why a spirit is such a little, little thing, that I have heard a man who was a great scholar say, that he'll dance ye a Lancashire hornpipe upon the point of a needle.

The opinions relative to apparitions which may be found in Jewish traditions, proceed upon the doctrine subsequently entertained by Christians, that the spirits of the dead were souls that had obtained a sort of temporary respite from the pains of purgatory, to which they had become subject after death. It was even supposed that the righteous were conducted through hell, that they might be completely purified in the fiery river Dinnur, before they could ascend into paradise. In conformity with this opinion, several ghost-stories are recorded by the Jews, relative to the conversations which the living had with the dead. A few of these I shall give; the first being a dialogue which took place between Turnus Rufus and the ghost of his father.

"It happened," say the Rabbins, "that the wicked Turnus Rufus met Rabbi Akkiva on a Sabbath-day; and he asked the Rabbi what the difference was between that day and another? Then did Rabbi Akkiva ask him, 'What difference there was between one man and another?' 'What is the difference,' says the Rabbin, 'between thee and another man, that thou art by thy Lord advanced to the dignity thou possessest, and that others are not so much esteemed?' Turnus Rufus replied, 'It was because his Lord would have it so.' Rabbi Akkiva replied,—' I also honour the Sabbath, because my lord will have it so: as it is the will of thy lord that thou shouldst be honoured; so it is the will of the King of kings that we should honour the Sabbath.' 'Why then,' demanded Turnus Rufus, ' doth this God of yours do any work on the Sabbath?' 'What work doth he do?'

said the Rabbin. Turnus Rufus replied, ' The very work he doth on other days: He maketh the wind to blow and the rain to fall, the clouds to ascend, the sun and moon to rise, and the fruits to ripen.' Whereupon Rabbi Akkiva said to him, ' I know well that thou art skilled in the laws of the Hebrews. When two live together in the same court, then doth the one give to the other the mutual token (or an instrument, by which they agree, according to the law, concerning the office of carrying to and from one another on the Sabbath,) and they are allowed to carry certain things from one place to another. But one who liveth alone in a court, though the court were as large as Antioch, carrieth in that court certain things to land again, because there is no other to take that office upon him. Now, heaven is the throne of the holy and blessed God, and the earth is his foot-stool, and the whole earth is full of his glory: And there is no power in his world for to contend with him. Moreover, those who did eat the manna in the wilderness were witnesses of the (distinction it pleased God to annex to the) Sabbath, because the manna fell every day on the week but on the Sabbath. But this is not all: For the river Sabbatjon clearly shews this distinction, since it floweth during the six days, but floweth not on the Sabbath.' Then, replied Turnus Rufus, ' Speak no more of the manna; for no such thing as its falling hath happened in our days. And for the river Sabbatjon, I do not believe it.' Then said Rabbi Akkiva to him, ' Go to the soothsayers and diviners, and they will convince thee: For on every day of the week but the Sabbath they can, each in his way, make their divinations hit well enough; but on the Sabbath they labour in vain. Get thee to thy father's grave for information; for thou shalt on every day but the Sabbath perceive a smoke to arise from it; but on the Sabbath thou shalt perceive no such matter. If the dead, then, can discern and distinguish the Sabbath, how comes it to pass that the living are ignorant of it and neglect it?'

" Upon this, Turnus Rufus went and beheld his father's grave, but could perceive no smoke to ascend from it. And he said to Rabbi Akkiva, ' Perhaps his punishment is at an end.' The Rabbi answered, ' Thou shalt see the smoke to-morrow.' And when Turnus Rufus saw, on the first day of the week, the smoke ascend from the grave, he caused his father to be raised out of his grave by necromancy; and he said to him, ' Thou didst not in thy life-time keep the Sabbath, but now thou art among the dead thou observest it. How long is it since thou turnedst Jew?' Then answered his father, ' My son, every one among you that keepeth not the Sabbath in a becoming manner, shall, when he cometh among us, observe it against his will.' Then asked Turnus Rufus, ' What is it ye do on the working days?' And his father answered, ' We are punished on every working-day; but on the Sabbath we have rest. On the eve of the Sabbath, a voice is heard from heaven, saying, ' Let the wicked out, that they may have rest.' And there is an angel, who is set over us, who punisheth us every day. And at the end of the Sabbath, when the Sedarim, or the Jewish form of prayers, is ended, the same angel calls aloud, saying, ' Ye wicked, get ye again into hell; for the Israelites have ended their form of prayer.'"*

A second ghost-story relates a dialogue of the Rabbi Akkiva with an individual, who was condemned after death to carry wood for fuel to the fire of hell. "It happened, that as Rabbi Akkiva, at a certain place, was going to a funeral, he met a man, who had a burden of wood upon his back, with which he run with the speed of a horse. Rabbi Akkiva stopt him, and said to him, 'My son, how cometh it to pass, that thou undergoest such heavy labour? if thou art a slave, and thy master yokes thee to this burden, I will purchase thy freedom, and deliver thee from him. If it be thy poverty that is the cause, I will enrich thee.' The man answered, 'My lord, suffer me to go on; for I must not stop.' Then did Rabbi Akkiva ask him, 'Art thou a devil or a human being?' And he was answered, 'I died, and am now obliged to fetch wood for fuel to the fire' (of hell, we suppose.) 'What,' said the Rabbin, 'was thy business in thy life-time?' And he was answered, 'I was an exciseman. I favoured the rich, and oppressed the poor. But that is not all: on the day of atonement I lay with a virgin, who was betrothed to me.' Then said Rabbi Akkiva, 'My son, hast thou ever heard from those that are set over thee in hell, whether there be any means by which thou mayest be delivered from thence?' And he was answered, 'Detain me no longer, lest my stay provoke my punishers to anger;

---

* Stehelin's Tradition of the Jews, vol. ii. p. 56.

for there is no help for me. Nor have I heard of any means that might procure my redemption, excepting one: They have said, if thou hast a son, who could stand in the congregation, and there say, 'Blessed be the blessed Lord, (words at the head of a certain Jewish prayer) thou wouldest be delivered from this punishment.' 'But I have not a son. Indeed, when I died, I left my wife with child; but I know not whether she bore a son or a daughter. And if she bore a son (and he be still living) there is no knowing for me, whether he be instructed in the law.' Then did Rabbi Akkiva ask him his name, and his wife's name, and the name of the city where he dwelt. He replied, 'My name is Akkiva, and my wife's name Susmira, and the city where I dwelt is called Alduca.' Then did Rabbi Akkiva lament for him.

"And the Rabbi went from city to city till he came to the city Alduca; and there he asked where the man and where his house was? And the people made answer, 'May his bones be bruised in hell.' And he asked after the man's wife, and was answered, 'Let her name be rooted out of the world.' Then he inquired after the man's son, and was answered, that the son was not circumcised, and that his parents had no regard to that covenant.

"Then took Rabbi Akkiva the lad, and made him sit before him, in order to instruct him in the law. But he could not be instructed, until, for his sake, Rabbi Akkiva had fasted forty days; when a voice came from heaven, saying, 'Fastest thou thus for his sake?' And he answered, 'Yea.' And then the lad read the alphabet, till Rabbi Akkiva had brought him to his house, and taught him the prayer at meat, and the shema, (*i. e.* the words in Deut. vi. 4. 'Hear, O Israel,') and the Prayer Book. Then did he (Rabbi Akkiva) place him properly; and the lad prayed, and said, 'Blessed be the blessed Lord for ever.' And in the same hour his father was freed from hell.'

"And the Father appeared in a dream to the Rabbi Akkiva, and said to him, 'May the rest of Paradise be thy portion, because thou hast rescued me from the punishment of hell.' Then began the Rabbi Akkiva to say, 'Thy name, O Lord, endureth for ever, and thy memorial, O Lord, throughout all generations.'"*

A third narrative, *farinæ ejusdem*, I shall give at length on account of the precept that the fable is intended to convey.

"There happened something remarkable in the holy community at Worms. It fell out that a Jew, whose name was Ponim, an ancient man, whose business was altogether about the dead, coming to the door of the school, saw one standing there who had a garland on his head. Then was Rabbi Ponim afraid, imagining it was a spirit. Whereupon he whom the Rabbi saw called to him, saying, 'Be not afraid, but pass forward: Dost not thou know me?' Then said Rabbi Ponim, 'Art not thou he whom I buried yesterday?' And he was answered, 'Yea, I am he.' Upon which Rabbi Ponim said, 'Why comest thou hither? How fareth it with thee in the other

---

* Stehelin's Tradition of the Jews, vol. ii. p. 64.

world?' And the apparition made answer, 'It goeth well with me, and I am in high esteem in Paradise.' Then said the Rabbi, 'Thou wert but looked upon in the world as an insignificant Jew. What good work didst thou that thou art esteemed?' The apparition answered, 'I will tell thee: The reason of the esteem I am in is, that I rose every morning early, and with fervency uttered my prayer, and offered the grace from the bottom of my heart; for which reason I now pronounce grace in Paradise, and am well respected. If thou doubtest whether I am the person, I will show thee a token that shall convince thee of it. Yesterday, when thou didst clothe me in my funeral attire, thou didst tear my sleeve.' Then asked Rabbi Ponim, 'What is the meaning of that garland?' The apparition answered, 'I wear it to the end the wind of the world may not have power over me; for it consists of excellent herbs of Paradise.' Then did Rabbi Ponim mend the sleeve of the deceased; for the deceased had said, that if it was not mended, he should be ashamed to be seen among others whose apparel was whole. And then the apparition vanished. Wherefore let every one utter his prayer with fervency, for then it will go well with him in the other world: and let care be taken, that no rent or tearing be left in the apparel in which the dead are interred."[*]

The opinions entertained by the early Christians respecting ghosts may now be noticed. Origen conceived that souls which had been guilty of flagrant

---

[*] Stehelin's Tradition of the Jews, vol. ii. p. 19.

crimes, and were not purged of their impurity, sometimes were lodged in buildings, or were attached to other places. Other theologians condemned all visions or apparitions that had not the unequivocal sanction of the Deity, our Saviour, or the angels. Athanasius maintained, that when souls were once released from their bodies, they held no more communion with mortal men. Augustine remarked, that if souls did actually walk and visit their friends, he was convinced that his mother, who had followed him by land and by sea, would have shewn herself to him, in order to inform him what she had learned in another state, as well as to give him much useful advice.

The notions regarding ghosts which were entertained during the Christian era, but more particularly during the middle ages, are very multifarious; yet these, with the authorities annexed to them, have been most industriously collected by Reginald Scot. His researches are replete with amusement and instruction. "And, first," says he, "you shall understand, that they hold that all the soules in heaven may come downe and appeare to us when they list, and assume anie bodie saving their owne: otherwise (saie they) such soules should not be perfectlie happie. They saie that you may know the good soules from the bad very easilie. For a damned soule hath a very heavie and sowre looke; but a saint's soule hath a cheerfull and a merrie countenance: these also are white and shining, the other cole black. And these damned soules also may come up out of hell at their pleasure, although Abraham made Dives beleeve the contrarie. They affirme, that damned soules walke oftenest: next unto them, the soules of purgatorie; and most seldome the soules of saints. Also they saie, that in the old lawe soules did appeare seldome; and after doomsdaie they shall never be seene more: in the time of grace they shall be most frequent. The walking of these souls (saith Michael Andræas) is a most excellent argument for the proofe of purgatorie; for (saith he) those soules have testified that which the popes have affirmed in that behalfe; to wit, that there is not onelie such a place of punishment, but that they are released from thence by masses, and such other satisfactorie works; whereby the goodnes of the masse is also ratified and confirmed.

"These heavenlie or purgatorie soules (saie they) appeare most commonlie to them that are borne upon Ember daies: because we are in best state at that time to praie for the one, and to keep companie with the other. Also, they saie, that soules appeare oftenest by night; because men may then be at best leasure, and most quiet. Also, they never appeare to the whole multitude, seldome to a few, and most commonlie to one alone: for so one may tell a lie without controlment. Also, they are oftenest seene by them that are readie to die: as Trasilla saw Pope Fœlix; Ursine, Peter and Paule; Galla Romana, S. Peter; and as Musa the maid sawe our Ladie: which are the most certaine appearances, credited and allowed in the church of Rome: also, they may be seene of some, and of some other in that presence not seene at all, as Ursine sawe Peter and Paule, and yet manie at that instant being present could not see anie such sight, but thought it a lie, as I do. Michael Andræas confesseth, that papists see more visions than protestants: he saith also, that a good soule can take none other shape than a man; manie a damned soule may and dooth take the shape of a blacke moore, or of a beaste, or of a serpent, or speciallie of an heretike."

Such is the account which Scot has given regarding the Popish opinion of departed spirits. In another part of his work, he triumphantly asks, " Where are the soules that swarmed in time past? Where are the spirits? Who heareth their noises? Who seeth their visions? Where are the soules that made such mone for trentals, whereby to be eased of their pains in purgatorie? Are they all gone into Italie, because masses are growne deere here in England?—The whole course may be perceived to be a false practise, and a counterfeit vision, or rather a lewd invention. For in heaven men's soules remaine not in sorow and care; neither studie they there how to compasse and get a worshipfull burial here in earth. If they did, they would not have foreslowed it so long. Now, therefore, let us not suffer ourselves to be abused anie longer, either with conjuring priests, or melancholicall witches; but be thankfull to God that hath delivered us from such blindness and error."*—This is the congratulation of a true protestant at an early period of the Reformation.

The early Popish church, as we might expect, has

---

* Scot's Discoverie of Witchcraft, book xv. chap. 39; also Discourse on Devils and Spirits, chap. 28.

favoured the world with numerous stories of apparitions, the subject of which is generally connected with the doctrine of Purgatory. I shall give Reginald Scot's abstract of one of these narratives, which was taken, as he assures us, " out of the rosarie of our ladie, in which booke do remaine (besides this) ninetie and eight examples to this effect, which are of such authoritie in the church of Rome, that all Scripture must give place unto them."

" A certeine hangman passing by the image of our ladie, saluted hir, commending himself to hir protection. Afterwards, while he praied before hir, he was called awaie to hang an offender; but his enemies intercepted him, and slew him by the waie. And lo! a certeine holie preest, which nightlie walked about everie church in the citie, rose up that night, and was going to his ladie, I should saie to our ladie church. And in the churchyard he saw a great manie dead men, and some of them he knew, of whome he asked what the matter was, and who answered, that the hangman was slaine, and the divell challenged his soule, the which our ladie said was hirs: and the judge was even at hand, coming thither to heare the cause, and therefore (said they) we are now come togither. The preest thought he would be at the hearing hereof, and hid himself behind a tree, and anon he saw the judicial seat readie prepared and furnished, where the judge, to wit, Jesus Christ, sate, who tooke up his mother unto him. Soon after the divels brought in the hangman pinioned, and proved by good evidence that his soule belonged to them. On the other side, our ladie pleaded for the hangman, proving that he, at the houre of death, commended his soule to hir. The judge hearing the matter so well debated on either side, but willing to obeie (for these are his words) his mother's desire, and loath to doo the divels anie wrong, gave sentence, that the hangman's soule should return to his bodie, until he had made sufficient satisfaction; ordeiring that the Pope should set foorth a publike forme of praier for the hangman's soule. It was demanded, who should do the arrand to the Pope's holiness. Marie, quoth our ladie, that shall yonder preest that lurketh behind the tree. The priest being called foorth, and injoined to make relation hereof, and to desire the Pope to take the paines to doo according to this decree, asked by what token he should be directed. Then was delivered unto him a rose of such beautie, as when the Pope saw it, he knew his message was true."

But although it is certain, that with the disbelief of a future state of purgatory, taught by the Romish church, the communication of the living with the dead became much less frequent, Protestants still continued to entertain numerous opinions on the subject of apparitions, which fully equalled in absurdity the superstitious notions of the church they so zealously opposed. A host of imaginary phantoms, the history of which I have attempted to trace, derived from Celtic and Teutonic mythologies, and even from eastern tales, gave rise to new fables, to new dreams, and to new spectral impressions. Scot, in his Discovery of Witchcraft, remarks on this subject, " And know you this, by the waie, that hertofor Robin Goodfellow and Hobgobblin were as terrible, and also credible, to the people, as hags and witches be now;—and, in truth, they that maintaine walking spirits, with their transformation, &c., have no reason to denie Robin Goodfellow, upon whom there hath gone as manie and as credible tales as upon witches; saving, that it hath not pleased the translators of the Bible to call spirits by the name of Robin Goodfellow, as they have termed diviners, soothsaiers, poisoners, and coseners, by the name of witches."

Nor did these opinions so soon lose ground; they were popular in all parts of Britain until the middle of the last century; and, even at the present day, the demoniacal influence of fairies, and other mythological sprites, is acknowledged in such sequestered districts as Wales, the Western Highlands of Scotland, Orkney, and Shetland. The notion, however, of souls revisiting our globe after death, has met with more extensive support, since it was a creed to which even philosophers were not ashamed to subscribe. To a volume, for instance, of Dr Archibald Pitcairn's Latin poems, which I have lately seen, are prefixed several MS. anecdotes relative to his family, which are from some one evidently on terms of intimacy with him. Among these, a dream of the doctor is recorded, the circumstances of which appear to have been dictated by himself. The narrative is as follows:—

" Robert Lindsay, grandchild, or great-grandchild, to Sir David Lindsay of ye Month, Lyon King at Arms, &c., being intimate condisciple with A. P., they bargained, *anno* 1671, that whoever dyed first should give account of his condition if possible. It happened that he dyed about the end of 1675, while A. P. was at Parise; and the very night of his death A. P. dreamed that he was at Edinburgh, where Lindsay attacked him thus:—' Archie,' said he, ' perhaps ye heard I'm dead?'—' No, Roben.'—' Ay, but they burie my body in the Greyfryers. I am alive, though in a place whereof the pleasures cannot be exprest in Scotch, Greek, or Latine. I have come with a well-sailing small ship to Leith Road, to carry you thither.'—' Roben, I'll go with you, but wait till I go to Fife and East Lothian, and take leave of my parents.'—' Archie, I have but the allowance of one tide. Farewell, I'll come for you at another time.' Since which time A. P. never slept a night without dreaming that Lindsay told him he was alive. And having a dangerous sickness, *anno* 1694, he was told by Roben that he was delayed for a time, and that it was properly his task to carry him off, but was discharged to tell when.*

But among the well-informed classes of Great Britain, the belief in apparitions would probably have ceased to exist about the commencement of the 18th century, if an important circumstance had not occurred, which was materially connected with the history of these illusions. Very loose, and even atheistical opinions, relative to a future state of existence, began to prevail, and hence arose that fashionable class of sceptics, who self-dubbed themselves *free-thinkers*. Numbers of persons, some of whom were

---

* For this curious ghost-story I am indebted to David Laing, Esq. of Edinburgh.

distinguished for their great attainments, then began to consider, if some additional arguments might not be produced to oppose the torrent of infidelity that prevailed, besides what they could procure from the sacred writings. In turning their attention to this subject, it was conceived that a direct evidence in favour of a future state might be advanced, if the Platonic notion could be established, that there existed an occasional intercourse between the spiritual denizens of another world and the living inhabitants of this earth. A speculation of this kind was accordingly revived; and from the time of Addison down to that of the author of Rasselas, we find the greatest names enrolled among its supporters. They wished, as Dr Johnson has frankly confessed, additional evidence besides what the Holy Bible contained, concerning a future state of existence.

This, then, was the true motive why so many idle stories relative to apparitions were fabricated at the commencement and the middle of the last century;— it was to supply the demand of those individuals who wished to confute with them the infidel opinions of the freethinkers. " For, says Mr Wesley, in the following remarkable confession, " it is true that the English in general, and indeed most of the men in Europe, have given up all accounts of witches and apparitions as mere old wifes' fables. I am sorry for it; and I willingly take this opportunity of entering my solemn protest against this violent compliment, which so many that believe the Bible pay to those who do not believe it. I owe them no such service. I take knowledge, these are at the bottom of the outcry which has been raised, and with such insolence spread throughout the nation, in direct opposition not only to the Bible, but to the suffrage of the wisest and best of men in all ages and nations. They well know (whether Christians know it or not) that the giving up witchcraft is, in effect, giving up the Bible. And they know, on the other hand, that if but one account of the intercourse of men with separate spirits be admitted, their whole castle in the air (deism, atheism, materialism,) falls to the ground. I know no reason, therefore, why we should suffer even this weapon to be wrested out of our hands. Indeed there are numerous arguments besides, which abundantly confute their vain imaginations. But we need not be hooted out of one,—neither reason nor religion requires this."

I have no other view in quoting the foregoing passage from Mr Wesley's works, than to shew the spirit with which he, and many other truly pious individuals, were impressed, when they wished to revive the belief in apparitions, which was evidently beginning to lose ground. The anxiety they manifested to listen to all stories of a supernatural cast, soon gave rise to a host of needy romance-writers, who got up " well-authenticated" ghost-stories as fast as the anti-freethinkers were able to swallow them. It was in this period that the exquisite story was invented of the ghost of Mrs Veal, who came into the world for no other purpose than to assure Mrs Bargrave, that, from her actual knowledge of another state of existence, " Drelincourt's book of death was the best on that subject ever written." Of course, the story of Mrs

Veal (a good bookseller's puff) naturally found its way into the preface to the translation of Drelincourt. Another romance of the same sort was the popular story of Lord Littleton's warning, said to have been received by him before death. But let us be thankful, that we live in an age when the truths which are contained in the Holy Scriptures need no additional confirmation from apparitions.

There were, again, other efforts made, but assuredly of the most ridiculous kind, for the purpose of confuting the freethinkers. These consisted of deputations, instituted even by John Aubrey, Esq. F. R. S. which were sent to the poor illiterate Highlanders, in order to procure all the evidence that could be collected from this superstitious source of intelligence respecting a future state of existence. "From the certainty of dreams, second sight, and apparitions," says Theophilus Insulanus, "follows the plain and natural consequence of the existence of spirits, immateriality, and immortality of the soul." The author then proceeds in a lavish abuse of atheists, deists, and freethinkers, " those adepts in science, that refine themselves into infidelity, who are the nuisances of society, and the disgrace of human nature,—who bring themselves on a level with the brute beasts that perish."

The general result, attending the researches of the gentlemen who consulted the Highlanders for the purpose of confuting the freethinkers, may now be stated. They found out that the visions of second sight were often of a prophetic nature. It is said, in one of the numerous illustrations given of this faculty, that " Sir Normand M'Leod, who has his residence in the isle of Bernera, which lies between the isle of North-Uist and Harries, went to the isle of Skye about business, without appointing any time for his return: his servants, in his absence, being altogether in the large hall at night, one of them, who had been accustomed to see the second sight, told the rest they must remove, for they would have abundance of other company that night. One of his fellow-servants answered, that there was very little appearance of that, and if he had seen any vision of company, it was not like to be accomplished this night; but the seer insisted upon it that it was. They continued to argue the improbability of it, because of the darkness of the night, and the danger of coming through the rocks that lie round the isle; but within an hour after, one of Sir Normand's men came to the house, bidding them provide lights, &c., for his master had newly landed." *

---

* The more frequent uncertainty, however, of these ghostly predictions, is not unaptly illustrated in the Table-Talk of Johnson. "An acquaintance," remarks Boswell, "on whose veracity I can depend, told me that, walking home one evening at Kilmarnock, he heard himself called from a wood, by the voice of a brother who had gone to America, and the next packet brought an account of that brother's death. Macbean asserted, that this inexplicable *calling* was a thing very well known. Dr Johnson said, that one day at Oxford, as he was turning the key of his chamber, he heard his mother distinctly calling *Sam*. She was then at Litchfield; but *nothing ensued*." This casual admission, which, in the course of conversation, transpired from a man, *him-*

But the discovery of Aubrey and others, that the visions of second sight disclosed future events, might have been readily anticipated, when we reflect that, from the remotest antiquity, there has scarcely existed a religious institution, of which prophets have not formed a component part. And when we consider that the Highlands were peopled both by a Celtic and Teutonic stock, it is far from improbable that the modern Gaelic seer is the genuine successor either of the Celtic bard or of the Northern Scald; his ecstatic illusions having been the most effective when they partook of the imagery which an early distracted state of the country would suggest.* But the time is past, when the gleaming swords of hostile clans stained the Highland plains with that blood which now is only shed for mutual defence.

In the next place, the praiseworthy individuals who undertook to prove " the existence of spirits, the immateriality and immortality of the soul," from the morbid as well as pretended visions of the Highland seer, learned (and how appalling to their sneering opponents must have been the knowledge of the important fact), that the spirit Brownie was a common object of second sight! " Sir Norman Macleod, and some others," say these delectable theologians, "playing at tables, at a game called by the Irish Falmer-

---

self strongly tainted with superstition, precludes many farther remarks on the prophetic nature of these impressions, which would now indeed be highly superfluous.

* See note 4.

more, wherein there are three of a side, and each of them throw the dice by turns, there happened to be one difficult point in the disposing of one of the tablemen. This obliged the gamester to deliberate before he was to change his man, since upon the disposing of it the winning or losing of the game depended. At last the butler, who stood behind, advised the player where to place his man, with which he complied, and won the game. This being thought extraordinary, and Sir Normand hearing one whisper him in the ear, asked who advised him so skilfully? He answered, it was the butler; but this seemed more strange, for he could not play at tables. Upon this, Sir Normand asked him how long it was since he had learned to play? and the fellow owned that he never played in his life; but that he saw the spirit Browny reaching his arm over the player's head, and touching the part with his finger on the point where the tableman was to be placed."

The last discovery which the theologians made who visited the Northern seers, was, that the second sight was " a thing very troublesome to them that had it; and that they would gladly be rid of it. For if the object was a thing that was terrible, they were seen to sweat and tremble, and shriek at the apparition. At other times they laughed and told the thing cheerfully, just according as the thing was pleasant or astonishing." They found that " it was ordinary with seers to see houses, gardens, and trees, in places void of all these;" that " some found themselves, as it were, in a crowd of people;" that visions were seen in night when colours could not otherwise be distinguished. This is in fact the only information that is worth any notice regarding the second sight of the Highlanders. But the active scientific gentlemen, who wished to silence the freethinkers by their researches, were not thus content. They found that children, horses, and cows, possessed the second sight; that the second sight might be communicated by sympathy; and *"that any person that pleased might get it taught him for a pound of tobacco."*

Really, it is impossible to seriously proceed any farther in describing this faculty of the gifted seer,—a faculty which so seriously engaged the contemplative mind of that great *colossus of literature* (as his admirers call him), Dr Johnson. Suffice it to say, that by the latest information derived from the Highlands, *Deuteroscopia* is now scarcely known. "To have circumnavigated the Western Isles," says Dr Macculloch, in the following excellent remarks, "without even mentioning the second sight, would be unpardonable. No inhabitant of St Kilda pretends to have been forewarned of our arrival; ceasing to be believed, it has ceased to exist. It is indifferent whether the propagators of an imposture, or of a piece of supernatural philosophy, be punished or rewarded. In either case the public attention is directed towards the agent; whether by the burning of the witch, or by the flattering distinction which attended the Highland seer. When witches were no longer burnt, witchcraft disappeared. Since the second sight has been limited to a doting old woman, or a hypochondrical tailor, it has been a subject for ridicule; and, in matters of this nature, ridicule is death."*

Thus, then, I have endeavoured to shew, that the commencement of the eighteenth century was a period in which, for special purposes, many ghost-stories were revived, and even new ones were fabricated. The author to whom I have alluded, styling himself Theophilus Insulanus, even affixes the term of *irreligious* to those who should entertain a doubt on the reality of apparitions of departed souls. " Such ghostly visitants," he gravely affirms, " are not employed on an errand of a frivolous concern to lead us into error." With due deference, however, to this anonymous writer, whom I should scarcely have noticed, if he had not echoed in this assertion an opinion which was at the time popular, I shall advert to the opposite sentiments expressed on the subject by a far more acute, though less serious author. The notion, for instance, of the solemn character of ghosts, and that they are never employed on frivolous errands, is but too successfully ridiculed by Grose. " In most of the relations of ghosts," says this pleasant writer, " they are supposed to be mere aerial beings without substance, and that they can pass through walls and other solid bodies at pleasure. The usual time at which ghosts make their appearance is midnight, and seldom before it is dark, though some audacious spirits have been said to appear even by daylight. Ghosts

---

* Description of the Western Isles, by Dr Macculloch, vol. ii. p. 32.

commonly appear in the same dress they usually wore when living, though they are sometimes clothed all in white; but this is chiefly the churchyard-ghosts, who have no particular business, but seem to appear *pro bono publico*, or to scare drunken rustics from tumbling over their graves. I cannot learn that ghosts carry tapers in their hands, as they are sometimes depicted, though the room in which they appear, if without fire or candle, is frequently said to be as light as day. Dragging chains is not the fashion of English ghosts; chains and black vestments being chiefly the accoutrements of foreign spectres, seen in arbitrary governments: dead or alive, English spirits are free. If, during the time of an apparition, there is a lighted candle in the room, it will burn extremely blue: this is so universally acknowledged, that many eminent philosophers have busied themselves in accounting for it, without ever doubting the truth of the fact. Dogs too have the faculty of seeing spirits."*

There are several other minute particulars respecting ghosts given by this author, for the insertion of which I have not room; yet it would be inexcusable to omit noticing the account which he has subjoined, of the strange mode in which spirits execute the awfully momentous errands upon which they are sent. " It is somewhat remarkable," he adds, " that ghosts do not go about their business like the persons of this

---

* " As I sat in the pantry last night counting my spoons," says the Butler, in the comedy of the Drummer, " the candle methought burnt blue, and the spay'd bitch look'd as if she saw something."

world. In cases of murder, a ghost, instead of going to the next justice of the peace, and laying its information, or to the nearest relation of the person murdered, appears to some poor labourer who knows none of the parties; draws the curtain of some decrepit nurse, or alms-woman; or hovers about the place where his body is deposited. The same circuitous mode is pursued with respect to redressing injured orphans or widows; when it seems, as if the shortest and most certain way would be, to go to the person guilty of the injustice, and haunt him continually till he be terrified into a restitution. Nor are the pointing out lost writings generally managed in a more summary way; the ghost commonly applying to a third person, ignorant of the whole affair, and a stranger to all concerned. But it is presumptuous to scrutinize far into these matters;—ghosts have undoubtedly forms and customs peculiar to themselves."*

---

* I find, in a recent publication of great merit, the incidents of a ghost-story, told by Clarendon, relative to the Duke of Buckingham, which are commented on in the following manner:— "This noble historian interrupts his narrative with a long story about the ghost of Sir George Villiers, the Duke's father, having given a warning of his son's fate no seldomer than three times. Like ghosts, in general, this was a very silly one; for, instead of going directly to his son, (was the spirit under the same sycophantish awe with the living followers of the Duke?) the phantom carried its errand to an officer of the wardrobe, whom in life it had paid attention to at school, but whose situation was too mean to warrant his going directly with the important intelligence to the favourite. The man neglected the warning till the third time, and

The view which Grose has taken of the character of most stories about departed spirits is pretty correct, although I have certainly read of some spirits whose errands to the earth have been much more direct. One ghost, for instance, has terrified a man into the restitution of lands, which had been bequeathed to the poor of a village. A second spirit has adopted the same plan for recovering property of which a nephew had been wronged; but a third has haunted a house for no other purpose than to kick up a row in it—to knock about chairs, tables, or other furniture. Glanville relates a story, of the date of 1632, in which a man, upon the alleged information of a female spirit, who came by her death foully, led the officers of justice to the pit where a mangled corpse was concealed, charged two individuals with her murder; and, upon the strength of this fictitious story, the poor fellows were condemned and executed, although

---

then he went to a gentleman to whom he was well known, Sir Ralph Freeman, one of the masters of the requests, who had married a lady nearly allied to the Duke, and prevailed with him to apply to his Grace to grant the officer of the wardrobe an opportunity of speaking with him privately on a subject of the utmost consequence to his Grace. The man gave sufficient information, which he had got from the ghost, relative to Buckingham's private affairs, to satisfy the Duke that he was no impostor, and the Duke was observed to be very melancholy afterwards. But to what all this warning tended, except to create uneasiness at some impending calamity, it is impossible to conceive, since the hint was too dark and mysterious to enable him to provide against the danger?"—*History of the British Empire, by George Brodie, Esq.* vol. ii, p. 209.

they solemnly persevered to the last in maintaining their innocence. It is but too evident, in this case, by whom the atrocious deed had been committed.

There is, however, another point of view in which apparitions have been considered. It has been said that they arise for special purposes connected with the extension of our holy religion. "These ghostly visitants," says Theophilus Insulanus, "are employed as so many heralds by the great Creator, for the more ample demonstration of his power, to proclaim tidings for our instruction; and, as we are prone to despond in religious matters, to confirm our faith of the existence of spirits (the foundation of all religions), and the dignity of human nature." Dr Doddridge, professing exactly similar sentiments, published in corroboration of them the remarkable story of Colonel Gardiner's conversion. "This memorable event," says the pious writer, "happened towards the middle of July, 1719. The Major had spent the evening (and, if I mistake not, it was the Sabbath) in some gay company, and had an unhappy assignation with a married woman, whom he was to attend exactly at twelve. The company broke up about eleven, and, not judging it convenient to anticipate the time appointed, he went into his chamber to kill the tedious hour perhaps with some amusing book or some other way. But it very accidentally happened, that he took up a religious book which his good mother or aunt had, without his knowledge, slipped into his portmanteau. It was called, if I remember the title exactly, The Christian Soldier, or Heaven taken by Storm; and it was written by Mr Thomas Watson.

Guessing by the title of it, that he would find some phrases of his own profession spiritualized in a manner which, he thought, might afford him some diversion, he resolved to dip into it; but he took no serious notice of any thing it had in it; and yet, while this book was in his hand, an impression was made upon his mind (perhaps God only knows how,) which drew after it a train of the most important and happy consequences.—He thought he saw an unusual blaze of light fall upon the book while he was reading, which he at first imagined might happen by some accident in the candle; but, lifting up his eyes, he apprehended, to his extreme amazement, that there was before him, as it were suspended in the air, a visible representation of the Lord Jesus Christ upon the cross, surrounded on all sides with a glory; and was impressed, as if a voice or something equivalent to a voice had come to him, to this effect, (for he was not confident as to the words,) 'Oh, sinner! did I suffer this for thee, and are these thy returns?' Struck with so amazing a phenomenon as this, there remained hardly any life in him; so that he sunk down in the arm-chair in which he sat, and continued, he knew not how long, insensible."

With regard to this vision,—the appearance of our Saviour on the cross, and the awful words repeated, can be considered in no other light than as so many recollected images of the mind, which probably had their origin in the language of some urgent appeal to repentance that the Colonel might have casually read or heard delivered. From what cause, however, such ideas were rendered as vivid as actual impressions, we have no information to be depended upon.* The illusion was certainly attended with one of the most important of consequences connected with the Christian dispensation—the conversion of a sinner. And hence, no single narrative has perhaps done more to confirm the superstitious opinion, that apparitions of this awful kind cannot arise without a divine fiat. Dr Doddridge, for instance, prefaces the story with the following striking appeal:—" It is with all solemnity that I now deliver it down to posterity, as in the sight and presence of God; and I choose deliberately to expose myself to those severe censures, which the haughty but empty scorn of infidelity, or principles nearly approaching it, and effectually doing its pernicious work, may very probably dictate upon the occasion, rather than to smother a relation which may, in the judgment of my conscience, be likely to conduce so much to the glory of God, the honour of the Gospel, and the good of mankind."

These are, indeed, most solemn words,—far more solemn perhaps than the occasion required. If Dr Doddridge had merely contented himself with expressing the satisfaction, which every Christian must necessarily feel at the happy effect which the vision ultimately had upon the mind of Colonel Gardiner, he would have done more real service to true religion than by considering it as a special interposition of

---

* A short time before the vision Colonel Gardiner had received a severe fall from his horse.—Did the brain receive some slight degree of injury from the accident, so as to predispose him to this spectral illusion?

Heaven. For, could this very learned author be ignorant, that apparitions no less genuine than the one which he has recorded have never failed, during every period of time, to sanction the grossest idolatry of the Heathens, or even of papal Rome? The Doctor was doubtless unaware that there was a vision on record, the authenticity of which no one can reasonably doubt, wherein a supernatural token, no less awful than that which appeared to Colonel Gardiner, and, to all appearance, no less sanctioned by Heaven, was sent to one of the most powerful enemies to Christianity that lived in the 17th century, encouraging him to publish the book in which his dangerous tenets were contained. This singular narrative is to be found in the Autobiography of Lord Herbert of Cherbury, which I shall give in this nobleman's own words.

"My book, *De Veritate, prout distinguitur à revelatione verisimili, possibili et à falso,* having been begun by me in England, and formed there in all its principal parts, was about this time finished; all the spare hours which I could get from my visits and negociations being employed to perfect this work, which was no sooner done but that I communicated it to Hugo Grotius, that great scholar, who, having escaped his prison in the Low Countries, came into France, and was much welcomed by me and Monsieur Tieleners, also one of the greatest scholars of his time, who, after they had perused it and given it more commendations than it is fit for me to repeat, exhorted me earnestly to print and publish it; howbeit, as the frame of my whole book was so different from any thing which had been written heretofore, I found I must either renounce the authority of all that had been written formerly concerning the method of finding out truth, and consequently insist upon my own way, or hazard myself to a general censure concerning the whole argument of my book; I must confess it did not a little animate me, that the two great persons above-mentioned did so highly value it; yet, as I knew it would meet with some opposition, I did consider whether it was not better for me a while to suppress it. Being thus doubtful in my chamber one fair day in the summer, my casement being open towards the south, I took my book, *De Veritate*, in my hand, and, kneeling on my knees, devoutly said these words:

" ' O thou eternal God, author of the light which now shines upon me, and giver of all inward illuminations, I do beseech thee, of thy infinite goodness, to pardon a greater request than a sinner ought to make; I am not satisfied enough whether I shall publish this book *De Veritate;* if it be for thy glory, I beseech thee give me some sign from heaven; if not, I shall suppress it.'

" I had no sooner spoken these words, but a loud, though yet gentle noise came from the heavens, (for it was like nothing on earth,) which did so comfort and cheer me, that I took my petition as granted, and that I had the sign demanded, whereupon also I resolved to print my book.

" This, how strange soever it may seem, I protest before the eternal God is true; neither am I any way superstitiously deceived herein, since I did not only clearly hear the noise, but in the serenest sky that ever I saw, being without all cloud, did to my thinking see the place from whence it came. And now I sent my book to be printed in Paris at my cost and charges, without suffering it to be divulged to others than to such as I thought might be worthy readers of it; though afterwards, reprinting it in England, I not only dispersed it among the prime scholars in Europe, but was sent to not only from the nearest but furthest parts of Christendome, to desire the sight of my book, for which they promised any thing I should desire by way of return."

On this narrative of Lord Herbert, Dr Leland, in his "View of the Deistical Writers," makes the following remarks:—" I have no doubt of his Lordship's sincerity in this account; the serious air with which he relates it, and the solemn protestation he makes as in the presence of the eternal God, will not suffer us to question the truth of what he relates; viz., that he both made that address to God which he mentions, and that, in consequence of this, he was persuaded that he heard the noise he takes notice of, and regarded as a mark of God's approbation of the request he had made; and accordingly this great man was determined by it to publish his book. He seems to have considered it as a kind of *imprimatur* given to it from Heaven, and as signifying the Divine approbation of the book itself, and of what was contained in it."

I shall now merely observe, that the inference which was drawn from Colonel Gardiner's story is completely neutralized by this counterpart to it; by the fact, that while one special sign warns a sinner of the awful consequence of slighting the gospel, another encourages a deist to publish a work, the design of which is to completely overturn the Christian religion. Such are the contradictions which a superstitious belief in apparitions must ever involve; and well may a late writer, to whom we are indebted for some excellent remarks on Lord Herbert's life, exclaim with astonishment,—" In what strange inconsistencies may the human mind entangle itself!"*

It must be admitted, however, that, at the close of the 18th and at the commencement of the 19th century, the wish to explain the occurrence of apparitions on superstitious principles evidently declined. Nicolai, in the memoir which he read to the Royal Society of Berlin, on the appearance of spectres occasioned by disease, remarked, that a respectable member of that academy, distinguished by his merit in the science of botany, whose truth and credibility were unexceptionable, once saw, in the very room in which they were then assembled, the phantasm of the late president Maupertuis. But it appears that this ghost was seen by a philosopher, and, consequently, no attempt

---

* Retrospective Review, vol. vii. page 328.—The following are the remarks made, in this well-conducted periodical work, on Lord Herbert's vision :—" It is highly singular that a writer, holding opinions like these, should, when doubtful as to the propriety of promulgating them, look for a special revelation of the Divine pleasure. In what strange inconsistencies will the human mind entangle itself! when, on the point of publishing a book which was to prove the inefficacy of revelation, Lord Herbert put up a prayer for an especial interposition of Heaven to guide him."

was made to connect it with superstitious speculations. Mr Coleridge, who has confessed to many mental illusions, informs us that a lady once asked him if he believed in ghosts and apparitions? " I answered," said he, " with truth and simplicity, *No, madam! I have seen far too many myself.*"*

But, before quitting entirely this subject, I ought to attempt a physical explanation of many ghost-stories which may be considered as most authentic. This is seldom, however, a very easy task. There is, for instance, a story related of Viscount Dundee, whose ghost, about the time he fell at the battle of Killiecranky, appeared to Lord Balcarras, then under confinement on the suspicion of Jacobitism at the castle of Edinburgh. The spectre drew aside the curtain of his friend's bed, looked steadfastly at him, leaned for some time on the mantle-piece, and then walked out of the room. The Earl, not aware at the time that he was gazing upon a phantasm, called upon Dundee to stop. News soon arrived of the unfortunate hero's fate. Now, regarding this and other stories of the kind, however authentic they may be, the most interesting particulars are suppressed. Of the state of Lord Balcarras's health at the time, it has not been deemed necessary that a syllable should transpire. No argument, therefore, either in support of, or in opposition to, the popular belief in apparitions, can be gathered from an anecdote so deficient in any notice of the most important circumstances upon which the development of truth depends. With re-

---

* The Friend, by S. T. Coleridge, Esq. vol. i. p. 248.

gard to the spectre of Dundee appearing just at the time he fell in battle, it must be considered that, agreeably to the well-known doctrine of chances, which mathematicians have so well investigated, the event might as well occur then as at any other time, while a far greater proportion of other apparitions, less fortunate in such a supposed confirmation of their supernatural origin, is quietly allowed to sink into oblivion. Thus, it is the office of superstition to carefully select all successful coincidences of this kind, and to register them in her marvellous volumes, where for ages they have served to delude and mislead the world.

Nor can another striking narrative, to be found in Beaumont's World of Spirits, meet with any better solution. I shall give it for no other reason than because it is better told than most ghost-stories with which I am acquainted. It is dated in the year 1662, and it relates to an apparition seen by the daughter of Sir Charles Lee, immediately preceding her death. No reasonable doubt can be placed on the authenticity of the narrative, as it was drawn up by the Bishop of Gloucester from the recital of the young lady's father.

" Sir Charles Lee, by his first lady, had only one daughter, of which she died in child-birth; and when she was dead, her sister, the Lady Everard, desired to have the education of the child, and she was by her very well educated, till she was marriageable, and a match was concluded for her with Sir William Perkins, but was then prevented in an extraordinary manner. Upon a Thursday night, she, thinking she saw a light in her chamber after she was in bed, knocked for her maid, who presently came to her; and she asked, ' why she left a candle burning in her chamber?' The maid said, she ' left none, and there was none but what she had brought with her at that time;' then she said it was the fire, but that, her maid told her, was quite out; and said she believed it was only a dream; whereupon she said, it might be so, and composed herself again to sleep. But about two of the clock she was awakened again, and saw the apparition of a little woman between her curtain and her pillow, who told her she was her mother, that she was happy, and that by twelve of the clock that day she should be with her. Whereupon she knocked again for her maid, called for her clothes, and when she was dressed, went into her closet, and came not out again till nine, and then brought out with her a letter sealed to her father; brought it to her aunt, the Lady Everard, told her what had happened, and declared, that as soon as she was dead it might be sent to him. The lady thought she was suddenly fallen mad, and thereupon sent presently away to Chelmsford for a physician and surgeon, who both came immediately; but the physician could discern no indication of what the lady imagined, or of any indisposition of her body; notwithstanding the lady would needs have her let blood, which was done accordingly. And when the young woman had patiently let them do what they would with her, she desired that the chaplain might be called to read prayers; and when prayers were ended, she took her guitar and psalm-book, and sat down upon a chair without arms, and played and sung so melodiously and admirably, that her musickmaster, who was then there, admired at it. And near the stroke of twelve, she rose and sate herself down in a great chair with arms, and presently fetching a strong breathing or two, immediately expired, and was so suddenly cold, as was much wondered at by the physician and surgeon. She died at Waltham, in Essex, three miles from Chelmsford, and the letter was sent to Sir Charles, at his house in Warwickshire; but he was so afflicted with the death of his daughter, that he came not till she was buried; but when he came, he caused her to be taken up, and to be buried with her mother at Edmonton, as she desired in her letter."

This is one of the most interesting ghost-stories on record. Yet, when strictly examined, the manner in which a leading circumstance in the case is reported, affects but too much the supernatural air imparted to other of its incidents. For whatever might have been averred by a physician of the *olden time,* with regard to the young lady's sound state of health during the period she saw her mother's ghost, it may be asked,— If any practitioner at the present day would have been proud of such an opinion, especially when death followed so promptly after the spectral impression?

> —————" There's bloom upon her cheek;
> But now I see it is no living hue,
> But a strange hectic—like the unnatural red
> Which autumn plants upon the perish'd leaf."

Probably the exhausted female herself might have unintentionally contributed to the more strict verification of the ghost's prediction. It was an extraordinary exertion which her tender frame underwent, near the expected hour of its dissolution, in order that she might retire from all her scenes of earthly enjoyment with the dignity of a resigned Christian. And what subject can be conceived more worthy the masterly skill of the painter, than to depict a young and lovely saint, cheered with the bright prospect of futurity before her, and before the quivering flame of life, which for the moment was kindled up into a glow of holy ardour, had expired for ever, sweeping the strings of the guitar with her trembling fingers, and melodiously accompanying the notes with her voice, in a hymn of praise to her heavenly Maker? Entranced with such a sight, the philosopher himself would dismiss for the time his usual cold and cavilling scepticism, and, giving way to the superstitious impressions of less deliberating by-standers, partake with them in the most grateful of religious solaces, which the spectacle was so well calculated to inspire.

Regarding the confirmation, which the ghost's mission is, in the same narrative, supposed to have received from the completion of a foreboded death,—all that can be said of it is, that the coincidence was *a fortunate one;* for, without it, the story would probably have never met with a recorder, and we should have lost one of the sweetest anecdotes that private life has ever afforded. But, on the other hand, a majority of popular ghost-stories might be adduced, wherein apparitions have either visited our world without any ostensible purpose and errand whatever, or, in the circumstances of their mission, have exhibited all the inconsistency of conduct so well exposed in the quotation, which I have given from Grose, respecting departed spirits.

With respect to some other apparitions which have been recorded, the difficulty is far less to satisfactorily account for them; they may be contemplated as the illusions of well-known diseases. Thus, there can be no hesitation in considering the following apparition, given on the authority of Aubery and Turner, as having had its origin in the Delirium Tremens of drunkenness. " Mr Cassio Burroughs," says the narrator of this very choice, yet, I believe, authentic story, "was one of the most beautiful men in England, and very valiant, but very proud and blood-thirsty. There was then in London a very beautiful Italian lady," [whom he seduced]. " The gentlewoman died; and afterwards, in a tavern in London, he spake of it," [contrary to his sacred promise], " and then going" [out of doors] " the ghost of the gentlewoman did appear to him. He was afterwards troubled with the apparition of her, even sometimes in company when he was drinking. Before she did appear, he did find a kind of chilness upon his spirits. She did appear to him in the morning before he was killed in a duel."

But it is now time to review the progress which has been made in this inquiry. I have endeavoured to trace the connexion of spectral illusions with certain diseased or irritable states of the system, and to demonstrate in what manner the subject of the apparitions thus produced has corresponded with the fanciful images, which have had their origin in various popular superstitions.

Our attention will now become exclusively confined to the different subordinate incidents, which are reported to have taken place during communications held with apparitions. We shall find, that the quality and form of these unearthly visitants, their strange errands to the earth, and their seemingly capricious conduct, are not the indications of a proper world of spirits, as pneumatologists have averred, but that they merely prove the operation of certain laws of the mind, modified by the influence of those morbific causes, which are capable of imparting an undue vividness to thought. But, in pursuing this investigation, I shall often have occasion to lament that many valuable facts, which intense excitements of the mind are calculated to develop, should have been, on the one hand, distorted by superstition,* or, on the other hand, totally concealed from the world for fear of ridicule. But Nicolai's interesting detail of his own case first shewed in what light spectral impressions ought to be considered: nor can I conclude this department of my researches more appropriately, than by holding out, as a memorable example, the motives by which he was induced to examine the mental phenomena under which he laboured, and to present them to the world with an accuracy, that must ever recommend his narrative to the attentive consideration of the physiologist and of the metaphysician. His words are as follows:

---

*See Note 5.

"Had I not been able to distinguish phantasms from phenomena, I must have been insane. Had I been fanatic or superstitious, I should have been terrified at my own phantasms, and probably might have been seized with some alarming disorder. Had I been attached to the marvellous, I should have sought to magnify my own importance, by asserting that I had seen spirits; and who could have disputed the facts with me? The year 1791 would perhaps have been the time to have given importance to these apparitions. In this case, however, the advantage of sound philosophy and deliberate observation may be seen. Both prevented me from becoming either a lunatic or an enthusiast; for with nerves so strongly excited, and blood so quick in circulation, either misfortune might have easily befallen me. But I considered the phantasms that hovered around me as what they really were, namely, the effects of disease; and made them subservient to my observations, because I consider observation and reflection as the basis of all rational philosophy."

PART IV.

AN ATTEMPT TO INVESTIGATE THE MENTAL
LAWS WHICH GIVE RISE TO
SPECTRAL ILLUSIONS.

PART IV.

CHAPTER I.

GENERAL OBJECT OF THE INVESTIGATION WHICH FOLLOWS.

> Next, for 'tis time, my muse declares and sings,
> *What* those are we call images of things,——
> By day they meet, and strike our minds, and fright,
> And show pale ghosts, and horrid shapes by night.
> CREECH's *Lucretius*.

A FIT opportunity now occurs for more explicitly stating the plan upon which this dissertation has been hitherto conducted, as well as its ultimate object.

In the first place, a general view was given of the particular morbid affections with which the production of phantasms is often connected. Apparitions were likewise considered as nothing more than ideas, or the recollected images of the mind, which had been rendered more vivid than actual impressions.

In another part of this work, my object was to

point out, that, in well-authenticated ghost-stories of a supposed supernatural character, the ideas which had been rendered so unduly intense as to induce spectral illusions, might be traced to such fantastical objects of prior belief as are incorporated in the various systems of superstition, which for ages have possessed the minds of the vulgar.

In the present and far most considerable part of this treatise, the research is of a novel kind. Since apparitions are ideas equalling or exceeding in vividness actual impressions, there ought to be some important and definite laws of the mind which have given rise to this undue degree of vividness. It was chiefly, therefore, for the purpose of explaining such laws that this dissertation was written.

An investigation of this kind the late Dr Ferriar had evidently in view, when he wrote the first pages of his work, entitled, *A Theory of Apparitions*. But it must be confessed, that this entertaining author has been far more successful in affording abundant evidence of the existence of morbid impressions of this nature, without any sensible external agency, than in establishing, as he proposed, a general law of the system, to which the origin of spectral impressions could be referred. " It is a well-known law," he remarks, " that the impressions produced on some of the external senses, especially on the eye, are more durable than the application of the impressing cause." This statement comprises the whole of the writer's theory of apparitions; and the brevity with which it is given is in exact conformity with the abruptness of its dismissal; for, after being applied to explain one or two cases only of mental illusions, numerous other instances of the kind are related, but the theory is not honoured with any farther notice. This neglect, which probably arose from the reasonable doubts subsequently entertained by the author himself, of the sufficiency of his hypothesis, or, rather, of the generality of its application, will render it the less necessary for me to bestow upon it any attention. The truth is, that a proper theory of apparitions embraces the consideration, not of one law only, but of many laws of the human mind; on which account, it will be absolutely impossible to proceed in this inquiry, until certain principles of thought are at the same time perspicuously stated. This object, therefore, I shall attempt, although, from the restricted nature of the present dissertation, it will be impossible for me to enter into any explanation and defence of the metaphysical views which may be advanced, in contradiction to opinions that deserve the highest respect, in deference to the names with which they are associated. Any one, also, conversant in the smallest degree with researches of this kind, will be but too well aware of the difficulties which they involve. For this reason, I must request every indulgence, whenever I shall have occasion to state, as briefly as the subject will allow me, certain primary laws of the mind, which, from the maturest consideration, I have been induced to advocate.

CHAPTER II.

INDICATIONS AFFORDED BY MENTAL EXCITEMENTS, THAT ORGANS OF SENSATION ARE THE MEDIUM THROUGH WHICH PAST FEELINGS ARE RENOVATED.

" Phantasma enim est sentiendi actus; neque differt a sensione, aliter quam *fieri* differt a *factum esse.*" HOBBES.

MY first object is to give validity to the conjecture which I threw out on a former occasion, that past feelings are renovated through the medium of organs of sense. It will, indeed, be impossible to proceed much farther in our researches, until this curious subject has met with due consideration.

In the commencement of these researches, I set out with stating the view of the late Dr Brown respecting the mind, namely, that it was simple and indivisible, and that every mental feeling was only the mind itself existing in a certain state.

Sensations were, at the same time, considered as states of the mind induced by objects actually present, and acting upon the organs of sense. I need scarcely add, that such mental states admit of various degrees of *intensity, vividness,* or *faintness ; first,* from the greater or less susceptibility of any sensitive structure to actual impressions ; and, *secondly,* from the greater or less force with which material causes act upon our organs of sense.

It has also been pointed out, that pleasurable feelings, from whatever source they may be derived, depend upon a freedom being given to the expansive power of the circulating mass, while pain is induced by any cause which tends to deprive it of this vital property. But regarding the instrumentality by which such changes are induced, I have already adverted to the conclusions of Dr Wilson Philip, deduced from his experiments, namely, that " the nervous system consists of parts endowed with the vital principle, yet capable of acting in concert with inanimate matter; and that in man, as well as in certain well-known animals, electricity is the agent thus capable of being collected by nervous organs, and of being universally diffused for purposes intimately connected with the animal economy throughout every part of the human system." But without founding any system on this particular view, I considered the nerves as not only the natural dispensers of that influence upon which the opposite qualities of pleasure and pain depend, but, likewise, as the natural source, whence all the degrees of vividness imparted through the medium of the circulating fluid to our various sensations, had their origin. At the same time it was shewn, that under certain morbid circumstances, substances affecting the blood, without the intervention of the nerves, had the same effect of exciting or even depressing the feelings of the mind. I shall therefore now add, that from the different circumstances of the circulating fluid, as it supplies different structures of the human frame, arise our various susceptibilities of sensation.

In what, then, consists a susceptibility to *ideas?* This question has been already in part answered. Since an idea is nothing more than a past feeling renovated with a diminution of vividness proportional to the intensity of the original impression, we are justified in entertaining the suspicion, that the susceptibility of the mind to sensations and ideas ought to refer to similar circumstances of corporeal structure. Accordingly, there can be little or no doubt, as I have before hinted, that organs of sense are the actual medium through which past feelings are renovated; or, that when, from strong mental excitements, ideas have become more vivid than actual impressions, this intensity is induced by an absolute affection of those particular parts of the organic tissue on which sensations depend. Thus, the mere idea of some favourite food is well known to occasionally excite the salivary glands no less than if the sapid body itself were actually present, and stimulating the papillæ of the fauces.

After this explanation, there can be little difficulty in understanding why strong mental excitements should occasionally, though rarely, restore impressions of touch, which are indeed seldom so proportionally vivid as renovated feelings of vision or of hearing. Such appears to have been the case when Sir Humphry Davy subjected himself to the vivifying influence of the nitrous oxide. He confesses to an increased sensibility of touch, and occasionally notices what he names a *tangible extension.* In Dr

Kinglake's case, this gas had the peculiar effect of reviving rheumatic pains in the shoulder and knee-joints, which had not previously been felt for many months.* Another gentleman, Mr James Thomson, speaks to nearly a similar fact. " I was surprised," he remarks, " to find myself affected, a few minutes afterwards, with the recurrence of a pain in my back and knees, which I had experienced the preceding day from fatigue in walking. I was rather inclined to deem this an accidental coincidence than an effect of the air; but the same thing constantly occurring whenever I breathed the air, shortly after suffering pain, either from fatigue or any other accidental cause, left no doubt on my mind as to the accuracy of the observation."†

From the facts thus advanced, we need not be surprised that the impression of muscular resistance or of blows should be occasionally blended with the incidents of ghost-stories. " After having dropped asleep," says a writer in Nicholson's Journal on Phantasms produced by Disease, " an animal seemed to jump on my back with the most shrill and piercing screams, which were too intolerable for the continuance of sleep." I have quoted a case of *delirium tremens*, where a man is said to have suffered even bodily pain from the severe lashing of an imaginary waggoner. In Wanley's Wonders of the Little World, I find a story, taken from Rosse's Arcana, to the following purport:—" There was an apparition

---

* Davy's Researches concerning Nitrous Oxide, p. 504.
† Ibid, 515.

(saith Mr Rosse) to Mr Nicholas Smith, my dear friend, immediately before he fell sick of that fever that killed him. Having been late abroad in London, as he was going up the stairs into his chamber, he was embraced (as he thought) by a woman all in white, at which he cried out; nothing appearing, he presently sickeneth, goeth to bed, and within a week or ten days died." Beaumont also remarks of the spirits which he saw,—" I have been sitting by the fire with others. I have seen several spirits, and pointed to the place where they were, telling the company they were there. And one spirit whom I heard calling to me, as he stood behind me, on a sudden clapped his finger to my side, which I sensibly perceived, and started at it; and as I saw one spirit come in at the door, which I did not like, I suddenly laid hold of a pair of tongs, and struck at him with all my force, whereupon he vanished."

But it is useless to multiply stories of this kind, at the hazard of stumbling upon narratives mixed up with mere fable; otherwise I might recount, how the familiar of one man struck him on the right or left ear as he did well or ill,—how to another individual an angel came with a similar purport,

" And whipp'd the offending Adam out of him;"

how a third visionary fancied he was scourged on a bed of steel by devils,—how a lad was killed by a spirit from a box on the ear,—and, in short, how numerous other phantasms have not been content with a bodiless form, but have occasionally put on, what the pneumatologists of the middle ages were wont to name, *caro non adamica;* and, under this garb, have demonstrated the miraculous force of their muscular exertions:

> " I've heard a spirit's force is wonderful;
> At whose approach, when starting from his dungeon,
> The earth does shake, and the old ocean groans,
> Rocks are removed, and towers are thunder'd down;
> And walls of brass and gates of adamant
> Are passable as air, and fleet like winds."*

In the next place, the retina may be shewn, when subjected to strong excitements, to be no less the organ of ideas than of sensations. This fact is illustrated in the following anecdote related by Nicolai:—"A person of a sound and unprejudiced mind, though not a man of letters, whom I know well, and whose word may be credited, related to me the following case:—" As he was recovering from a violent nervous fever, being still very weak, he lay one night in bed, perfectly conscious that he was awake, when the door seemed to open, and the figure of a woman entered, who advanced to his bed-side. He looked at it for some moments, but as the sight was disagreeable, he turned himself and awakened his wife; on turning again, however, the figure was gone."† Now, in this incident, the real sensation of a closed door, to which the axis of vision had been previously directed, was followed by the fantastical representation of a door being opened by a female figure. The question then

---

* Tragedy of Œdipus, by Lee and Dryden.
† Nicholson's Journal, vol. vi. p. 174.

is, if those very points of the retina on which the picture of the real door had been impressed, formed the same part of the visual organ on which the idea or past feeling that constituted the phantasm was subsequently induced:—or, in other words, did the revival of the fantastic figure really affect those points of the retina which had been previously impressed by the image of the actual object? Certainly there are grounds for the suspicion, that when ideas of vision are vivified to the height of sensations, a corresponding affection of the optic nerves accompanies the illusion. A person, for instance, labouring under spectral impressions, sees the form of an acquaintance standing before him in his chamber. Every effect in this case is produced, which we might expect from the figure being impressed on the retina. The rays of light issuing from that part of the wall which the phantasm seems to obscure, are virtually intercepted. But if impressions of vision are really renewable on the retina, their delineation ought to be always remarkable for accuracy. The author of a paper on the phantasms produced by disease, (inserted in Nicholson's Journal), remarks, that the phantastical representations of some books or parchments, exhibited either manuscript or printed characters, agreeably to the particular subject of his previous thoughts.

But the question, which I have been thus disposed to answer in the affirmative, has, since the publication of the first edition of this work, met with a most remarkable confirmation from one of the most eminent philosophers of the present day. Dr Brewster, in some remarks which he has published of his own experience in these mental impressions, informs us, that, " when the eye is not exposed to the impressions of external objects, or when it is insensible to these impressions, in consequence of the mind being engrossed with its own operations, any object of mental contemplation which has either been called up by the memory, or created by the imagination, will be seen as distinctly as if it had been formed from the vision of a real object. In examining these mental impressions," he adds, " I have found that they follow the motions of the eyeball exactly like the spectral impressions of luminous objects, and that they resemble them also in their apparent immobility when the eyeball is displaced by an external force. If this result (which I state with much diffidence, from having only my own experience in its favour) shall be found generally true by others, it will follow that the objects of mental contemplation may be seen as distinctly as external objects, and will occupy the same local position in the axis of vision, as if they had been formed by the agency of light.* Hence all the phenomena of apparitions may depend upon the relative intensities of these two classes of impressions, and upon their manner of accidental combination. In perfect health, when the mind possesses a control over its powers, the impressions of external objects alone occupy the atten-

---

* Dr Brewster, in a note subjoined to his paper, has honoured me by observing, that these results, and several others that he intends to explain in another paper, (which, I understand, will be published in the 5th Number of the *Edinburgh Journal of Science*,) confirm, in a remarkable manner, the views that have been given in this work.

tion, but in the unhealthy condition of the mind, the impressions of its own creation either overpower, or combine themselves with the impressions of external objects; the mental spectra in the one case appearing alone, while in the other they are seen projected among those external objects to which the eyeball is directed."*

In the same interesting paper from which the foregoing extract has been made, there are other particulars given relative to phantoms which I cannot resist quoting. The author, in opposing the view of Mr Charles Bell, that there is an immobility of the spectral impression when the eye is displaced by the pressure of the finger, thus proceeds:—" This spectrum is by no means immoveable. It is quite true that it moves through a very small space; but this space, small as it is, is the precise quantity through which it ought to move according to the principles of optics; and the explanation of this fact leads us to investigate the difference between the vision of external objects and that of impressions upon the retina.

" In order to understand this difference, let A in the following figure be the eye of the observer, and O an external object, whose image at P is seen along the axis of vision POM. Let the eye be pushed upwards, suppose one-tenth of an inch, into the position B, the

---

* See the Edinburgh Journal of Science, conducted by Dr Brewster, vol. ii. p. 1. in a paper by the editor, entitled "Observations on the Vision of Impressions on the Retina, in reference to certain supposed Discoveries respecting Vision announced by Mr Charles Bell."

external object O remaining fixed. The image of O upon the retina will now be raised from P to Q in the elevated eye at B. Hence the object O will now be seen in the direction QON, having descended by the elevation of the eye from M to N.

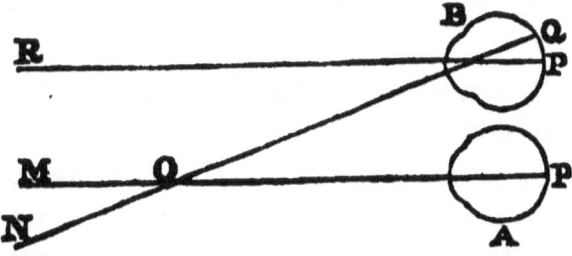

"Let the eye be now brought back to its original position A, and let the object O be the lamp with ground glass used by Mr Bell. The spectral impression will therefore be made upon the retina at P, and will remain on that spot till it is effaced. If the eye A is now raised to B, the impression will still be at P in the elevated eye, and it will be seen in the direction PR parallel to PM, having risen only one-tenth of an inch, or the height through which the eye has been raised by pressure. This small space is not very visible to an ordinary observer, when his head is at liberty to move; but if the head is carefully fixed, the motion of the spectrum becomes quite apparent. Hence it is obvious, that Mr Bell has been first misled by not observing the motion of the spectrum, and, secondly, by supposing that the vision of an impression followed the same law as the vision of an external object. The difference between these two cases of vision which Mr Bell has overlooked, consists in this, that in *ordinary vision* the object forms a new image upon a new part of the retina, after the eye is pushed up; whereas in *spectral vision* the original object has nothing to do with it after the eye is displaced, the spectrum itself, which retains its place on the retina, being now the only object of perception."

I shall next observe, that there can be little or no doubt but that the ear is likewise the medium through which the past feelings of sound are renovated. In a case of *delirium tremens* which fell under my own observation, the patient, during his convalescence, was at intervals assailed, as from an adjoining closet, by imaginary voices, distinctly articulating certain expressions to him; and when thus addressed, he shewed the same impatience at being prevented by the clamour from listening to some conversation that was going on in the room, as if he had been disturbed by real sounds.

These are the few remarks I have to offer on the indications afforded during intense excitements of the mind, that our susceptibility to sensations and ideas depends upon similar circumstances of organic structure; and hence, that past feelings are renovated through the medium of organs of sensation. But a question may be put, if the same notion does not lurk among other systems of metaphysical philosophy which have been taught? " Idea, in the old writers," says Dr Brown, " like the synonimous word *perception* at present, was expressive, not of one part of a process, but of two parts of it. It included, with a certain vague comprehensiveness, the organic *change* as well as the *mental*,—in the same way as *perception* now implies a certain change produced in our organs of sense, and a consequent change in the state of the mind."

The last question that may be asked is, What description of ideas, whether of sight, of hearing, or of touch, most frequently gives rise to spectral illusions? Certainly, the majority of apparition-stories on record indicaets, that ghosts are more frequently seen or heard, than absolutely felt.

False impressions of vision are decidedly more numerous than those of any other faculty. Thus Macbeth very properly exclaims, when in doubt respecting the nature or purport of the imaginary dagger he saw before him,—

" Mine eyes are made the fools o' the other senses,
Or else worth all the rest."

The ideas which have their origin in the affections of our muscular frame much less frequently delude us than those of vision or of hearing. In fact, those modifications of the sense of external resistance, which bear reference to our muscular contractions, (whence are derived all our notions of hardness, softness, roughness, smoothness, solidity, liquidity, &c.) often (but certainly not always) afford the very means by which we ascertain whether an apparition is true or false. When Macbeth sees the air-drawn dagger before his eyes, and finds that it does not resist the muscular contractions of his fingers, or, in less formal metaphysical language, that it eludes his grasp, he asks in amazement,—

> " Art thou not, fatal vision, sensible
> To feeling as to sight ? Or art thou but
> A dagger of the mind ; a false creation,
> Proceeding from the heat-oppressed brain ?"

Occasionally the trial has served to deter an intended imposture. Thus, when a friar personated an apparition, and haunted the chamber of the Emperor Josephus of Austria, a relation of the monarch seized hold of the substantial phantasm, and flinging him out of the window, *laid* him pretty effectually.*

---

* " In most of the relations of ghosts," says Grose, " they are supposed to be mere aerial beings, without substance, and that they can pass through walls and other solid bodies at pleasure. A particular instance of this is given, in relation the 27th, in Glanvil's Collection, when one David Hunter, neat-herd to the Bishop of Down and Connor, was for a long time haunted by the apparition of an old woman, whom he was by a secret impulse obliged to follow whenever she appeared, which, he says, he did for a considerable time, even if in bed with his wife ; and because his wife could not hold him in his bed, she would go too, and walk after him till day, though she saw nothing ; but his little dog was so well acquainted with the apparition, that he would follow it as well as his master. If a tree stood in her walk, he observed her always to go through it. Notwithstanding this seeming immateriality, this very ghost was not without some substance ; for, having performed her errand, she desired Hunter to lift her from the ground, in the doing of which, he says, she felt just like a bag of feathers."

There can be little doubt, but that the circumstance of our muscular feelings of resistance being less liable to delusion than those of sight, has given rise to a variety of notions which, from a very early period, have been entertained on the nature of spiritual beings. Thus, Lucretius, as he is translated by Creech:

> " Nor must we think these are the blest abodes,
> The quiet mansions of the happy gods,
> Their substance is so thin, so much refin'd,
> Unknown to sense, nay, scarce perceiv'd by mind;
> *Now, since these substances can't be touch'd by man,*
> They cannot touch those other things that can;
> For whatsoe'er is touch'd, that must be touch'd again.
> Therefore, the mansions of those happy pow'rs
> Must be all far unlike, distinct from ours;
> Of subtle natures suitable to their own;"

(and, as the translator quaintly adds,)

> " All which, by long discourse, I'll prove anon."

Lastly, I might observe, that the olfactory organs may occasionally be the medium through which ideas of smell are so intensely excited, as to give rise to mental illusions. Burton, on the authority of Petrus Forestus, relates, that " a minister, through precise fasting in Lent, and over much meditation, became desperate, thought he saw divells in his chamber, and that he could not be saved. He smelled nothing, as he said, but fire and brimstone, and was already in hell, and would aske them still if they did not smell as much. I told him he was melancholy, but he laughed me to scorne, and replied that hee saw divells, talked with them in good earnest, and would spit in my face, and aske me if I did not smell brimstone."

CHAPTER III.

THE VARIOUS DEGREES OF EXCITEMENT, OF WHICH IDEAS, OR THE RENOVATED FEELINGS OF THE MIND, ARE SUSCEPTIBLE.

" Men must acquire a very peculiar and strong habit of turning their eye inwards, in order to explore the interior regions and recesses of the MIND—the hollow caverns of deep thought—the private seats of fancy—and the wastes and wildernesses, as well as the more fruitful and cultivated tracts of this obscure climate."

WE are now literally entering on the investigation of what the French metaphysicians name *ideology*, a subject which, from the manner it has been treated, has recently incurred a censure that it too well deserves. " Ideology is, no doubt, a part of human physiology; but it has far outgrown its parent science in point of extent, and is still far inferior to it in the means of verification. Let the metaphysician always avail himself of the experiments of physiology as far as he is able; but let not the physiologist imagine that he can ever derive a reciprocal assistance from metaphysics. It is possible, however, to transfer credulity from one extreme to the other;—to yield a faith as implicit to the *probabilities* of the scientific physiologist, as is usually required for the dogmas of pneumatology."*

These are, indeed, excellent remarks, from the just severity of which I can scarcely flatter myself with the prospect of an entire escape. The discussion will be, however, hazarded.

This investigation has hitherto been conducted upon the principle, that the various degrees of vividness of which our mental states are susceptible correspond to certain conditions of the sanguineous system; and that the natural source of the excitement which is imparted to the circulation, and of the corresponding vividness which the feelings of the mind receive, is attributable to the influence of the brain and nerves.

In the next place, several proofs were adduced in support of the conclusion, that organs of sensation were the common medium through which actual impressions were induced, and past feelings or ideas were renovated.

According, then, to this view, every organ of feeling, which is no less the organ of ideas than of sensations, must be considered as supplied with its own vital fluid, and as more or less influenced by nervous matter. To the various stimulated conditions, therefore, incidental to the vascularity of each organ of feeling, the vividness of sensations and ideas corresponds.

---

* Notes on Magendie's Physiology, by Dr Milligan. See his translation of this work, page 423.

I shall now attempt a description of the various degrees of excitement incidental to ideas, when exclusively rendered intense, premising, however, that such gradations are to be chiefly distinguished when the vision is affected.

1st Stage of Excitement.

By a principle of the mind, *purely intellectual*, the impressions which may at any time be induced on the seat of vision, suggest the notion of groups of sensible figures, each varying in hue and intensity, and each included in a distinct outline. While this mental operation is going on, each affected point of the retina becomes subject to a law (the consideration of which would detain us too long), whereby its vividness is considerably modified. The effect is as follows:—

The nerves which impart their influence to visual sensations, first render more vivid those impressed points of the retina which give rise to the outlines of forms, and then extend their influence to the interior and central points of each figure. Thus, when we survey a landscape composed of such multifarious objects as woods, mountains, houses, or lakes, it will be found that the outlines of each of these visible forms first become distinct, or bright, and that this distinctness or vividness is in each of them gradually propagated to the interior or central parts of the figure.

In a short time, however, the outlines of each form which may have been impressed on the retina, become less clear to the vision, while the interior impressed points become more distinct. This fact indicates, that the vivifying influence has extended to the centre of the visual form. The process of excitement then gradually subsides. The faintness which has commenced at the outline of the figure, extends itself to the interior, so as to convey the notion of a gradual evanescence, until a more general indistinctness becomes the ultimate result.

Such is the vivifying influence imparted by the nerves to actual impressions; we may therefore advert to their apparent action, when past feelings are renovated on the surface of the retina.

Past feelings never begin to be renovated upon the surface of the retina, until the outlines of such figures as are formed by the actual impressions of luminous bodies have become evanescent. It is therefore on such parts of the seat of vision as have ceased to be affected by particles of light, that the recollected images of the mind may be traced. Hence, when any morbific stimulus gives an undue degree of intensity to the nerves which assist in renovating past feelings, the outlines of such ideal figures as arise by the law of association appear to be formed on the fading outlines of sensible forms. "I do not remember," says a writer on phantasms produced by disease, in a paper which I have before quoted, "by what gradation it was, that the frequently changing appearances before the sight gave place to another mode of delusive perception, which lasted for several days. All the irregularly figured objects, such as the curtains or clothes, were so far transformed, that they seemed to afford outlines of figures, of faces, animals, flowers, and other objects, perfectly motionless, somewhat in the manner of what fancy, if indulged, may form in the clouds or in the cavity of a fire; but much more complete and perfect, and not to be altered by steady observation or examination. They seemed to be severally as perfect as the rest of the objects with which they were combined, and agreed with them in colour and other respects." *

2d Stage of Excitement.

A second stage of excitement is induced when the nerves, upon which the renovation of past feelings depends, have exerted such an influence upon a revived figure, that the vividness has been gradually extended, until, upon the faded outlines of sensible forms, a complete fantastical image has been formed.

But it would appear, that in this stage of excitement, ideas are the most easily vivified, when the retina is not at the same time affected by sensible objects. This is, indeed, a fact which may be very readily anticipated, when we consider how vividly ideas of vision are represented in the minds of those individuals, who, after having long experienced the enjoyment of light, become affected with blindness. I recollect taking a journey in company with a gentleman thus circumstanced, than whom no one, in the complete possession of the faculty of vision, could be more interested with learning the general features of the country through which he passed, the form of its

---

* Nicholson's Journal, vol. xv. page 293.

hills, the course of its rivers, or the style of architecture displayed by various edifices. He often remarked, that the ideas communicated to him, although in the ordinary course of conversation, were so vivid, that he was convinced they must almost equal the sensations of perfect vision. On the general principle, then, that ideas of visible objects are the most readily excited during a seclusion from actual impressions, the operation of a morbific cause in inducing spectral illusions will be exerted with the greatest force in complete darkness, or during the closure of the eyelids. Yet it is at the same time a distinctive character of this inferior stage of excitement, that *the ideas which, during darkness, are unduly vivified, may be easily dispelled by an exposure to strong sensations of light.*

I shall now give a few illustrations of phantasms of this class.

Dr Crichton, in his excellent Treatise on Mental Derangement, has remarked, " that patients, when they first begin to rave in fevers, only do so when the room is darkened, or when they shut their eyes, so as to exclude the light of external objects."—" Then immediately they see, as it were, a crowd of horrid faces, and monsters of various shapes, grinning at them, or darting forward at them. As soon as they open their eyes, or upon being allowed to see a good deal of light, all these phantasms vanish."

This stage of excitement meets with another illustration in the interesting account which Nicolai has given of the state of his ideas, during the attack of a bilious remittent. " I found myself," he observes, frequently in a state between sleeping and waking, in which a number of pictures of every description, often of the strangest forms, shew themselves, change, and vanish. In the year 1778, I was afflicted with a bilious fever, which, at times, though seldom, became so high as to produce delirium. Every day, towards evening, the fever came on, and if I happened to shut my eyes at that time, I could perceive that the cold fit of the fever was beginning, even before the sensation of cold was observable. This I knew by the distinct appearance of coloured pictures of less than half their natural size, which looked as in frames. They were a set of landscapes, composed of trees, rocks, and other objects. If I kept my eyes shut, every minute some alteration took place in the representation. Some figures vanished, and others appeared. But if I opened my eyes all was gone; if I shut them again I had a different landscape. In the cold fit of the fever, I sometimes opened and shut my eyes every second for the purpose of observation, and every time a different picture appeared, replete with various objects, which had not the least resemblance to those that appeared before. These pictures presented themselves without interruption as long as the cold fit of the fever lasted. They became fainter as soon as I began to grow warm, and when I was perfectly so all were gone. When the cold fit of the fever was entirely past, no more pictures appeared; but if, on the next day, I could again see pictures when my eyes were shut, it was a certain sign that the cold fit was coming on.*

---

* Nicholson's Journal, vol. vi. page 175.

Another illustration is the case of the late Dr Ferriar, which he has reported of himself. " I remember," says this writer, " that about the age of fourteen, it was a source of great amusement to myself, if I had been viewing any interesting object in the course of the day, such as a romantic ruin, a fine seat, or a review of a body of troops, as soon as evening came on, if I had occasion to go into a dark room, the whole scene was brought before my eyes, with a brilliancy equal to what it had possessed in daylight, and remained visible for several minutes. I have no doubt, that dismal and frightful images have been presented to young persons after scenes of domestic affliction, or public horror."*

Now, with regard to the last illusion, I shall remark, that an affection of this kind is by no means so liable to occur to young persons as, from the foregoing narrative, we might be led to suppose; and hence there is every reason for the suspicion, that some slight morbific cause, operating on the vividness of ideas, might have so increased the usual degree of intensity, which pleasurable emotions are known to impart to youthful feelings, as, by a joint influence of this kind, to have disposed the mind to spectral impressions.

3d Stage of Excitement.

It has been supposed by some metaphysicians, that when spectral illusions of vision occur during the seclusion from any sensible impressions of the retina, they

---

* Ferriar on Apparitions, page 16.

may be always dispelled upon the introduction of light. This is, however, a mistake. The examples last given certainly prove, that ideas of vision are liable to acquire an additional degree of intensity when the retina is least exposed to actual sensations; for which reason, phantasms very frequently occur during the darkness or complete stillness of night. But we shall often find, that during the time when the mind is actually under the influence of a spectral illusion, the single or combined influence of its conspiring causes may be so far increased, that the restoration of light, and the counteracting power it exercises, will be found totally inadequate to the proposed expulsion of the phantasm. Hence the reason which I have for inferring, that phantasms appear under very different degrees of vividness, and that they thereby indicate corresponding stages of mental excitement. This view meets with support from the experience of Nicolai, whose remarks on some spectral figures which he saw are as follows:—" It is to be noted, that these figures appeared to me at all times, and under the most different circumstances, equally distinct and clear, whether I was alone or in company, by broad daylight equally as in the night time, in my own as well as in my neighbour's house. When I shut my eyes, sometimes the figures disappeared, sometimes they remained even after I had closed them. If they vanished, as in the former case, on opening my eyes again, nearly the same figure appeared which I had seen before."*

Again, in opposition to the assertion, that visual il-

---

* Nicholson's Journal, vol. vi. p. 268.

lusions are always dispelled by light, a philosophical writer, whose lively phantasms were occasioned by symptomatic fever, has given the result of his own experience. "It was in my recollection," he remarks, "that Hartley, in his work upon man, adopts a theory, that the visions of fever are common ideas of the memory, recalled in a system so irritated, that they act nearly with the same force as the objects of immediate sensation, for which they are mistaken; 'and therefore it is,' says he, 'that when delirium first begins, if in the dark, the effect may be suspended by bringing in a candle, which, by illumination, gives the due preponderance to the objects of sense.' This, however, I saw was manifestly unfounded."*

But it is now proper to advert more particularly to the very curious circumstance, that when Nicolai's disorder was at its greatest height, the figure of a deceased person which he saw should remain unchanged during both the shutting and the opening of the eyelids. This fact would indicate, that his ideas of vision, thus unduly vivified, exceeded in their degree of intensity those of actual impressions; for which reason they could not be annihilated by the operation of common sensible objects. One character, then, of the third stage of mental excitement is, that the illusions which are incidental to it are not dispelled by light, but may remain during the operation of sensations of an ordinary degree of intensity.

It must be admitted, however, that the persistence of phantasms is less durable when such sensible ob-

---

* Nicholson's Journal, vol. xv. p. 292.

jects are opposed to the organ of vision as are calculated by their vivifying influence to divert the attention of the individual from the particular subject of his spectral impressions. " When my attention," observes a philosophical *seer*, " was strongly fixed on the idea of an absent place or thing, the objects of sensation and of delirium were less perceived or regarded. When the mind was left in a passive or indolent state, the objects of delirium were most vivid, and the objects of sensation, or real objects in the room, could not be seen. But when, by a sort of exertion, the attention was roused, the phantasms became as it were transparent, and the objects of sensation were seen as if through them. There was not the least difficulty in rendering either object visible at pleasure, for the phantasms would nearly disappear while the attention was steadily fixed on the real objects."*

The transparency of these phantasms was evidently owing to their ceasing in part to affect the sensibility of the seat of vision, and to those points of the retina which were impressed by vivid objects actually present, being mingled with the dim and fading images that had been renovated.

Many of the phantasms which Nicolai saw ceased to haunt him during the influence of such pleasurable and vivifying objects as were connected with social intercourse; for he remarks, that, when he was at any other person's house, the phantasms with which he was beset were less frequent, and when he walked the public street they very seldom appeared.

---

* Nicholson's Journal, vol. xv. p. 292.

I may lastly observe, that when any sensible object, calculated by its casual and vivifying influence to arrest the attention of a seer, has been opposed to that part of the retina which was the object of a spectral illusion, an apparent interception of the phantasm has indicated that its persistence has been overcome; or, in other words, that the intensely vivid idea, of which the apparition consisted, had faded away, and had been succeeded by an actual impression. Thus, when the axis of vision has been directed to some particular part of a room where a phantasm was conceived to be present, and when between the eye and the phantasm some luminous object has afterwards been placed, so that rays reflected from it might impinge on the same points of the retina which were affected by the spectre, the consequence has been, that, like the phenomena of intercepted sensible impressions, actual rays of light have succeeded in effacing feelings which were ideal. This fact was proved in the case of an inhabitant of the Scottish metropolis. He was constantly annoyed by a spectral page, dressed like one of the Lord Commissioner's lacqueys, whom he always saw following close to his heels, whatever might be the occupation in which he was engaged. But to this attendant soon succeeded another no less unremitting, but far more unwelcome retainer, in the form of a frightful skeleton. An eminent medical practitioner of Edinburgh was the exorcist properly called in, who, in the course of his interrogatories, inquired, if at that very moment his patient saw the spectre? The man immediately pointed to a particular corner of the room where he alleged his familiar was keeping guard. To this spot, therefore, the learned gentleman walked.— "Now, do you see the skeleton?" he asked. "How can I," was the reply, "when you are interposed between us?" Here, then, was a satisfactory indication, not only that the retina had been actually impressed by the imaginary phantasm, but that the real object at present engaging the attention of the seer had overcome the persistence of the apparition. Soon, however, Fancy began her work again; for, with a sudden tone of exclamation that even inspired the philosopher himself with momentary alarm, the man suddenly exclaimed,—"Ay, now I see the skeleton again, for at this very moment he is peeping at me from behind your shoulders!"

But frequently, phantasms which appear without any assignable reason as arbitrarily vanish. Thus, it is recorded of one of the presidents of the Swiss cantons, that "he had occasion to visit the library of the establishment. Entering it about two o'clock in the afternoon, what was his amazement to see the former president of the same body, his deceased friend, sitting in solemn conclave in the president's chair, with a numerous list of ' great men, dead,' assisting him in his deliberations! He hastened from the place in fear, and went to some of his brethren in office to advise upon the most speedy measures to divorce the usurpers of their stations; but on returning with a re-enforcement of trembling associates, he found the long table in *statu quo*, the chairs empty, and every mark of the mysterious deliberators vanished into air."*

These remarks conclude what I have to say on the subject of the present chapter. It would appear, that when ideas of vision are rendered unduly intense, three stages of excitement may give rise to spectral impressions.

In the *first* stage of excitement, nothing more than the outlines of the recollected images of the mind are rendered as vivid as external impressions.

In the *second* stage, ideas are vivified during darkness so as to produce phantasms of a perfect form; but these are easily expelled by a strong exposure to light.

In the *third* stage of excitement, the illusions incidental to it are *not* dispelled by light, but may subsist during the influence of sensations of an ordinary degree of intensity.

---

* This story I have quoted from a late work, the Edinburgh Literary Gazette. It is the report of an anecdote related by Sir Walter Scott, on the occasion when I read a paper to the Royal Society, which has given rise to the present expanded dissertation.

CHAPTER IV.

AN INQUIRY INTO THOSE LAWS OF MENTAL CONSCIOUSNESS WHICH GIVE RISE TO THE ILLUSIONS OF DREAMS.

―――――― I talk of dreams,
Which are the children of an idle brain,
Begot of nothing but vain phantasy,
Which is as thin of substance as the air,
And more inconstant than the wind.—SHAKSPEARE.

THERE is, perhaps, no one familiar with the various apparition-stories which have from time to time been published, who is not strongly inclined to suspect that many of them are mere dreams. Whether this conjecture be well-founded or not, it is often difficult to determine. On this account it will be necessary to investigate the phenomena of sleep with some degree of care.

In reference to this inquiry it may be observed, that the excitability of the sanguineous fluid, upon which the vividness of our mental feelings depends, has, in a healthy condition of the system, its due limits. The power possessed by the blood of augmenting the heart's systole or diastole cannot be too long kept up. After a certain degree of excitation, a tendency is shewn to an opposite state of debility, when the feelings of the mind gradually decrease in their degree of vividness. Thus, there are periodical laws which govern our hours of slumber, and which, at the same time, are conducive to the regular exercise of the important functions of assimilation.

Some philosophers have supposed, that in sleep there is a temporary suspension of thought; others (the Cartesians in particular) have much more reasonably conceived that thought continues without any intermission. For, upon the principle inculcated by the late Dr Brown, that all our mental feelings are nothing more than the mind itself existing in different states, it is difficult to imagine in what way this relation of the mind to the body can possibly be suspended or dissolved, as long as the vitality of our frame subsists. When, likewise, it is considered, that we cannot entertain the least conception of any other states of the mind, than those which must necessarily include sensations or renovated feelings, the hypothesis becomes extremely plausible, that mental feelings of this kind, though certainly of extreme faintness, do actually occur in sleep, or even during deliquum.

This theory may be viewed in connexion with certain states of the circulating system, upon which those of the mind depend. The vividness of our mental feelings is regulated by the force and duration of each systole and diastole of the heart. Should these actions be too short and feeble, a corresponding faintness in the affections of the mind is the result, as is the case during the tremulous fluttering pulsations which are characteristic of syncope; also, if objects of sensation are uniform in their impressions, the vividness of our mental states will be no less diminished. Hence the promotion of sleep by the unchanged feelings of touch, which are induced by a horizontal position of the body during rest; hence also the somniferous effect of monotonous sounds. The continuation of sleep is likewise favoured by the exclusion of all impressing objects of vision.

After these preliminary remarks, I shall attempt a strict scrutiny of the states of the mind peculiar to sleep, as they are to be distinguished from those which occur during our waking hours.

According to the definition which I have given of sensations, they are states of the mind induced by objects *actually present*, and acting upon the organs of sense, while ideas are the renewals of *past* sensations. A question then, which, as we shall soon find, is most intimately connected with this inquiry, may be asked, By what law we thus arrive at our notions of the *present* and the *past?*

When, by the repetition of any sensation, those feelings are recalled with which they were before associated, such past feelings are renovated in a less vivid state, and hence acquire the name of *ideas;* that is, *images* of prior-sensations. It is, then, from nothing more than the comparative degrees of vividness which distinguish sensations and ideas, that the mind becomes intuitively susceptible of certain relative feelings of *succession* that subsist between them; which feelings of succession we express by such terms as *the present* and *the past*. This notion of a *succession* of mental states is in fact acquired by an ultimate law of our nature. The *more vivid* or *sensible* affection is contemplated as *present* to the mind, while the *less vivid*, or *ideal* state, is considered as *past*.

But it is essential to this knowledge of *succession*, that it should at the same time bear a reference to *the identity of the mind;* and, accordingly, this conviction is suggested, whenever we think of *the present* and *the past*. The late Dr Brown was the first to successfully explain this last-mentioned principle of the human intellect. " In all the varieties of our feelings," he remarks, " we believe that it is *the same mind* which is thus variously affected;" or, as this metaphysician has elsewhere explained himself, " that " the mind, which is capable of existing in various states, is felt by us as *one* in all its varieties of feelings."—" The belief flows from a principle of intuition, and it is in vain to look for evidence beyond it. We have an irresistible belief in our identity as long as we think of *the present* and *the past*."*

In correspondence, then, with this view, I shall consider mental consciousness as that intellectual feeling of the mind *suggested*† by a succession of sensations and renovated feelings, whereby *it acquires a notion of the present* and of *the past, and of one and the same*

---

* Dr Brown, in his Physiology of the Human Mind, likewise remarks, that, " in accordance with the belief in our identity, we use the personal pronoun *I* to express the whole series of these feelings to one self as the permanent subject of them."

† This is a very appropriate word employed by Dr Brown. I am sorry, however, that a difference of views on certain subjects will not always allow me to apply the term in the exact sense in which this eminent author meant it should be used.

mind, which is capable of existing in a succession of states. After this definition, we shall be better prepared to consider what are the proper mental phenomena which distinguish sleep.

I have already pointed out the extreme difficulty of supposing, that the relation which the immaterial principle of the mind bears to the human frame should be suspended during the periodical repose allotted to the body. This relation consists in the mind being made susceptible of certain successive states. As we can therefore conceive of no succession of states that does not necessarily include sensations and renovated feelings, it is certainly a reasonable hypothesis, that, during our moments of slumber, actual impressions and ideas should occur, although in a state of extreme faintness. But as it must be at the same time granted, that there exists no mental consciousness during *perfect sleep,* or that state of sleep which is free from dreams, we are now, I trust, sufficiently prepared to overcome any objections on this score to the theory proposed. For, while it is almost impossible to imagine that, during the vitality of the body, such essential states of the mind as sensations and ideas should not occur, there is not, on the other hand, the least difficulty in supposing, that a suspension may take place, during perfect sleep, of that particular law of *suggestion,* which merely furnishes the *connecting links,* as it were, that properly subsist between those actual impressions which arise by the organs of sense, and those renovated feelings, or ideas, which the law of association calls forth. When the operation of this connecting principle is for a time suspended, there no longer arises that new description of feelings which we express under the term *consciousness ;*—there no longer arises that intuitive and intellectual impression of the mind relative to the present and the past, as well as to the belief in its own identity.

Thus, then, we have endeavoured to establish the doctrine, that in perfect sleep the organs of sense are still impressed, though faintly, by external objects, and that feelings no less faint become the proper states of the mind;—also, that past feelings are renovated agreeably to the law of association, though in a state far less vivid, when compared with those which occur during our waking hours. Our investigation, therefore, now becomes limited to this sole object,—to determine under what circumstances that particular law is suspended, whereby the mind begins to lose all knowledge of the present and of the past, as well as of its own identity; or, in other words, our proper business is to inquire, Under what circumstances *mental unconsciousness* takes place?

Upon the approach of sleep, all organs of sense become less and less affected by their usual stimuli; and, with this diminution of sensibility, the degree of vividness in our mental affections keeps an uniform pace. But it is an important fact, that sensations and ideas are each susceptible of different extremes of faintness. Ideas cannot, by any known causes, be rendered so faint as actual impressions; they therefore, much sooner than sensations, acquire their own definite and extreme degree of faintness. It follows, therefore, that *the cause which induces the state of sleep is to be considered as a cause tending to make sensations more faint than ideas.*

The knowledge of this law is of the utmost importance in all our inquiries relative to the phenomena of sleep. But, first, it may be remarked, that if the cause of sleep render sensations more faint than ideas, it must evidently happen, that, in the course of this transition, sensations will, at some interval of time, arrive at the same degree of faintness as ideas. When, therefore, it is considered, that the human mind can form no notion of the present and the past, but from the comparative degree of vividness which, during our waking hours, subsists between sensations and ideas, and that the notion of present and past time necessarily enters into our definition of consciousness, it must follow, that when the cause of sleep has reduced sensations to the same degree of faintness as ideas, a state of mental unconsciousness must necessarily be the result.

There are still other circumstances to be taken into consideration concerning sleep. A certain degree of vividness in our various feelings is necessary to the production of mental consciousness; or, in other words, consciousness cannot be induced after the states of the mind have acquired a certain extreme degree of faintness. From the operation, then, of this law, which takes place while the cause that induces sleep is tending to make sensations more faint than ideas, that state of unconsciousness, which first arises when there is an uniformity of vividness in sensations and ideas, becomes so far prolonged, as to include in its duration the usual period of sound and healthy repose.

During the particular interval, when sensations are becoming more faint than ideas, so powerful is the agency of sleep, that, as we well know, very strong impressions made upon the organs of sense often fail in imparting to the affections of the mind that degree of intensity upon which watchfulness depends. Ideas, on the contrary, after having undergone a certain extreme degree of faintness, cease much sooner than sensations to become obnoxious to the power of sleep. We must therefore, at present, contemplate sleep as chiefly employed in enfeebling sensations, while ideas, or renovated feelings, are less under its influence.

This investigation will, I trust, prepare us to theorize with far greater facility on the subject of dreams.

The causes of our most common dreams have, during our waking hours, an inferior influence in rendering more vivid the states of the mind. They are, for instance, connected with such trivial affections as indigestion, or with the remissions of inflammatory or febrile attacks, where a repose, more or less disturbed by visions, is afforded to the wearied frame. In sleep, therefore, such causes have little power in increasing the vividness of sensations. For it is but too evident, that if the organs of sense were capable of being affected by slight stimuli, our states of repose, which are so important to the functions of assimilation, would be materially interrupted. Ideas, however, which are more removed from the enfeebling influence of sleep, are in a greater degree liable to be affected by causes that impart to our mental affections various degrees of vividness.

I shall therefore observe, that when, by some cause affecting the state of the circulation, the ideas of *perfect sleep* have been excited to a certain degree of vividness, the mind then acquires a knowledge of the present and the past, and of its own identity; or, in other words, consciousness begins, and, with it, the state of dreaming. It will therefore be a very interesting research, to ascertain what may be the modifications which the usual phenomena of the mind undergo, from the operation of those laws that more immediately relate to consciousness?

We must once more recall our attention to the principle so fully demonstrated, that the usual comparative degree of vividness which subsists between sensations and ideas alone suggests the notion of *present* and *past* time; the more vivid feeling being considered as *present*, and the less vivid feeling, or idea, being contemplated as *past*. This law, in fact, continues to operate, after renovated feelings alone have become the subject of consciousness. When, therefore, it is considered, that ideas of themselves partake of various degrees of vividness, it must be evident that, in our dreams, the more vivid idea would be contemplated as a *present* feeling, while the least vivid one would be considered as *past*. By this means, various recollected images of the mind protrude themselves, as it were, from the train of thought going on, and though fainter than sensations, have still the power of suggesting a false conviction of actual impressions.

In reference to the same law of consciousness, may be explained the illusions of many spectral impressions which occur during our waking hours. That principle in our nature by which mental feelings of various degrees of vividness suggest a notion of the present and of the past, is continually influencing the mind; hence, the moment that ideas become more vivid than sensations, they are contemplated as present, or as actual impressions; while the least vivid feeling suggests the notion of past time.

The partial resemblance of spectral impressions to dreams will now, I trust, be sufficiently apparent. There is still a difference to be noticed in the circumstances under which they are severally produced. Before spectral impressions can arise, the vivid ideas of our waking hours must be raised to an unusually high degree of intensity; but during our moments of mental repose, a very slight degree of vividness imparted to the faint ideas of perfect sleep is sufficient to excite a similar illusion. Hence the images of spectral impressions differ from those of dreams, in being much more vivid.

CHAPTER V.

PHANTASMS MAY ARISE FROM IDEAS OF WHICH THE MIND MIGHT OTHERWISE HAVE BEEN EITHER CONSCIOUS OR UNCONSCIOUS.

"The difficulty is this :—Consciousness being interrupted always by forgetfulness, there being no moment of our lives wherein we have the whole train of our past actions before our eyes in one view; but even the best memories losing the sight of one part while they are viewing another." LOCKE.

I SHALL now attempt to explain other laws of consciousness, which are materially involved in the circumstances under which phantasms arise. The investigation, however, is difficult; a proof of which is, that, from not prosecuting it, considerable disturbance seems to have been given to the speculations of those who have endeavoured to explain, upon established metaphysical principles, the origin of apparitions.

Nicolai, the philosophical seer of Berlin, who was long under the influence of spectral impressions, offers the following remarks on his own case :—

"I observed these phantasms of the mind with great accuracy, and very often reflected on my previous thoughts, with a view to discover some law in the association of ideas by which exactly these or other figures might present themselves to the imagination. Sometimes I thought I had made a discovery, especially in the latter period of my visions; but, on the whole, I could trace no connexion which the various figures that thus appeared and disappeared to my sight, had either with my state of mind, or with my employment and the other thoughts which engaged my attention. After frequent accurate observations on the subject, having fairly proved and maturely considered it, I could form no other conclusion on the cause and consequence of such apparitions, than that, when the nervous system is weak, and at the same time too much excited, or rather deranged, similar figures may appear in such a manner as if they were actually seen and heard; for these visions in my case were not the consequence of any known law of reason, of the imagination, or of the otherwise usual association of ideas."*

Such were the difficulties that pressed themselves upon the mind of Nicolai, in endeavouring to account for the mysterious introduction of the fantastic visitants, by whom he was almost hourly surrounded. In the attempt, therefore, which I shall make to obtain some satisfaction on this head, it will be first necessary to inquire how far we are entitled, on every occasion, to seek for an explanation of such phenomena in the well-known law of the association of ideas.

It has been before shewn, that when a number of sensations occur in succession, the repetition of any

---

* Nicholson's Journal, vol. vi. p. 167.

one of them would recall in their original order, yet in a less vivid state, the feelings by which they were followed. To this law was affixed the usual term of *the association of ideas.* But a question now arises, If ideas, of which we are at any one moment of time totally unconscious, be still liable to recur agreeably to the law of association? The *hypothetical* answer which I should be disposed to give is this, That past feelings, even should they be those of our earliest moments of infancy, never cease to be under the operation of this principle, and that they are constantly liable to be renovated, though they should not be the object of consciousness, at the latest period of our life. According to this view, any past impression of the mind never becomes, as it were, extinct. Yet, amidst the incalculable quantity of ideas which are rapidly succeeding to each other, the amount of those that are vivified to such a degree as to be the object of consciousness, must fall far short of the actual number of such, as, from their extreme faintness, are no longer recognised.

After these remarks, I shall advert to another principle of the mind deserving consideration, which is this: *Feelings of any particular description or subject are liable to be frequently renovated, and there is a natural tendency in the same feelings, on each occasion of their renewal, to become gradually more and more faint.** The law which *partially* counteracts this tendency will be explained in the next chapter.

---

* A tendency of this kind differs in degree in different individuals. Thus, in the Psychological Magazine of Germany, there

I shall now suppose, that certain sensations have been induced sufficiently vivid to excite mental consciousness; and that the renovated feelings, named *ideas*, which correspond to them, sustain, upon each occasion of their renewal, a gradual diminution from their original degree of vividness. The result which, agreeably to the general doctrine I have inculcated, will ensue, may be readily anticipated. Any train of ideas must, in the course of its undisturbed depression, be eventually reduced to states far too faint to be the object of our consciousness.

In order, however, to render this law as intelligible as possible, I subjoin the following tabular view, in which the lower numbers in the scale represent the more faint or least vivid of our feelings, and the higher numbers the more excited states of the mind.

---

is the narrative of a girl, whose ideas must have declined very slowly from their original state of vividness. After having listened but once to the longest song, she could repeat it *verbatim*, and with equal accuracy could not only rehearse the whole of any sermon she might hear at church, but was even found to preserve the recollection of it after the interval of a year had expired.—The memory of Bishop Jewel was very remarkable. It is stated in Clark's Mirror, that " he could readily repeat any thing that he had penned after once reading: and therefore, usually, at the ringing of the bell, began to commit his sermons to heart, and kept what he had learned so firmly, that he used to say, That if he were to make a speech premeditated, before a thousand auditors, shouting or fighting all the while, yet could he say whatsoever he had provided to speak. Sir Francis Bacon, reading to him only the last clauses of ten lines in Erasmus his paraphrase in a confused and dismembered manner, he, after a small pause, rehearsed all those broken parcels of sentences the right way, and the contrary, with-

TABULAR VIEW.

Mode in which a Train or Association of Ideas, uninterrupted by Sensations, is supposed to uniformly decrease in Vividness.

	Degrees of Vividness and Faintness	Previous Sensation	Associated Train of Ideas.					
			1st Stage of Depression.	2d Stage of Depression.	3d Stage of Depression.	4th Stage of Depression.	5th Stage of Depression.	6th Stage of Depression.
Vivid Feelings of which we are conscious.	7	Sensation						
	6	. .	Ideas					
	5	. .	. .	Ideas				
	4	. .	. .	. .	Ideas			
Feelings too faint to be the Object of mental Consciousness.	3	. .	. .	. .	. .	Ideas		
	2	. .	. .	. .	. .	. .	Ideas	
	1	. .	. .	. .	. .	. .	. .	Ideas

Such is the mode in which a train of past feelings would decrease in vividness, if the original sensations, of which they are revivals, had possessed any uniform degree of vividness, and if there had been no excitements influencing at the time the ideas of the mind. But I ought to add, that from so many disturbing causes, which have a tendency to irregularly vivify the recollected images of thought, no actual illustration can be afforded of this principle, that in a strict sense is exempt from sources of fallacy.

From an inspection of the foregoing table, the law which I have laid down may be explained in terms somewhat different to those which I have used, and, perhaps, with some advantage to the proper subject of our inquiry.

It has been repeatedly stated, that, upon the repetition of any definite sensation, there is not only a renewal of the past feelings with which this sensation was formerly associated, (their renovation taking place agreeably to their prior order,) but that the number of ideas thus renewable may be prolonged to an incalculable extent. I may now add, that the train which is induced only meets with interruption from some new sensation, and with it, from some new succession of renovated feelings. It may therefore be observed, that *there is*, cæteris paribus, *a general tendency in every uninterrupted association of ideas to decrease in vividness, the diminution keeping pace with the extent to which the train is prolonged.*

This law will explain the purport of our next investigation, which relates to such incidents of spectral illusions as are connected with the natural tendency of the ideas that form an associated train to gradually fade, or, in other words, to become more faint. I shall therefore proceed upon the general view, that if a train of ideas be not prematurely interrupted, the close of it will always be found to consist of renovated feelings that are too faint to be the object of consciousness.

Such being the subject of our present inquiry, a second reference may be made to the foregoing tabular view, which is merely intended to convey a very general notion of the principle I would establish,—that there is a tendency in ideas to fade, the diminution of vividness keeping pace with the extent to which a series of revived impressions is prolonged. But by consulting the table, it will be seen, that when a train of uninterrupted ideas is, as it were, lengthened out, it must naturally include two varieties of renovated feelings.

Of one variety of ideas the mind is absolutely conscious. This particular variety forms the first, or preceding part of a sequence of renovated feelings.

Of another variety of ideas the mind is unconscious, and this faint description of them is to be found in the remaining part of the train.

I shall next remark, that a cause of mental excitement, adventitious, or truly morbific, may commence its vivifying influence upon the mental feelings during any interval of time that the mind is not susceptible of actual impressions. This operation may then involve any one of the two following circumstances of excitement:

First, An exciting cause may commence its influence, when the ideas, which form the concluding part of an uninterrupted train of renovated feelings, are becoming so faint as to cease being the object of consciousness.

Secondly, An exciting cause may commence its influence more prematurely; or before a train of ideas can have so much decreased in vividness as to cease being the object of consciousness.

These two circumstances of excitement will be considered in succession.

RISE TO SPECTRAL ILLUSIONS.

Section 1.

The Influence of vivifying Causes upon Ideas, of which we should otherwise have been unconscious.

I shall now suppose, that a cause of mental excitement has commenced its influence upon a sequence of ideas, but not until the train has gradually sunk into a degree of faintness so extreme, as to cease being the object of consciousness. A table, the exact reverse of the last given, will then shew the mode in which the concluding part of this train of renovated feelings is liable to such an excitement, as at length to be the object of consciousness.

TABULAR VIEW,

Explaining the Influence of a vivifying Cause upon the concluding Part of a Train of Ideas, of which we should otherwise have been unconscious.

	Degrees of Faintness and Vividness.	State to which Ideas were depressed before the Excitement.	Operation of a vivifying Cause.					
			1st Stage of Excitement.	2d Stage of Excitement.	3d Stage of Excitement.	4th Stage of Excitement.	5th Stage of Excitement.	6th Stage of Excitement.
Vivid feelings of which we are conscious.	7	...	...	...	...	...	...	Ideas
	6	..	...	...	...	...	Ideas	
	5	...	.	...	...	Ideas		
Too faint to be the object of consciousness.	4	...	...	...	Ideas			
	3	...	...	Ideas				
	2	...	Ideas					
	1	Ideas.						

I trust the above table will sufficiently explain the progressive mode, in which a morbific cause of excitement may restore to a vivid state of consciousness faint ideas, of which we should otherwise have been unconscious.

But this effect of a mental excitement will meet with a striking illustration, when we connect it with a law to which I have just adverted, namely, that past feelings, even should they be those of our earliest moments of infancy, never cease to be under the influence of the law of association, and that they are constantly liable to be renovated, even to the latest period of our life, although they may be in so faint a state as not to be the object of consciousness.

It is evident then, that a cause of mental excitement may so act upon a sequence of extremely faint feelings, as to render ideas of which the mind had long been previously unconscious, vivid objects of consciousness. Thus, it is recorded of a female in France, that while she was subjected to such an influence, the memory of the Armorican language, which she had lost since she was a child, suddenly returned.

With the knowledge of the foregoing fact before us, we shall now imagine, that certain definite ideas are arising in the mind in so vivid a state, that the order of succession in which they formerly occurred as sensible impressions may be distinctly traced. If, then, such ideas are succeeded, no less agreeably to the law of association, by another train, which, having long faded into extreme faintness, are, in the present instance, so morbidly excited as to again become the subject of consciousness,—such revived feelings will appear to arise in a sort of insulated manner, since their original connexion with recognised sensations may have been long since forgotten. Accordingly this was the case when certain of Nicolai's ideas met with an unexpected renewal of their long-lost vividness;—they appeared to be totally unconnected with the regular train of his thought. "I must observe," says this author, "that when I either think deeply on a subject, or write attentively, particularly when I have exerted myself for some time, a thought frequently offers itself, which has no connexion with the work before me, and this at times in a manner so lively, that it seems as if expressed in actual words."

We have next to consider, that the faded ideas of Nicolai's mind, when again becoming the subject of consciousness, had acquired such an extreme degree of vividness as to frequently induce the illusions of phantasms; when, therefore, all knowledge was lost of the original sensations that corresponded to such spectral impressions, no wonder that this writer should express himself after the following manner:— "None of the phantasms of my illness were of known places, objects, or persons." And, lastly, when the same metaphysician conducted his inquiry on the principle, that no ideas but those of which we are conscious were subject to the law of association, no small share of disappointment could fail to ensue, when he found himself unable to trace the origin of his phantasms to former impressions made in the usual manner upon his senses.

Section II.

The Influence of vivifying Causes upon Ideas of which we are conscious.

In the last section I endeavoured to shew, that an exciting cause may commence its influence after the ideas which composed the concluding part of an uninterrupted train of renovated feelings had ceased to become the object of consciousness; and that the effect of such an influence might be to revive the remembrance of long-forgotten ideas, and, as in Nicolai's case, to conjure up phantasms which the perplexed metaphysician could not refer to the law of association.

My next object is to point out other circumstances, under which a cause of mental excitement may vivify ideas. I have stated, that it may commence its action more prematurely, or before a train of ideas has so much decreased in vividness as to cease being the object of consciousness. But this circumstance of mental excitement has been so frequently illustrated in the course of this dissertation, that it requires little comment. The effect must be, that the order in which phantasms occur will be traced to the order of association in which ideas arise.

It is almost unnecessary to illustrate this vivifying action by the tabular view which is annexed.

TABULAR VIEW.

	Degrees of Vividness.	Previous State of Ideas.	A Train of Ideas of which we are conscious subjected to Excitement.			
Vivid feelings of which we are conscious.	9	. . .	. . .	. . .	. . .	Ideas.
	8	. . .	. . .	. . .	Ideas.	
	7	. . .	. . .	Ideas.		
	6	. . .	Ideas.			
	5	Ideas.				

But Nicolai has conceived, that the circumstances under which phantasms arise are not referable to the law by which past feelings are renovated.

Other philosophical seers, however, as I have shewn, have been more successful in tracing their phantasms to ideas vivified in the natural order of their association; and, in this case, it is almost unnecessary to repeat a remark I made, that such spectres could have been nothing more than highly-excited ideas, which had not antecedently ceased to be objects of consciousness. Indeed, Nicolai himself affords us a curious narrative of a gentleman, whose vivid recollections of the conversation which he might have heard in the course of the day, were morbidly revived in the evening, but in states of intensity far exceeding those of the original impressions. " My much-lamented friend, Moses Mendelsohn," he observes, " had, in the year 1792, by too intense an application to study, contracted a malady which also abounded with particular psychological apparitions. For upwards of two years he was incapacitated from doing any thing; he could neither read nor think, and was rendered utterly incapable of supporting any loud noise. If any one talked to him rather in a lively manner, or if he himself happened to be disposed to lively conversation, he fell in the evening into a very alarming species of catalepsis, in which he saw and heard every thing that passed around him, without being able to move a limb. If he had heard any lively conversation during the day, a Stentorian voice repeated to him, while in the fit, the particular words or syllables that had been pronounced, with an impressive accent, or loud emphatic tone, and in such a manner that his ears reverberated."

CHAPTER VI.

THE EFFECT OF MORBIFIC EXCITEMENTS OF THE MIND WHEN HEIGHTENED BY THE VIVIFYING INFLUENCE OF HOPE AND FEAR.

"Spem mihi nescio quam vultu promittis amico."—OVID.

> " Thou to whom the world unknown
> With all its shadowy shapes is shown;
> Who seest, appall'd, the unreal scene,
> While Fancy lifts the veil between,
>   Ah, Fear! ah, frantic Fear!
>   I see, I see thee near."   COLLINS.

OUR inquiry into the effect produced on mental consciousness by strong excitements of the mind, is at length so far advanced, that a fit opportunity occurs for noticing the phenomena attending other occasions besides those which are morbid, on which various degrees of vividness are imparted to our feelings.

In the last chapter I took occasion to remark, that when any sensation is renewed, it has a tendency to become on each occasion of its repetition less vivid, and when followed by a revival of the feelings with which it was before associated, such revived feelings evince a similar tendency on each occasion of their recurrence to become fainter and fainter. A question then may be asked, *In what consists that principle of the mind, which in a partial degree is counteracting this tendency?* Dr Brown has clearly shewn that there is (to use his own words) " a principle by which it is impossible for us not to believe that the course of nature has been uniform in all the simple sequences that have composed or may hereafter compose it, and that the same antecedents, therefore, have always been followed, and will continue to be followed by the same consequents;—that whatever we observe becomes at once, by the influence of this principle, representatives to us of the past and of the future as well as of the present." Such are the functions of the anticipating faculty of the mind,—that faculty whereby we are enabled to contemplate present and past feelings in the relation of the present and the future, or in the relation of the past and the future. Whenever, therefore, this anticipating principle is thus exercised, various degrees of pleasure or pain are contemplated as future events; and, in proportion to the amount of the pleasure or pain thus anticipated, and to the probability of the event anticipated taking place, a renovation of vividness is given to feelings that would otherwise have ceased in time to be the object of consciousness. In this point of view, the anticipating faculty of the mind is the counteracting principle, which is calculated to prevent many of our feelings from becoming on each occasion of their recurrence less and less vivid.

I need now scarcely add, that when good or evil is thus anticipated, the emotions thereby induced, which are always productive of vivid renewals of pleasure or pain, we express by the terms *hope* or *fear*.

These are the very few remarks which I can stay to offer on that principle of our nature which is constantly more or less counteracting the tendency of sensations and ideas to become, on each occasion of their recurrence, fainter and fainter. But the power of this anticipating faculty to revive our feelings must be considered as limited in its operations, since the greatest proportion of our mental states is allowed to so decrease in vividness, as to cease in time being the object of consciousness.

After these observations, we shall be prepared to expect, that in all spectral impressions palpable evidence will be afforded of the share which Hope and Fear had in the illusion;—that is, the illusion will be either increased or diminished in proportion to the form of the prospective affections of the mind which it excites. Of this fact a few examples may be given.

The first illustration which I shall offer is from the autobiography of Benvenuto Cellini. This surprising man, during his confinement in a vile loathsome dungeon, underwent a series of cruelties that had produced a morbid habit of body which stimulated, to the highest degree of excitement, feelings that were of themselves naturally vivid. He, therefore, continually fancied himself in the presence of an invisible guardian. Soon afterwards he was removed to the deepest subterranean cell of the castle in which he was immured, when the intense feeling of hope which he cherished of returning from darkness to the full brightness of day, not only dictated the subject of his spectral impressions, but greatly conspired to increase their vividness. Having prayed that he might once more behold the light of the sun, he suddenly fell into a sort of ecstacy, in which he fancied that he beheld the object of his fervent wish. But the exclamation which he uttered, and the glorious changes which this orb underwent, are best told in his own words:

" O wonderful power! O glorious influence divine! how much more bounteous art thou to me than I expected! The sun, divested of his rays, appeared a ball of purest melted gold. Whilst I gazed on this noble phenomenon, I saw the centre of the sun swell and bulge out, and, in a moment, there appeared a Christ upon the cross, formed of the self-same matter as the sun; and so gracious and pleasing was his aspect, that no human imagination could form so much as a faint idea of such beauty. As I was contemplating this glorious apparition I cried out aloud, A miracle! A miracle! O God! O clemency divine! O goodness infinite! what mercies dost thou lavish on me this morning! At the very time I thus meditated, and uttered these words, the figure of Christ began to move towards the side where the rays were concentered, and the middle of the sun swelled and bulged out as at first: the protuberance having increased considerably, was at last converted into a figure of the beautiful Virgin Mary, who appeared to sit with her son in her arms, in a graceful attitude, and even to smile; she stood between two angels of so divine a beauty, that imagination could not even form an idea of such perfection. I likewise saw in the same sun, a figure dressed in sacerdotal robes; this figure turned its back to me, and looked towards the blessed Virgin, holding Christ in her arms. All these things I clearly and plainly saw, and, with a loud voice, continued to return thanks to the Almighty. This wonderful phenomenon having appeared before me about eight minutes, vanished from my sight, and I was instantly conveyed back to my couch."

Of the vivifying effect of fear in conspiring, along with morbific agents, to heighten the intensity of mental illusions, numerous examples might be cited. But I shall first remark, that false impressions of sound are calculated in a particular manner to create surprise and alarm :—

> " This is no mortal business, nor no sound
> That the earth owes."

" The ear," says a writer on this subject, who himself experienced very strange illusions of sound, " is much more an instrument of terror than the eye. Diseased perceptions of sight are more common than those of hearing, and they are in general born with more tranquillity. A few simple sounds usually constitute the amount of what the ear unfaithfully presents; but when incessant half-articulated whispers, sudden calls, threats, obscure murmurs, and distant tollings, are heard, the mind is less disposed to patience and calm philosophy."*

A good example of the power of Fear to add to the vividness of apparitions, is afforded in the remarkable

---

* Nicholson's Journal, vol. xv. p. 296.

confession of John Beaumont, the Platonic philosopher.† "I would not," he says, " for the whole world, undergo what I have undergone, upon spirits coming twice to me; their first coming was most dreadful to me, the thing being then altogether new, and consequently more surprising, though at the first coming they did not appear to me, but only called to me at my chamber-windows, rung bells, sung to me, and played on music, &c.; but the last coming also carried terror enough; for when they came, being only five in number, the two women before mentioned, and three men, (though afterwards there came hundreds,) they told me they would kill me if I told any person in the house of their being there, which put me in some consternation; and I made a servant sit up with me four nights in my chamber, before a fire, it being in the Christmas holidays, telling no person of their being there. One of these spirits, in woman's dress, lay down upon the bed by me every night; and told me, if I slept, the spirits would kill me, which kept me waking for three nights. In the meantime, a near relation of mine went (though unknown to me) to a physician of my acquaintance, desiring him to prescribe me somewhat for sleeping, which he did, and a sleeping potion was brought me; but I set it by, being very desirous and inclined to

---

† " Had this man," says Dr Ferriar, " instead of irritating his mental disease by the study of Platonic philosophers, placed himself under the care of an intelligent physician, he would have regained his tranquillity, and the world would have lost a most extraordinary set of confessions."

sleep without it. The fourth night I could hardly forbear sleeping; but the spirit, lying on the bed by me, told me again, I should be killed if I slept; whereupon I rose and sat by the fireside, and in a while returned to my bed; and so I did a third time, but was still threatened as before; whereupon I grew impatient, and asked the spirits what they would have? Told them I had done the part of a Christian, in humbling myself to God, and feared them not; and rose from my bed, took a cane, and knocked at the ceiling of my chamber, a near relation of mine lying then over me, who presently rose and came down to me about two o'clock in the morning, to whom I said, ' You have seen me disturbed these four days past, and that I have not slept: the occasion of it was, that five spirits, which are now in the room with me, have threatened to kill me if I told any person of their being here, or if I slept; but I am not able to forbear sleeping longer, and acquaint you with it, and now stand in defiance of them; and thus I exerted myself about them; and notwithstanding their continued threats, I slept very well the next night, and continued so to do, though they continued with me above three months, day and night."

Again, in the case of Nicolai,—it would appear, that, notwithstanding his boasted calmness, the spectres which he saw were not always without the power of creating in his mind a little uneasiness, as the effort which he evidently made in order to preserve his composure betrays what was the real state of the philosopher's feelings. "After I had recovered," he observes, " from the first impression of terror, I never felt myself particularly agitated by these apparitions, as I considered them to be what they really were, the extraordinary consequences of indisposition; on the contrary, *I endeavoured as much as possible to preserve my composure of mind*, that I might remain distinctly conscious of what was passing within me." As it is evident, from this admission, that Nicolai's phantasms had occasionally some little power in disturbing him, we shall inquire into the effect that the agitation had upon his mind:—" In the afternoon," says Nicolai, " or a little after four o'clock, the figure which I had seen in the morning again appeared. I was alone when this happened,—a circumstance which, as may easily be conceived, could not be very agreeable. I went therefore to the apartment of my wife, to whom I related it. But thither also the figure pursued me. Sometimes it was present, sometimes it vanished, but it was always the same standing figure. A little after six o'clock, several stalking figures also appeared, but they had no connexion with the standing figure. I can assign no other reason for this apparition than that, though much more composed in my mind, I had not been able so soon entirely to forget the cause of such deep and distressing vexation, and had reflected on the consequences of it, in order, if possible, to avoid them; and that this happened three hours after dinner, at the time when digestion just begins.

" At length I became more composed with respect to the disagreeable incident which had given rise to the first apparition; but though I had used very excellent medicines, and found myself in other respects perfectly well, yet the apparitions did not diminish, but, on the contrary, rather increased in number, and were transformed in the most extraordinary manner."*

It is apparent from this confession, as well as from that of Beaumont, that when any phantasm has the effect of exciting strong emotions of the mind, the illusion may not only be prolonged, but repeated. The latter result occurs when the recollected ideas of former spectral impressions are subjected to a fresh morbific excitement, and when this effect is increased by the vivifying influence of the particular Hope or Fear, which the remembrance of the apparition may have induced.

An illustration to this effect is given by a writer on phantasms produced by disease, the account of which appeared in Nicholson's Journal:—" I know a gentleman," he says, " in the vigour of life, who, in my opinion, is not exceeded by any one in acquired knowledge and originality of deep research; and who, for nine months in succession, was always visited by a figure of the same man, threatening to destroy him, at the time of his going to rest. It appeared upon his lying down, and instantly disappeared when he resumed the erect posture." It is evident, from this narrative, that the most vivid idea in this individual's mind at his time of going to rest, was the remembered impression of the phantasm; and hence the same illusion was most likely to be renewed by a subsequent morbific cause of excitement.

The foregoing remarks will probably afford us an explanation of many cases of apparitions, in which an

* Nicholson's Journal, vol. vi. page 166.

individual has been haunted for many years by a similar description of phantasm, as by a good or evil genius, or by some supposed emissary from Satan, under the name of a *familiar*. In short, ideas which may be vivified by Hope or Fear, are, by the co-operation of morbific excitements, most easily converted into apparitions. They are then dispelled with considerable difficulty, and are rendered the more liable to return.

CHAPTER VII.

THE ILLUSIONS WHICH HOPE AND FEAR ARE CAPABLE OF EXCITING INDEPENDENTLY OF THE CO-OPERATION OF MORBIFIC CAUSES.

> " Then, led by thee to some wild cave remote,
> My taste I ply—the study of myself.
> Or, should the silver moon look kindly down,
> The vision'd forms of ages long gone by
> Gleam out from piled rock, or dewy bush—
> Mellow to kinder light the blaze of thought,
> And sooth the maddening mind to softer joy."
> *Lord* LEVESON GOWER's *Faust.*

AN apparition is, in a strict sense, a past feeling, renovated by the aid of morbific agents with a degree of vividness, equalling, or exceeding, an actual impression. If the renewed feeling should be one of vision, a form may arise perfectly complete; if of sound, a distinct conversation may be heard: or, if of touch, the impression may be no less complete. The question then is,—What illusions are Hope and Fear capable of exciting independently of the co-operation of morbific causes?

In this investigation a preliminary remark may be made, that all emotions which arise from such innate causes of them, as by their durable influence on our selfish and social dispositions or habits, have acquired the name of *moral*, are indicated by the same general effects on the circulation that result from the action of foreign agents introduced into the system, such as the particular gases to which I have alluded. For, while pleasurable excitement arising from sources of mental vividness is indicated by an increasing expansibility of the vital fluid, by a corresponding state of the diastole of the heart, and by a fulness and force of the arterial pulse, affections of a painful nature are manifested by an opposite tendency of the blood to reduce its volume; when a hard pulse, as well as that constricted state of the capillaries is induced, which bears the name of the *cutis anserina*. Such circumstances, then, are essential to the general susceptibility of the human frame to be affected in a definite manner, agreeably to the selfish and social nature of man.

I would next observe, that on laws connected with the various combinations of matter that more or less forcibly impress our sensitive organs, depend the *occasions* on which different susceptibilities of feeling are called forth. Particular hard or soft substances; for instance, luminous particles, sapid bodies, &c., in impressing with greater or less force any particular organ of sense, bear a reference to the definite susceptibility of the sensitive part to receive such impressions; and, accordingly, definite qualities of pleasure or of pain are produced in different states of vividness.

Again, when we contemplate man as a social being, we shall find, that his innate and individual susceptibilities of pleasures or of pain are liable to be still farther modified: that all his moral propensities or dispositions depend upon ultimate laws, determining on what definite occasions of social intercourse, various degrees of vividness shall be dispensed to the state of the mind.

After this general notice of the primary laws by which our emotions are governed, it may be briefly added, that in any train of sensations and ideas, the more any particular feelings are vivified by an occasion calculated to inspire hope or fear, the less vivid are all other impressions rendered which occur in the same train of feelings. But it is impossible for me, in this limited treatise, to enter into a full explanation of the principles which modify our natural emotions. I shall therefore remark, that one of them is alluded to after the following manner by Dr Brown; though I ought to premise, that he uses the word *perception* where others would use the term *sensation*, and *conception* where an idea or renovated feeling is evidently meant. His observations are to this effect:—
" The phantasms of the imagination in the reveries of our waking hours, when our external senses are still open and quick to feel, are, as mere conceptions, far less vivid than the primary perceptions from which they originally flowed: and yet, under the influence of any strong emotion, they become so much more bright and prominent than external things, that to the impassioned muser on distant scenes and persons, the scenes and persons truly around him are almost as if they were not in existence."

This, then, is the effect of Hope and Fear,—to reduce the vividness of all impressions that are not connected with the occasion which gave birth to the emotion, so as to render such impressions scarcely the object of consciousness. And thus it is, that in each train of thought, while every idea connected with a particular occasion of hope or fear becomes subject to a strong excitement, all other impressions, which bear no reference to the occasion, become proportionally faint. By this means the illusion must be increased. How well is this fact illustrated in the emotions which are excited, when, through the medium of the retina, an idea is intensely renovated upon the faded outlines of such forms as have been induced by the partial gleams of light which diversify woods, rocks, or clouds! In proportion as hope, or superstitious awe, impart an undue degree of vividness to the spectral outline which may thus be traced, all other parts of the natural objects which are unconnected with the form of the phantasm grow proportionally dim. The spectre then acquires an undue prominence in the imagination, and appears to start from the familiar objects of which, in reality, it merely forms a portion. This principle of our nature cannot perhaps be better exemplified than by a quotation from the Œdipus of Lee and Dryden:—

> " When the sun sets, shadows that shew'd at noon
> But small, appear most long and terrible ;
> So when we think fate hovers o'er our heads,
> Our apprehensions shoot beyond all bounds :
> Owls, ravens, crickets, seem the watch of death ;
> Nature's worst vermin scare her godlike sons ;
> Echoes the very leavings of a voice,

> Grow babbling ghosts, and call us to our graves.
> Each molehill thought swells to a huge Olympus;
> While we fantastic dreamers heave and puff,
> And sweat with an imagination's weight."

Such is the law which unduly vivifies the renovated outlines of figures that have been the subject of past feelings, and which renders all other parts of the sensible forms impressing the retina proportionally faint and obscure. But a much less sublime illustration of this principle is afforded in a well-told anecdote by Dr Ferriar in his Theory of Apparitions.

" A gentleman was benighted, while travelling alone, in a remote part of the highlands of Scotland, and was compelled to ask shelter for the evening at a small lonely hut. When he was to be conducted to his bed-room, the landlady observed, with mysterious reluctance, that he would find the window very secure. On examination, part of the wall appeared to have been broken down to enlarge the opening. After some inquiry, he was told that a pedlar, who had lodged in the room a short time before, had committed suicide, and was found hanging behind the door in the morning. According to the superstition of the country, it was deemed improper to remove the body through the door of the house; and to convey it through the window was impossible, without removing part of the wall. Some hints were dropped, that the room had been subsequently haunted by the poor man's spirit.

" My friend laid his arms, properly prepared against intrusion of any kind, by the bed-side, and retired to rest, not without some degree of apprehension. He was visited, in a dream, by a frightful apparition, and, awaking in agony, found himself sitting up in bed, with a pistol grasped in his right hand. On casting a fearful glance round the room, he discovered, by the moonlight, a corpse dressed in a shroud, reared erect against the wall, close by the window. With much difficulty he summoned up resolution to approach the dismal object, the features of which, and the minutest parts of its funeral apparel, he perceived distinctly. He passed one hand over it; felt nothing; and staggered back to the bed. After a long interval, and much reasoning with himself, he renewed his investigation, and at length discovered that the object of his terror was produced by the moonbeams forming a long bright image through the broken window, on which his fancy, impressed by his dream, had pictured, with mischievous accuracy, the lineaments of a body prepared for interment. Powerful associations of terror, in this instance, had excited the recollected images with uncommon force and effect."

CHAPTER VIII.

MENTAL EXCITEMENTS DISTINGUISHED AS PARTIAL OR GENERAL.

> " Behold from far a breaking cloud appears,
> Which in it many winged warriors bears:
> Their glory shoots upon my aking sense:—
> Thou, stronger, may'st endure the flood of light."—DRYDEN.

IN the earlier chapters of this part of the dissertation, some examples were adduced of spectral illusions, in which I had merely occasion to treat of ideas, and the excitements to which they alone may be subject from morbific agents. Little or no notice was taken of the important fact, that, in some instances, both actual impressions, and renovated feelings or ideas, may be simultaneously rendered unduly intense. I shall therefore now observe, that, in certain cases of phantasms originating from disease, it is evident that an exciting action is exclusively confined to the vivifying of renovated feelings. And, again, in that more complete illusion which is named an *ecstacy*, it is no less evident, that sensations as well as ideas are affected; the spectral illusions incidental to this state being far more vivid than when ideas are exclusively excited, and never failing to be accompanied with intense actual impressions,—such as acuteness of touch, and intolerance of light or sound.

To what causes this diversity of action is chiefly owing it is difficult to say. The nerves connected with the production of sensations are never excited but when the organ which they supply comes in actual contact with external matter. On the other hand, the nerves which give rise to ideas do not impart their peculiar influence, unless excited by that ultimate law of the mind, which ordains, that the repetition of a definite sensation shall be followed by a renovation of the past feelings with which it was before associated. If, then, the nerves, which are considered as instrumental to actual impressions or sensations, derive their origin from the external surface of the organ which they supply, and then influence the circulation, various morbid phenomena connected with the state of the memory no less indicate, that to other nerves, the peculiar function of which is the renovation of past feelings, a different origin may with some reason be assignable; that such nerves may first rise from the brain, and be afterwards distributed to each vascular organ. On this hypothesis may be probably explained the curious fact, that in certain morbid affections, the peculiar seat of which is in the brain, ideas only are excited; and hence, that spectral impressions may be unattended by any such increased sensibility of touch, hearing, vision, &c., as is common to ecstatic illusions.

But i may be now asked, Under what circumstances are sensations and ideas *conjointly* affected by morbific excitements? In attempting an answer to this question, it is rather difficult to conceive of a cause which, by acting immediately on the whole of the nervous system, can simultaneously vivify both actual and renovated impressions; but it is not so difficult to conceive of an agent, such as the nitrous oxide, which can communicate a general influence to each organ of feeling through the medium of the circulating system, upon the varied condition of which the vividness of sensations and ideas has a more direct dependence. By this means, therefore, an adventitious or morbific agent can prove the substitute for a general nervous influence; and whenever the blood is in this state of excitement, the phenomena of various ecstacies indicate, that while sensations and ideas are severally increased in intensity, the influence upon which the renovation of past feelings depends, is in proportion more freely and forcibly communicated than that which is connected with actual impressions.

There are, again, other circumstances to be considered in the vivifying actions of morbific causes. A true ecstacy, which is characterized by the simultaneous excitement of sensations and ideas, is often persistent. But when ideas are exclusively vivified, the action is seldom continued for a long time without remission. Thus, in a case of *delirium tremens*, which came under my notice, the intense revivals of past feelings of touch, or the distinct tones of voice which vibrated in the morbid ear, " like no mortal sounds," or the

" Forms without bodies, and impassive air,"

that flitted before the sight, were not uninterruptedly

continued, as during an ecstacy, but impressed the senses with evident remissions. The patient had therefore an opportunity of comparing his phantasies with the place in which he was stationed, and with the objects around him, so as to obviate the force of his illusion by the faculty of judgment. Nicolai possessed the same self-collection. " I was always able," he observes, " to distinguish, with the greatest precision, phantasms from phenomena. I knew extremely well, when it only appeared to me that the door was opened and a phantom entered, and when the door really was opened and any person came in." In many instances, however, the illusion has not been so easily corrected.

Nor do causes which exclusively vivify the recollected images of the mind constantly occupy the entire surface of any particular organ of feeling. It is in general only a few objects in a renovated landscape which usurp corresponding portions of the seat of vision. A detached figure may hold a place among natural and real objects, partaking with them of a similar degree of vividness, and hence be mistaken for an actual impression.

Having at length explained the phenomena by which partial and general excitements are distinguished, I shall, in the ensuing chapters, confine myself to the consideration of those agents which diffuse their influence so generally throughout the system as to act at one and the same moment of time, though in different proportions, both on sensations and ideas, producing what are named *ecstatic illusions*.

CHAPTER IX.

GENERAL MENTAL EXCITEMENTS CONSIDERED AS THE RESULT OF MORBIFIC CAUSES CO-OPERATING WITH MORAL AGENTS.

> "For I am sick, and capable of fears."
> *King John.*

I HAD occasion to remark in a preceding chapter, that feelings of pleasure and pain acknowledge certain innate laws, which may be regarded as arising from the particular constitution of the human frame. Thus, it is implanted in our nature, that certain external objects, as of touch, sound, colour, taste, smell, &c. should communicate to every individual definite pleasurable or painful effects.

The particular susceptibility of feeling, however, possessed by each part of the body, may materially differ in degree; and this difference may result from the extent of influence imparted by the brain and nerves to the various organs of sense, or it may arise from some particular condition of the organs themselves, by which the mental effect resulting from the nervous system is more or less modified. Nay, more— such various susceptibilities of feeling may even be occasioned by some unknown peculiarity of the immaterial mind itself, by which, in its relation to the structure of the human frame, it is rendered more liable to one particular state than to another. From any one, therefore, of these several causes, or even from a co-operation of two or more of them, there may, in the same person, be an innate tendency to receive a more vivid degree of pleasure from sound than from colour; or a degree of vividness, no less disproportionate, may be imparted to the sensations connected with the gustatory organs. Even with regard to feelings of the same kind, a variety of predilections may subsist. One tint of colour or shade may naturally give more delight than another, and the same observation may apply to particular odours, tones, &c. Lastly, this constitutional variety of susceptibilities evinced in the several organs of the body, may again differ in different individuals.

In the next place, when we contemplate man as a social being, we shall find, that his innate and individual susceptibilities of pleasure or of pain are liable to be still farther modified. Moral laws exist which determine on what occasions of social intercourse particular hopes and fears shall be excited. Such definite occasions are connected with the acquisition or privation of knowledge, of power, of society, of the means of evincing gratitude, of the means of resentment, and of the esteem of our fellow-creatures.

These remarks lead me to attempt the explanation of a very important law, relative to the manner in which the mind may be influenced. A morbific cause, whether pleasurable or painful, can only co-operate with moral agents endowed with a similar specific power. Thus, if we allow the nitrous oxide to be a morbific cause, (which the utmost range of its action certainly shews,*) it does nothing more than *single out*, as it were, all sensations and ideas which are of themselves morally pleasurable, but has no immediate effect on the painful feelings with which they are naturally mingled. For this reason, it is easy to suppose, that when Sir Humphrey Davy imbibed a large quantity of the gas, all the ideas connected with his favourite chemical researches would be among the first to be affected by this powerful agent. And, accordingly, on one occasion, he remarks, " I gradually began to lose the perception of external things, and a vivid and intense recollection *of some former experiments* passed through the mind." Again, in the opposite effects arising from the febrile miasma, this powerful agent imparts no additional degree of vividness to the quality of any feelings, but such as, from the previous operation of moral agents, are, of themselves, painful. The action of various other morbific causes admits of a similar explanation.

---

* Orfila, in his history of poisons, remarks, that the nitrous oxide dissolves with great promptitude in the veins of animals into which it is injected, but produces no apparent change in the arterial blood. When gradually injected, it does not at first give rise to any observable effect; but if the injections are multiplied, they are followed by phenomena, like those attending copious inhalations, and to these death may supervene, which (as he supposes) begins by the brain. If injected in a large quantity at once, it occasions the distension of the pulmonary portion of the heart, and is likewise fatal.

In contemplating, then, the co-operation of morbific causes with moral agents, there must evidently subsist two varieties of ecstacy.

One variety of ecstacy must occur when the cause of mental excitement, to which the affection is referable, has added to the vividness of pleasurable feelings, but has proportionally diminished that of painful feelings.

Another, and a second variety of ecstacy must occur, when the cause of mental excitement, to which the affection is referable, has added to the intensity of painful feelings, but has proportionally diminished the vividness of pleasurable feelings.

These two varieties of ecstacy will be constantly kept in view in the ensuing chapters.

CHAPTER X.

THE FREQUENT EFFECT OF GENERAL MORBIFIC EXCITEMENTS IN RENDERING THE MIND UNCONSCIOUS EITHER OF PLEASURABLE OR PAINFUL FEELINGS.

―――――――――" What is mortal man?
So changeable his being, with himself
Dissimilar; the rainbow of an hour!"
THOMPSON's *Progress of Sickness.*

BEFORE explaining a very important law of the mind relative to consciousness, which is materially connected with the object of the present dissertation, I shall briefly glance at the progress that has been made in the metaphysical part of this inquiry.

Sensations and ideas having been considered as nothing more than states of the immaterial mind, I proceeded upon the hypothesis, that, as long as vitality subsisted, a succession of such states, even during syncope and sleep, was continually recurring. It was next shewn, that the comparative degree of vividness which subsists between sensations and ideas, suggests to the mind the intellectual feelings of the present and of the past; and, along with this relation of time, the identity of *one mind*, as existing in a succession of states; and that, when ideas are rendered more vivid than sensations, a revival of past feelings is contemplated as the result of actual impressions. A further observation was made, that the notion of the present and of the past, as well as of the proper identity of the mind, necessarily enters into our definition of *consciousness;* and that mental consciousness cannot be induced until sensations and ideas have attained a certain degree of vividness. Hence the unconsciousness attending the faint impressions of sleep. It was also pointed out, that a morbific agent capable of exciting the feelings of the mind, exerted a specific power over some particular quality of the feelings; and that it could only impart a definite addition of pleasure or pain to feelings which, from the paramount influence of moral agents, were of themselves either pleasurable or painful.

The law, then, to be explained is this: *When a morbific agent adds to the general vividness of our pleasurable feelings, every feeling of an opposite or painful quality is, in an inverse proportion, rendered less vivid;* and, vice versa, *the same law holds good when a morbific agent adds to the vividness of all our painful feelings.*

It follows, then, that as consciousness is never excited until sensations and ideas have attained a certain degree of vividness, the intensity imparted to pleasurable states of the mind may be so great, that, from the extreme of faintness to which affections of an opposite quality will be proportionably reduced, every mental consciousness of painful feelings may be destroyed. And, in like manner, the action of a morbific agent, when intensely exciting all our painful affections, may, in the course of its operation, annihilate every consciousness of pleasurable emotions. I need scarcely remark how well this general effect is displayed in the actions of the gases to which I have so often alluded. Under the influence of the nitrous oxide, an inhaler is conscious of no feelings, or is under the influence of no mental illusions but those which impart to him delight. While under the influence of the febrile miasma, every blissful emotion is stifled in the overwhelming dejection which ensues, and in the horrid spectral images with which the unhappy patient is haunted.

In contemplating, then, the operation of the laws which I have explained, the following is a summary of the states of consciousness during each of the two varieties of ecstacy which I have enumerated.

In the first variety of ecstacy, where the particular cause of mental excitement to which the affection is referable has added to the vividness of pleasurable feelings, but has proportionally diminished that of painful feelings, the general result is, that pleasurable feelings are rendered inordinately intense, while painful feelings become so faint as to cease being the object of mental consciousness.

But in the second variety of ecstacy, where the particular cause of mental excitement to which the affection is referable has added to the intensity of painful feelings, but has proportionally diminished

x

the vividness of pleasurable feelings, the general result is, that painful feelings are rendered inordinately intense, while pleasurable feelings become so faint as to be no longer the object of mental consciousness.

CHAPTER XI.

THE INFLUENCE OF ANY PREVAILING MORAL DISPOSITION MAY BE SO INCREASED BY A MORBIFIC EXCITEMENT, AS TO BE PRODUCTIVE OF SPECTRAL IMPRESSIONS OF A CORRESPONDING CHARACTER.

> " The lunatic, the lover, and the poet,
> Are of imagination all compact."—SHAKSPEARE.

BEFORE proceeding in this investigation, a summary may be presented of some of the conclusions to which we have arrived in the foregoing chapters.

Morbific excitements of the mind were, in their operations, considered as either *partial* or *general*.

The indications of partial morbific excitements are manifested by the renovation of past feelings only in an intense state; actual impressions continuing in general unaffected. Nor are the illusions which follow to be traced to affections common to every organ of sensation. Phantasms of vision, for instance, may accrue without being necessarily attended by equally intense ideas of sound or of touch.

The indications of a *general* morbific excitement, or ecstacy, are manifested by actual impressions as well as recollected images of the mind having been rendered unduly intense; ideas, however, being more vivid than sensations. With respect to the illusions which follow, they are of so complete a nature as to indicate, that every organ of sensation has been more or less affected by the excitement.

It was also explained, that hope and fear possessed a powerful vivifying influence, and that all mental illusions, whether arising from partial or general morbific excitements, were heightened in their effect, in proportion to the intensity of the natural emotions of hope or fear which the subject of them was calculated from moral causes to excite.

These moral causes, therefore, it will be my present object to consider with more attention, but particularly with reference to the *occasions* on which the susceptibility of the human mind to its various affections is manifested.

All the moral propensities or dispositions of man depend upon ultimate laws, determining on what definite occasions various degrees of vividness shall be dispensed to the pleasurable and painful feelings of the mind. Such definite occasions are connected with the acquisition or privation, 1*st*, of knowledge; 2*dly*, of power; 3*dly*, of society; 4*thly*, of the means of evincing gratitude; 5*thly*, of the means of resentment; 6*thly*, of the esteem of our fellow-creatures. A sense of the acquisition of any of these objects is in each individual attended with a more or less vivid degree of pleasure; and a sense of the privation of any of them is attended with a more or less vivid degree of pain. Nor is it less favourable to the enjoyments of social intercourse, that there should exist a law by which the congratulations of sympathizing friends should add to the vividness of the joys we experience, or that their condolence should allay the poignancy of the most bitter affliction.

But with regard to the particular constitutional circumstances of the human system, which may be deemed necessary for the development of laws upon which the moral character of man depends, I shall offer no opinion. I have already hinted, that the susceptibility possessed by our mental feelings of various degrees of pleasure and pain may not depend upon one circumstance only connected with the animal economy, but may involve the co-operation of many causes far beyond the reach of human inquiry. It may depend in some measure upon certain peculiarities of the nervous system, contemplated as the source whence various degrees of mental vividness are derived; or it may depend upon the greater or less tendency of vascular organs to be affected by the nervous influence; or, lastly, it may involve some characteristic of the immaterial mind itself.

Having explained the moral occasions upon which our feelings are excited, it may be added, that their vivifying influence extends to all impressions which may be connected with them in any known relationship. But as all pleasurable or painful trains of feeling, when renewed, shew a tendency, on each occasion of their recurrence, to become fainter and fainter, the anticipation of good or evil, which vivifies our feelings, excites them in a degree proportional to the natural susceptibility of the mind to receive more or less pleasure and pain on various moral occasions, and proportional to the probability or improbability of an expected possession or privation; the affections thus induced being those which we express by the terms *Hope* and *Fear*.

These observations being premised, I shall now confine my attention far less to partial morbific causes of mental excitement, than to those general ones which conjointly influence both actual impressions and the renovated feelings of the mind.

It was demonstrated, that during every ecstacy, or general excitement of the mind, either pleasurable feelings were excited and painful ones depressed, or, *vice versa*, painful feelings were excited, and pleasurable ones depressed. Now, in each of these cases, the depressed feelings might be rendered so faint as to cease being the object of mental consciousness.

But it was likewise observed, that a morbific cause, in imparting a pleasurable or painful addition to the vividness of our feelings, possesses nothing more than a *co-operating* influence; the proper quality of our feelings being previously determined by natural objects of sensation, which, from the various modes in which they act, give to the different dispositions of mankind their peculiar character, and, thereby, come to be regarded in the light of moral agents. If a morbific cause, therefore, when operating on the states of the mind, should be endowed for the time with a pleasurable power, it merely *singles out* (as it were) and vivifies all the sensations and ideas which are of themselves naturally pleasurable, but has no direct influence on feelings of an opposite quality; and, *vice versa*, the same rule holds good with a morbific cause capable of rendering painful feelings more vivid.

According to this view, we must regard each morbific agent as very limited in its operations; it may, for instance, be capable of adding to the vividness of pleasurable feelings, and consequently of depressing painful ones; or, *vice versa*, of exciting painful feelings and depressing pleasurable ones. But, as long as moral agents are paramount in their vivifying influence to such as are adventitious or morbific, it must always happen, that those feelings which may be connected with a definite occasion of moral excitement will be rendered more disproportionally vivid than others of similar quality, whether pleasurable or painful, which may be unconnected with the same moral occasion. A good general illustration of this effect is afforded by Burton, when speaking of patients whose temper and pursuits are evidently frivolous, but all of which may be so acted upon by morbific causes as to be rendered pre-eminently vivid. Patients of this kind " vary," says Burton, " upon every object heard or seen. If they see a stage-play, they run upon that a week after; if they hear music or see dancing, they have nought but bagpipes in their brains; if they see a combat, they are all for arms; if abused, an abuse troubles them long after; if crossed, they cross. Restless in thoughts, and continually meditating. More like dreamers than men awake; they wake as others dream, and such, for the most part, are their imaginations and conceits; absurd, vain, foolish toys, yet they are most curious and solicitous continually. As serious in a toy as it were a most necessary business of great moment, and still thinking of it. Though they do talk with you, and seem to be otherwise employed, and to your thinking very intent and busy, still that toy runs in their mind, *that fear, that suspicion, that abuse, that vexation, that castle in the air, that pleasant walking dream,* whatever it is."

I shall likewise, on this occasion, repeat the remark which I made, that when Hope and Fear act on the mind without the co-operation of any morbific excitement, the tendency of these emotions is to render more vivid all the feelings of the mind that are actually connected with the moral occasion which gave irth to them, and to reduce to as opposite a state of faintness all feelings of the mind that fail in being connected with the same moral occasion. Owing, then, to this principle, which no morbific agent is capable of resisting, it is impossible that any quality of sensations and ideas, pleasurable or painful, can be excited or depressed with the least degree of uniformity.

I shall now illustrate this law by that passion which forms the chief theme of poets. In this instance, every idea of the object of the lover's hopes is unduly vivified, while every other object, particularly if it be ungrateful to the mind, appears to fade from the recollection. But no one has better described this effect than Dryden, in the truly affecting and natural strain of verse which he has put into the mouth of a heroine of one of his dramas:—

> " I am not what I was since yesterday;
> My food forsakes me, and my needful rest:
> I pine, I languish, love to be alone,
> Think much, speak little, and, in speaking, sigh :
> When I see Torrismond, I am unquiet;
> And when I see him not I am in pain.

"They brought a paper to me to be sign'd;
Thinking on him, I quite forgot my name,
And writ, for *Leonora*, Torrismond.
I went to bed, and to myself I thought
That I would think on Torrismond no more;
Then shut my eyes, but could not shut out him.
I turn'd, and tried each corner of my bed,
To find if sleep was there; but sleep was lost:
Fev'rish for want of rest, I rose and walk'd,
And by the moonshine to the windows went;
There, thinking to exclude him from my thoughts,
I cast my eyes upon the neighb'ring fields,
And, ere I was aware, sigh'd to myself,
There fought my Torrismond."*

With this illustration before us, (faithfully copied from nature, as most of my readers will, I think, admit,) it is easy to foresee the effect which must arise, when the vividness of a strong affection is increased by morbific causes of excitement. " A young man," says Pinel, " who had lost his reason amid the pangs of disappointed love, was influenced by so powerful an illusion, that he mistook every female visitor for his Mary Adelina, the object of his unfortunate attachment."†

But this investigation becomes of considerable moment, when we reflect upon the permanent effects which may result from the paramount influence of moral laws, when viewed in connexion with the subordinate, yet co-operating, influence of morbific excite-

---

* Spanish Fryer.
† Pinel on Insanity, translation by Dr Davis, page 144.

ments. Pinel has stated, that, out of one hundred and thirteen lunatic patients, the exciting causes of thirty-four of them might be traced to domestic misfortunes. Twenty-four had met with matrimonial obstacles, thirty had suffered from political events occasioned by the revolution, and twenty-five were disturbed by religious fanaticism.

These are all the remarks I have to offer on the cooperation of morbific and moral agents in their influence on the states of the mind. We are, therefore, I trust, entitled to expect, that when any quality of mental feelings, pleasurable or painful, is subjected to a vivifying action, an uniformity of excitement is by no means to be expected, and that the most intense ideas which may give rise to spectral illusions will be often found attributable to the predominant vivifying action of moral causes. But of this fact I shall now adduce several remarkable

ILLUSTRATIONS.

In the first place, the force of the sexual and parental ties will be often indicated by the subject of these visions. "When I accidentally fell into the sea," says a writer on the phantasms, to which he was subject from disease, "and, after swimming a certain time without assistance, began to despair of my situation, the image of my dwelling, and the accustomed objects, appeared with a degree of vividness little differing from that of actual vision. Mr Stuart, M. P. when greatly in danger some years ago, by being wrecked in a boat on the Eddystone rocks, relates, in an account which appeared in the papers, that his family appeared to him in this extremity. 'He thought he saw them.'"*

A vision of the same general character (though some little doubt may be expressed whether it was not a dream) occurred to Ben Jonson. But it is probable that, in this case, the poet's mental excitement had resulted from a plethoric state of the system, the consequence of too generous a diet, which had co-operated with parental anxiety for the safety of a son, whom he had left exposed to a contagious fever raging at the time in London. Drummond was told by Jonson, " that when the King came to England, about the time that the plague was in London, he, being in the country at Sir Robert Cotton's house with old Cambden, saw in a vision his eldest son, then a young child and at London, appear unto him with the mark of blood upon his forehead, as if it had been with a sword, at which, amazed, he prayed unto God, and in the morning he came unto Mr Cambden's chamber to tell him, who persuaded him it was but an apprehension, at which he should not be dejected. In the meantime, there came letters from his wife of the death of that boy in the plague. He appeared to him, he said, of a manly shape, and of that growth, he thinks, he shall be at the resurrection."

Many other narratives, exhibiting indications of a similar excitement of feelings, may be found in various biographies, where they have only found a place, be-

---

* Nicholson's Journal, vol. xv. p. 295.

cause a fortuitous coincidence with the subject of the phantasm and subsequent events, has served to countenance the popular views entertained regarding the sacred mission of apparitions.* Of such a character was the well-known illusion of Dr Donne. This eminent poet married, against her father's consent, Anne, daughter of Sir George Moore; and to this lady he felt an attachment, which the verses of no poet have ever recorded in more fervent terms. And, that his declarations were no less sincere, numerous anecdotes, recorded of his life, have fully corroborated. The persecution which he suffered from his father-in-law on account of the marriage preyed upon a constitution naturally delicate, and excited to an intense degree a temperament evidently melancholic; so that it was far from remarkable, that, during such a state of mental excitement, spectral impressions should have resulted. Nor can it create much surprise, that the subject of his mental illusion should be a wife, whom, in an elegy which he composed upon parting from her, before he accompanied Sir Robert Drury to Paris, he has thus affectionately commemorated:—

> Oh, Fortune!   *   *   *   *
> Rend us in sunder, thou canst not divide
> Our bodies so, but that our souls are ty'd,
> And we can love by letters still and gifts,
> And thoughts, and dreams: Love never wanteth shifts.
>   *   *   *   *   *

---

* See Note 6.

Be ever then yourself, and let no woe
Win on your health, your youth, your beauty so;
Declare yourself base Fortune's enemy;
Nor less by your contempt than her inconstancy;
That I may grow enamour'd of your mind,
When my own thoughts I here neglected find.
And this, to th' comfort of my dear, I vow,
My deeds shall still be what my deeds are now;
The poles shall move to teach me ere I start,
And when I change my love I'll change my heart."

It is evident, from the foregoing lines, under what frame of mind Dr Donne yielded to Sir Robert Drury's importunity to accompany him to Paris, and quitted the object of his connubial attachment. The fear that any woe should " win upon her health, her youth, and beauty," must have resulted from the circumstance, that he had left her when she was not far from her expected confinement,—in an ill habit of body, and so unwilling to part with him, that, as it is added, " her divining soul boded some ill in his absence."

Two days after Dr Donne had arrived in Paris, he was left alone in a room, where he had been dining with Sir Robert Drury and a few companions. Sir Robert returned about an hour afterwards. He found his friend in a state of ecstacy, and so altered in his countenance that he could not look upon him without amazement. The doctor was not able for some time to answer the question, *What had befallen him?*—but, after a long and perplexed pause, at last said, " I have seen a dreadful vision since I saw you;—I have seen my dear wife pass twice by me through this room, with her hair hanging about her shoulders, and a dead child in her arms. This I have seen since I saw you." To which Sir Robert answered,—" Sure, sir, you have slept since I went out; and this is the result of some melancholy dream, which I desire you to forget, for you are now awake." Donne replied,—" I cannot be more sure that I now live, than that I have not slept since I saw you; and am as sure that at her second appearing she stopped, looked me in the face, and vanished."

The poet's biographer (Isaac Walton) then adds, that a servant was dispatched to Drury-house, to know if Mrs Donne was living, and, if alive, in what condition; who brought back word, that he found and left this lady very sad and sick in bed; and that, after a long and dangerous labour, she had been delivered of a dead child. It is also stated, that the abortion took place on the same day, and about the same hour, that the spectral impression occurred.

Other subjects of spectral illusions are those which have been excited by strong friendship. Illustrations of this fact are familiar to most readers of the marvellous. The celebrated apparition of Ficinus was seen by Michael Mercato the elder, in consequence of an agreement made between these two friends, that the first who died should acquaint the other with his final condition. This survivor was studying in his closet. He heard the trampling of a horse's feet, which suddenly ceased at the door of his house. The well-known voice of Ficinus then vociferated in his ears, " O, Michael! Michael! those things are true!" Mercato immediately turned to the window, and had just time to behold his friend, dressed in white, and galloping off on a pale horse, when he was seen no more. At that very moment (says Baronius) Ficinus died at Florence.

Regarding this story, of which I have given a brief abstract, Dr Ferriar, in his Theory of Apparitions, offers the following remarks:—" Many attempts have been made to discredit it, but I think the evidence has never been shaken. I entertain no doubt that Mercato had seen what he described: in following the reveries of Plato, the idea of his friend, and of their compact, had been revived, and had produced a spectral impression, during the solitude and awful silence of the early hours of study."*

In co-operation with morbific causes, RESENTMENT, when highly excited, has contributed to produce spectral impressions. This fact is strikingly illustrated in the life of the most undaunted of champions that was ever opposed to the enemies of the Protestant cause. " Martin Luther's life," says Atterbury, " was a continual warfare; he was engaged against the united forces of the papal world, and he stood the shock of them bravely, both with courage and success." In freely subscribing, however, to pay this great man the homage he so richly deserves from posterity, for the successful display of most of those eminent virtues which were essential to the sacred cause that oc-

---

* Another apparition of the same kind, sent likewise into the world upon a similar errand, is that of Des Fontaines, as recorded by the Abbé de St Pierre.—See remarks in Note 7.

cupied his mind, it cannot be concealed, that he possessed an irritable temper of resentment, too little softened by the mild tenets of Christianity. This impetuousness, therefore, which often incorporated itself with purer motives of zeal, was unluckily fed by the unmerited cruelties he met with from the Romish church. Thus, in Captain Bell's translation of Luther's Table-talk, there is the following self-confession of this great reformer :—" When I (said Luther) write against the Pope, I am not melancholie; for then I labour with the brains and understanding, then I write with joie of heart; insomuch, that, not long since, Doctor Reisenpusch said unto mee, I much marvel that you can be so merrie; if the case were mine, it would go near to kill me: whereupon I answered him, and said, Neither the Pope, nor all his shaven retinue, can make me sad ; for I know that they are Christ's enemies; therefore I fight against him with joyful courage."

But Luther's resentment was not wholly concentrated against the assumed successor of St Peter. For, in the true spirit of the reforming age, he had considered the Pope as invoking the aid of the devil to dissipate the dawning light of religious truth. And when a temporary plethoric state of the system, occasioned by the sudden change from a spare to a generous diet, had given to this vivid image of his fancy an apparent form and substance, his resentment against Satan resembled that which he had harboured against the pontifical coadjutor of the fiend ;—it was not merely spiritual, but even personal. "As I departed from Worms," said Luther, " and not far from

Eisenach, was taken prisoner; I was lodged in the castle of Wartzburg, my Patmos, in a chamber far from people, where none could have access unto me, but only two boyes that twice the daye brought me meat and drink; now, among other things, they brought me hazel-nuts, which I put into a box, and sometimes I used to crack and eat of them. In the night times, my gentleman, the devil, came and got the nuts out of the box, and cracked them against one of the bed-posts, making a great noise, and a rumbling about my bed; but I regarded him nothing at all. When afterwards I began to slumber, then he kept such a racket and rumbling upon the chamber stairs, as if many emptie hogsheads and barrels had been tumbled down; and although I knew that the stairs were strongly guarded with iron bars, so that no passage was either up or down, yet I arose and went towards the stairs to see what the matter was; but finding the door fast shut, I said,—' Art thou there? so be there still;'—I committed myself to Christ, my Lord and Saviour, of whom it is written, *Omnia subjecisti pedibus ejus.*"

There is likewise another narrative told of this reformer to the same effect. "At such time," said Luther, "when I could not be rid of the devil without uttering sentences out of the Holie Scripture, then I made him flie with jeering and ridiculous words and terms: I have recorded my sins in thy register. I said likewise unto him, 'Devil, if Christ's blood, which was shed for my sins, be not sufficient, then I desire thee that thou wouldst pray to God for me.' When he findeth me idle," said Luther, "and that I have nothing in hand, then he is very busy,—and before I am aware, he wringeth from me a bitter sweat; but when I offer him the pointed spear, that is, God's word, then he flieth,—yet before he goeth he maketh me bloody armed, or else giveth me a grievous hurricane. When at the first I began to write against the Pope, and that the Gospel went on, then the devil laid himself strongly therein, he ceased not to rumble and rage about, for he willingly would have preserved purgatory at Magdeburg, and *discursum animarum.*"*

On occasions of ambition, also, which give rise to a desire for the acquisition of power, various degrees of vividness are imparted to the feelings of the mind. —Another cause of mental vividness is connected with the love of knowledge. Ashmole was constantly visited by a phantasm that solved his most intricate problems, the answers to which are said to still exist

---

* Upon the subject of Luther's visions Mr Coleridge makes the following excellent comment:—" Had Luther been himself a prince, he could not have desired better treatment than he received during his eight months' stay in the Wartzburg; and in consequence of a more luxurious diet than he had been accustomed to, he was plagued with temptations both from the ' flesh and the devil.' It is evident from his letters, that he suffered under great irritability of his nervous system, the common effect of deranged digestion in men of sedentary habits, who are, at the same time, intense thinkers; and this irritability adding to and vivifying the impressions made upon him in early life, and fostered by the theological systems of his manhood, is abundantly sufficient to explain all his apparitions, and all his mighty combats with evil spirits."— *Friend, by S. T. Coleridge, Esq. vol. ii. p.* 236.

in one of his manuscript volumes, under the title of *Responsum Raphealis*.

In the *last* place, an anxiety for the esteem, or a fear for the reprobation of mankind, is a natural vivid affection which always influences our actions, and which often gives a corresponding character to the subject of spectral impressions. Thus, among visionaries who boast of divine missions, we trace, in the subject of their illusions, a lurking ambition to maintain, by this means, a conspicuous rank among their fellow-mortals. " The Rev. John Mason, a clergyman of Water-stratford, near Buckingham," remarks Dr Crichton, " was observed to speak rationally on every subject that had no relation to his wild notions of religion. He died in 1695, soon after he fancied he had seen our Saviour, fully convinced of the reality of the vision, and of his own divine mission. He was perfectly persuaded in his own mind that he was Elias, and that he was destined to announce the coming of Jesus, who was to begin the millennium at Water-stratford."

CHAPTER XII.

WHEN MORAL AGENTS WHICH EXERT A PLEASURABLE INFLUENCE ARE HEIGHTENED IN THEIR EFFECTS BY THE CO-OPERATION OF MORBIFIC EXCITEMENTS OF A SIMILAR PLEASURABLE QUALITY, THE MIND MAY BE RENDERED TOTALLY UNCONSCIOUS OF OPPOSITE OR PAINFUL FEELINGS.

> " Sweetly oppress'd with beatific views,
> I hear angelic instruments, I see
> Primeval ardours, and essential forms."
>
> THOMPSON's *Progress of Sickness.*

I NOW trust that the view with which I set out is nearly established,—that the action of all morbific causes, capable of influencing the states of the mind, merely consists in an *addition* being made to the vividness of such qualities of our feelings, as had previously been rendered pleasurable or painful by the various objects which, from infancy, impress in a definite manner our several organs of sense. There is indeed no cause of mental excitement which, in this respect, exerts a more extensive influence over the mind than the nitrous oxide. This gas cannot absolutely change the quality of those mental states, which, from constitutional causes, are more or less painful, but its effect is to add an intensity of pleasure to feelings which are themselves grateful, and thereby to diminish the vividness of painful sensations and ideas. Thus, we have traced its influence in rendering all painful feelings so faint as to cease being the object of consciousness.

The law by which mental consciousness is regulated, meets with an ample illustration in the effects imparted to our various feelings, by many of the morbific causes of mental vividness which I have enumerated. That peculiar cause inducing insanity, for instance, which is referable to a highly-excited state of the sanguine temperament, gives an additional degree of vividness to the pleasurable feelings of the mind; hence impressions of pain are so proportionally enfeebled, that the mental consciousness of them is not excited. This fact is exemplified in those individuals who, according to Burton, " are commonly ruddy of complexion and high-coloured, who are much inclined to laughter, witty, and merry, conceipted in discourse, pleasant, if they be not too farre gone ;" who, if they should happen to take such a delight in dramatic scenes as the maniac recorded by Aristotle, are amused the whole day long with imaginary actors.

But it is instructive, in contemplating the cause of any pleasurable excitement, to confine our attention to its effect in diminishing the intensity of painful impressions made on sensitive organs. Sir Humphrey Davy has stated, that the nitrous oxide, in its extensive operation, is capable of destroying physical pain, and we know, that the cause of that variety of amentia which is distinguished by pleasurable fancies and reveries has a similar effect. Indeed, the insensibility of the maniac, during the greatest height of a paroxysm, to actual impressions, has been long a subject of remark. " The skin," says one writer, " is sometimes as it were benumbed; the patients feel every thing like cotton; they do not feel punctures, blisters, or setons." About three or four centuries ago, when lunatics were unprotected by charitable asylums, this diminished or almost obliterated consciousness of sensations, was, unfortunately for these hapless beings, too frequently put to the test, and thus became a subject of popular observation and notoriety. The cruel deprivation to which they were liable resulted from the dissolution of the religious houses, which took place at the time of the Reformation. Maniacs, or *Abraham-men,* as they were then named, had no longer the benefit of those hospitals which, during the papal establishment, were instituted for their relief. Deserted also by their friends, who superstitiously attributed the cause of their disorder to the possession of devils, they were allowed to ramble about the country almost naked, and exposed to every hardship which could result from famine and the inclemencies of the weather. Thus despised and shunned, they were compelled, in order to procure the sustenance necessary to satisfy the cravings of their hunger, to use not only prayers, but force; and this practice at length suggested to idle and dissolute beggars the advantage to be derived from feigning madness, as a cloak for the compulsion which they might find it equally requisite to use in the collection of alms. But, in order to give a proper colouring to such a counterfeit, it was found necessary that the insensibility to suffering which these poor Abraham-men evinced, should be also imitated.* Thus, in Decker's Bellman of London, we have the following account of one of these dissembling madmen :—" He swears he hath been in bedlam, and will talk frantickly of purpose; you see pins stuck in sundry places of his naked flesh, especially in his arms, which pain he gladly puts himself to (being indeed no torment at all, his skin is either so dead with some foul disease, or so hardened with weather) only to make you believe he is out of his wits." The disguise of one of these feigned bedlamites is assumed by Edgar in King Lear, who finds it no less necessary to imitate the maniac's corporeal insensibility :—

> " The country gives me proof and precedent
> Of bedlam-beggars, who, with roaring voices,
> Stick in their numb'd and mortified bare arms
> Pins, wooden pricks, nails, sprigs of rosemary;
> And with this horrible object, from low farms,
> Poor pelting villages, sheep-cotes, and mills,
> Some time with lunatic bans, some time with prayers,
> Inforce their charity." †

---

* From this imitation arises the cant-term *to sham Abraham*, in use among the sailors.

† It is scarcely in connexion with this subject to remark, that the horn which wandering madmen formerly carried about with them has excited much of the attention of antiquaries. Mr Douce, in his Illustrations of Shakspeare, observes, that Edgar, in order to be dressed properly, should, in the words of Randle Holme, " have a long staff and a cow or ox horn by his side, and be madly decked and dressed all over with ribbons, feathers, cuttings of

I shall, lastly, observe, that the symptomatic fever, named *hectic*, has the power of imparting so grateful an addition of vividness to our pleasurable emotions as to render the mind unaffected by painful emotions. Thus, in Phthisis Pulmonalis, how eloquently, yet faithfully, has a late eminent medical practitioner, Dr Parr, described the unconsciousness of pain, which, in the face of the most imminent and fatal symptoms, enables the patient to soar above despondency. " In the advanced stages," he remarks, " the irritation of the cough is incessant, the heat or perspiration almost constantly distressing, and when these are absent, the life seems exhausted from debility. What, then, affords the cheering ray of expected relief? Such, however, is afforded; for ingenuity invents every fallacious mode of eluding inquiries, and of giving the most favourable view of every symptom. The patient sinks to the grave with the constant assurances of having attained greater strength, and a relief from every dangerous symptom; with eager expectations of another year, when life is limited by another day. Such, we would say, is the kind interposition of Providence, was the same cheerfulness found in every disease, and was not, in many, the gloom as distressing to the patient as the ill-founded expectation of the consumptive victim is to the well-informed anxious friend. This cheerfulness is said to be owing

---

cloth, and what not." The same excellent antiquary also remarks, " That about the year 1760, a poor idiot, called Cuddie Eddie, habited much in the same manner, and rattling a cow's horn against his teeth, went about the streets of Hawick in Scotland."

to the absence of pain; but pain is not always absent: and the difficulty of breathing, the incessant cough, the burning heats, the deluging perspirations, would appear worse than the most poignant pain. Yet these are disregarded, represented as trifles, lessened in the report to the most inconsiderable inconveniences: it is truly singular."*

It must inevitably follow from the foregoing remarks, that the quality of all spectral illusions, whether distinctly pleasurable,—distinctly painful,—or alternately pleasurable and painful, must depend upon the particular nature and excitability of its morbific cause. For we have seen that in the symptomatic fever, named *hectic,* a morbific cause vivifies every pleasurable feeling which can possibly connect itself with a favourable prognosis. And if we grant, that this illusive hope of an immediate state of convalescence arises indiscriminately in the breast of the consumptive patient, what reason is there, that an expectation equally extravagant should not extend to a probable state after death: that scenes connected with the prospect of a blessed immortality should not rise before him, with all the vivid colouring that a hectic affection is so capable of imparting to the images of fancy, or that spectral impressions of angel-visits, incidental to a morbidly-excited state of hope, should not alike be cherished by the good man as by the slave of vice? The truth is, that the guardian spirits, who honour the beds of dying patients with a visit, adopt a line of conduct never to be depended upon for consistency.

---

* Parr's London Medical Dictionary, vol. ii. p. 398.

As harbingers to heaven, they shew the same readiness in offering their services of introduction to sinners as to saints. This fact still continues to meet with confirmation from many modern superstitious narratives, the subjects of which are the visible tokens of salvation, and beatific visions (if they may be so called,) enjoyed by the most dissolute and abandoned of human beings at their hour of death; and it is amusing to observe, how scriptural authority is in mysterious language wrested from its plain and evident meaning, to account for an inconsistency so glaringly opposed to all the conditions on which the joys of heaven are promised; namely, that they should be the reward of virtuous integrity.

These are all the illustrations which I have to offer on the first variety of general mental excitements that I took occasion to explain, where the cause to which the affection may be referable, is found to add to the vividness of pleasurable feelings, but proportionally to diminish that of painful feelings: the general result being, that pleasurable feelings are by this means rendered inordinately intense, while painful feelings become so faint as to cease being the object of mental consciousness.

CHAPTER XIII.

WHEN MORAL AGENTS WHICH EXERT A PAINFUL INFLUENCE ARE HEIGHTENED IN THEIR EFFECTS BY THE CO-OPERATION OF MORBIFIC EXCITEMENTS OF A SIMILAR PAINFUL QUALITY, THE MIND MAY BE RENDERED TOTALLY UNCONSCIOUS OF OPPOSITE OR PLEASURABLE FEELINGS.

" Mark how he trembles in his ecstacy."
Comedy of Errors.

I SHALL now consider the effect of those morbific agents, which exert a contrary influence on the states of the mind; which impart an additional degree of vividness to painful ideas, and thereby render proportionally faint all feelings of a pleasurable nature. When, from a highly-excited state of the melancholic temperament, a paroxysm of actual insanity is induced, the hideous phantoms incidental to it are not to be dispelled by the vividness of a single pleasurable emotion:

" The darken'd sun
Loses his light: the rosy-bosom'd Spring
To weeping Fancy pines: and yon bright arch
Contracted, bends into a dusky vault.
All nature fades, extinct."

Burton, when speaking of persons " melancholy *à toto copore*," observes, " that the fumes which arise from this corrupt blood, disturbe the minde, and make them fearful and sorrowfull, heavy-hearted as the rest, dejected, discontented, solitary, silent, weary of their lives, dull, and heavy. And if farre gone, that which Apuleius wished to his enemy, by way of imprecation, is true in them; dead men's bones, hobgoblins, ghosts, are ever in their mindes, and meet them still in every turne: all the bugbeares of the night and terrors, and fairy-babes of tombes and graves are before their eyes, and in their thoughts."

The foregoing remarks of this very accurate describer of the symptoms of melancholy but too plainly shew, how completely the undue excitement of painful ideas can reduce to an unconscious degree of faintness all joyous thoughts. And how well is this fact illustrated in the too correct, yet very uncharitable description of a melancholic scholar, as depicted by an early popular writer. " A melancholy man," says Sir Thomas Overbury, " is a stranger from the drove: one that nature made a sociable, because she made him man, and a crazed disposition has altered. Impleasing to all, as all to him; straggling thoughts are his content, they make him dream waking, there's his pleasure. His imagination is never idle, it keeps his mind in a continuall motion, as the poise of the clocke: he winds up his thoughts often, and as often unwindes them; Penelope's webbe thrives faster. He'le seldom be found without the shade of some grove, in whose bottome a river dwels. Hee carries a cloud in his face, never faire weather: his outside is framed to his inside, in that hee keepes a *decorum*, both unseemly. Speake to him; he heares with his eyes, eares follow his mind, and that's not at leysure. He thinkes businesse, but never does any: he is all contemplation, no action. He hewes and fashions his thoughts, as if hee meant them to some purpose; but they prove unprofitable, as a piece of wrought timber of no use. His spirits and the sunne are enemies; the sun bright and warme, his humour blacke and cold: variety of foolish apparitions people in his head, they suffer him not to breathe, according to the necessities of nature; which makes him sup up a draught of as much aire at once as would serve at thrice. Hee denies nature her due in sleepe, and nothing pleaseth him long, but that which pleaseth his own phantasies: they are the consuming evils, and evil consumptions that consume him alive. Lastly, he is a man onely in shew, but comes short of the better part; a whole reasonable soule, which is man's chief pre-eminence, and sole marke from creatures sensible."*

Another interesting elucidation of the view which I have attempted to explain, is afforded in a case related by Pinel, where it is evident that the feelings which a general state of mental excitement had morbidly affected, were, from the same principle of selection, vivified to a most painful degree. The patient was a young gentleman, endowed with a most vivid imagination, who came to Paris to study the law. His application was said to have been laborious and painful in the extreme, the consequence of which was, that, along with frequent bleeding at the nose, spasmodic

---

* Sir Thomas Overbury, His Wife, 14th edit. A. D. 1630.

oppressions of the chest, wandering pains of the bowels, and a troublesome flatulence, he was seized with great depression of spirits, and a morbidly enervated sensibility. These symptoms daily increased, until, as a French physician adds, " complete lunacy at length established its melancholy empire. One night, he bethought himself that he would go to the play, to seek relief from his own unhappy meditations. The piece which was presented, was ' The Philosopher without knowing it.' He was instantly seized with the most gloomy suspicions, and especially with a conviction, that the comedy was written on purpose, and represented to ridicule himself. He accused me with having furnished materials for the writer of it, and the next morning he came to reproach me, which he did most angrily, for having betrayed the rights of friendship, and exposed him to public derision. His delirium observed no bounds. Every priest and monk he met in the public walks he took for comedians in disguise, despatched there for the purpose of studying his gestures, and of discovering the secret operations of his mind. In the dead of the night he gave way to the most terrific apprehensions,—believed himself to be attacked sometimes by spies, and at other times by robbers and assassins. He once opened his window with great violence, and cried out murder and assistance with all his might."

It is evident, that, in the foregoing example, the morbific cause of the young gentleman's insanity had imparted such an additional degree of vividness to his painful feelings, as to render all pleasurable thoughts so proportionally faint, that a perfect unconsciousness of them ensued. A general gloom, therefore, darkened all his reflections and emotions.

The continuation of this patient's case has no immediate relation to the object of our inquiry, yet its interest is too great to be withheld. It appears that the young man was sent, under the protection of a proper person, to an asylum belonging to a little village in the vicinity of the Pyrenees. " Greatly debilitated both in mind and body," continues Pinel, " it was some time after agreed upon that he should return to his family residence, where, on account of his paroxysms of delirious extravagance, succeeded by fits of profound melancholy, he was insulated from society. Ennui and insurmountable disgust with life, absolute refusal of food, and dissatisfaction with every thing, and every body that came near him, were among the last ingredients of his bitter cup. To conclude our affecting history, he one day eluded the vigilance of his keeper, and, with no other garment on than his shirt, fled to a neighbouring wood, where he lost himself, and where, from weakness and inanition, he ended his miseries. Two days afterwards he was found a corpse. In his hand was the celebrated work of Plato on the Immortality of the Soul."*

These are all the examples which I have to offer in illustration of the second variety of ecstacy that I have noticed, where the cause of mental excitement, to which the affection is referable, has added to the intensity of painful feelings, but has proportionally di-

---

* Pinel's Treatise on Insanity. Trans. by Dr Davis, page 57.

minished the vividness of pleasurable feelings; the general result being, that painful feelings are rendered inordinately intense, while pleasurable feelings become so faint as to be no longer the object of mental consciousness.

CHAPTER XIV.

PROOFS THAT, DURING INTENSE EXCITEMENTS OF THE MIND, NO LESS THAN DURING SYNCOPE AND SLEEP, THE CAUSES WHICH EXCLUSIVELY ACT UPON ORGANS OF SENSATION EVENTUALLY EXTEND THEIR VIVIFYING INFLUENCE TO THE RENOVATION OF PAST FEELINGS.

" Perturbations and passions which trouble the phantasie, though they dwell between the confines of sense and reason, yet they rather follow sense than reason, because they are drowned in corporeal organs of sense." *Anatomy of Melancholy.*

AT the present day, it would appear the most idle of tasks to attempt a serious answer to a question as seriously proposed,—Why the ideas of sleep or of syncope, which are so faint as not to be the object of consciousness, may be rendered vivid by stimuli that act intensely on organs of sensation? Ancient metaphysicians, however, thought very differently of the matter. They often puzzled their brains to explain, why blows, for instance, which affected organs of touch only, should, in a fainting fit, occasion the full activity of thought. They conceived of such agents as stimulating the blood in its purification and overheating,—a process supposed to take place in the heart,— whereby the vital fluid was the sooner enabled to throw off subtle vapours, which passed immediately to the cavities of the brain. These fumes or animal spirits, as they were commonly named, then put into movement the little cerebral gland, which is the seat of the soul, and thereby recalled or revived such species or ideas of things as had been seen or heard formerly, and were there in a manner buried. Hence the rationale of the plan which Ralpho pursued, when he endeavoured to recover Hudibras from a fit into which he had fallen. He inflicted some severe blows on the knight's breast, which had the effect of stirring up or of stimulating the blood nearest the heart, whereby animal spirits were the sooner concocted and enabled to make their escape from this fluid to the brain, so as to act upon the pineal gland, and assist it in resuscitating and liberating a few ideas:—

> " Then Ralpho gently raised the knight,
> And set him on his end upright:
> To rouse him from lethargic dump,
> He tweak'd his nose; with gentle thump
> Knock'd on his breast, as if't had been
> To raise the spirits lodg'd within:
> They, waken'd with the noise, did fly
> From inward room to window eye,
> And gently opening lid, the casement,
> Look'd out, but yet with some amazement."

But, after all, it is a question of some importance to our present investigation, Why, during syncope or sleep, the causes which exclusively excite organs of sensation should eventually extend their vivifying influence to the renovation of past feelings? Now this effect can only be explained by an irritating cause, which primarily operates upon organs of sensation eventually influencing the whole of the circulation,—to the varied conditions of which the general vividness of sensations and ideas holds a more immediate correspondence than to states of the nervous system.

Nor is a simple explanation of this kind without its use. It may assist us in reconciling the plan resorted to for a recovery from very vivid as well as from faint states of the mind, which, *prima facie*, seems to involve a contradiction. For it is very remarkable, that the self-same means should, under certain circumstances, be employed, not exclusively for the excitation, but even for the depression of intense mental states.

Two illustrations in proof of this fact may be now adduced. The first of these is from an old dramatic author, who, from the incidents of common life, has but too faithfully depicted the rough practices, not altogether unknown at the present day, that are employed for the purpose of stimulating the faint feelings of syncope:—

> *Rut.* Come, bring him out into the air a little:
> There set him down. Bow him, yet bow him more,
> Dash that same glass of water in his face:
> Now tweak him by the nose. Hard, harder yet:
> If it but call the blood up from the heart,
> I ask no more. See, what a fear can do!
> Pinch him in the nape of the neck now; nip him, nip him.
>   *Item.* He feels, there's life in him.
>   *Palate.* He groans and stirs.
>   *Rut.* Gi' him a box, hard, hard on his left ear.
>   *Interest.* O!
>   *Rut.* How do you feel yourself?
>   *Interest.* Sore, sore!

Rut. But where?
Interest. I' my neck.
Rut. I nipt him there.
Interest. And i' my head.
Rut. I box'd him twice or thrice to move those sinews.
Bias. I swear you did.
Polish. What a brave man's a doctor,
To beat one into health! I thought his blows
Would e'en ha' kill'd him: he did feel no more
Than a great horse.*

With Doctor Rut's plan of exciting feelings, when in an extreme languid state, may be compared the mode, apparently self-same, that Cardan successfully employed, but with the opposite view of reducing his mental excitement, and thereby of dispelling the ecstatic illusions to which he was almost daily subject. " I have found out," he observes, " that I cannot exist without a certain degree of pain; for when it altogether ceases, I feel so impetuous a fury seize my mind, that a moderate quantity of voluntary pain is much more safe, and renders me much more respectable. For this reason I bite my lips, distort my fingers, pinch my skin, and the tender fleshy part of the left arm, even to tears. Thus have I been able to ive without reproach."

From these two illustrations, it is now, I trust, sufficiently evident, that whether an increase of mental vividness be meditated, as in the attempt to rouse the languid feelings of syncope,—or, on the contrary, whether a reduction of the intense ideas of ecstatic illusions be the object of medical treatment, one com-

---

* Magnetic Lady, by Ben Jonson, act 3, scene 4.

mon mode of practice appears to be equally successful. But before this apparent anomaly can meet with an explanation, we must be compelled to admit, that, during intense excitements of the mind, no less than during syncope or sleep, an irritating cause, which confines its action to organs of sensation, must eventually influence the whole of the circulation,—to the varied conditions of which (as I have before observed) the general vividness of sensations and ideas, when conjointly excited, holds a more immediate correspondence than to states of the nervous system. And thus the general effect must be, that the additional agents, which during an ecstacy exclusively excite organs of sensation, must, through the medium of the circulation, eventually extend their vivifying influence to the renovation of past feelings.

It will also be expedient, in completing my explanation of this anomaly, to recall the attention to a law, lately noticed, regarding the effect which mental excitements have upon consciousness. The law was thus stated:—When a cause of mental excitement adds to the general vividness of our pleasurable feelings, every feeling of an opposite quality is in an inverse proportion rendered less vivid; and, *vice versa;* the same law holds good when a morbific agent adds to the vividness of all our painful feelings.

It follows, then, that we must necessarily regard such causes as may act upon organs of sensation during an ecstacy, and may, by this means, impart an additional degree of vividness to renovated feelings under two distinct points of view.

In the first place, an ecstacy may be pleasurable,

while the cause, which during its continuance imparts an additional degree of intensity to actual impressions, may also be pleasurable; or, again, an ecstacy may be painful, while the cause, which, during its continuance, imparts an additional degree of intensity to actual impressions, may also be painful. Now, in each of these instances, it is almost unnecessary to add, that the effect must be, that the force or violence of the ecstacy will be increased.

In the *second place*, the peculiar influence imparted by any cause, which acts during an ecstacy upon organs of sensation, may be of the same pleasurable or painful kind as that class of feelings may possess, which has been rendered so faint as to be no longer the object of consciousness. In this case, then, a different result will ensue; for, by virtue of the law to which I have often adverted, when any exciting cause of this kind, during a continuous operation, extends its vivifying influence to such *pleasurable* feelings as may have been rendered in an extreme degree faint, all intense feelings of an opposite or *painful* quality must be proportionally rendered less vivid; and, again, when any exciting cause of the same irritating nature extends its vivifying influence to such *painful* feelings as may have been rendered in an extreme degree faint, all intense feelings of an opposite or *pleasurable* quality must, in a similar manner, be proportionally rendered less vivid. It is evident, then, that the revival of one quality of feelings, which has been rendered unduly faint, will be followed by the reduction of the other quality of feelings which has been rendered unduly intense; and by this means an ecstacy will be eventually removed. Of this principle, then, Cardan, whose case has suggested these remarks, evidently availed himself. This remarkable man, who was born at Pavia in the year 1501, and was professor of mathematics at Milan, possessed a temperament which partook strongly of the sanguine description; and this, no doubt, was a predisposing cause, which, with an excess of nervous irritability, materially conspired to render him liable to the trances, which form the subject of the remarkable narrative that he has published in his curious work, *De Vita Propria*. The symptoms preceding each trance, were those which so very frequently usher in many of the mental paroxysms that we have traced in other diseases, and the pathology of which is so well illustrated by the action of the nitrous oxide or febrile miasma. There was an increased intensity of pleasurable sensations. A peculiar feeling was experienced in the head, which gradually diffused itself from this organ to other parts of the system along the course of the spinal cord. He perceived, as he observes, a kind of separation from the heart, like the issuing forth of the soul, while so serious a departure was felt by the whole body, as if a door had opened; and hence the impression which arose, that he was visited by supernatural impulses. Shortly afterwards, he was less sensible of actual impressions, while spectral illusions of the most vivid kind became the sportive objects of his imagination. The words of those who discoursed to him were but faintly heard, and in time were imperceptible. His organs of touch became less and less sensible to pain, until, at length, he felt neither pullings nor pinches, nor was he in the least degree conscious of gouty tortures, but only of such causes as were without the body. And, as he adds, when he had naturally no pain, he would excite it by whipping himself with rods, by biting his lips and arms, or by squeezing his fingers. But he acted thus to prevent a greater evil; for, in this complete state of insensibility to painful impressions, he felt such violent sallies of the imagination, and peculiar affections of the brain, as were more insupportable to him than any corporeal suffering which he could inflict upon himself. His pleasurable excitements could therefore be only subdued by exciting acute sensations of an opposite or painful quality.

The general inference to be deduced from the illustrations which I have given is briefly this:—If we would impart to the faint feelings of sleep and syncope a degree of vividness, such as subsists in our cool waking hours, it is immaterial whether the acute impressions to which the organs of sense are subjected be pleasurable or painful. But if, on the contrary, our view should be the depression of intense feelings, this object can be effected in no other way than by opposing to them the influence of acute sensations, similar in their quality of pleasure or pain to such states of the mind as, during the ecstacy, have been rendered proportionally faint and languid.

CHAPTER XV.

WHEN MORBIFIC CAUSES OF MENTAL EXCITEMENT EXERT TO THEIR UTMOST EXTENT THEIR STIMULATING POWERS, THEY OFTEN CHANGE THE QUALITY OF THEIR ACTION, AS FROM PLEASURE TO PAIN, OR FROM PAIN TO PLEASURE.

" Pleasure and pain are convertible and mixed:"—" that which is now pleasure, by being strained a little too far, runs into pain, and pain, when carried far, creates again the highest pleasure, by mere cessation, and a kind of natural succession."
Lord SHAFTSBURY's Characteristics.

I SHALL now make a few remarks on those morbific agents, which, when exerting their utmost influence over the states of the mind, have the effect of alternately increasing the vividness of pleasurable and painful feelings. The natural consequence of this action is, that the unconsciousness of grateful and ungrateful ideas undergoes a corresponding alternation. Alcohol possesses a subordinate influence of this kind. To a particular preparation of opium used in the East, the power is ascribed not only of rendering the mind by turns unconscious of pleasure or of pain, but of eventually inducing proper ecstatic illusions. The traveller Chardin, while recounting the effects of a certain drink prepared with a decoction of the head and seeds of the poppy, remarks, that " there is a decoction" [of this kind] " called *Coquenar*, for the sale of which there are taverns in every quarter of the town, similar to coffee-houses. It is extremely amusing to visit these houses, and to observe carefully those who resort there for the purpose of drinking it, both before they have taken the dose, before it begins to operate, and while it is operating. On entering the tavern, they are dejected, sad, and languishing; soon after they have taken two or three cups of this beverage, they are peevish, and find fault with every thing, and quarrel with one another; but, in the course of its operation, they make it up again, and each one giving himself up to his predominant passion, the lover speaks sweet things to his idol; another, half-asleep, laughs in his sleeve; a third talks big and blusters; a fourth tells ridiculous stories; in one word, a person would believe himself to be really in a madhouse. A kind of lethargy and stupidity succeeds to this unequal and disorderly gaiety; but the Persians, far from treating it as it deserves, call it an ecstacy, and maintain that there is something supernatural and heavenly in this state. As soon as the effect of the decoction diminishes, each one retires to his own house."

That peculiar insanity which is connected with a melancholic temperament presents analogous phenomena. " This progresse of melancholy," says Burton, " you shall easily observe in them that they have been so affected; they goe smiling to themselves at first, at length they laugh out; at first solitary, at last they can endure no company; or if they doe, they are now dizards, past sense and shame, quite moped; they are not what they say or doe, all their actions, words, gestures, are furious or ridiculous. Upon a sudden, they whoop and hollow, or run away, and sweare they see or heare players,* divells, hobgoblins, ghosts, strike or strut, and grow humorous in the end."

From this last illustration it is evident, that when there is an intense excitement of the melancholic temperament, painful and pleasurable feelings become alternately affected by the undue vivifying influence. During the interval that painful feelings are rendered intense, there is a perfect unconsciousness of pleasurable feelings; and (*vice versa*) during the interval that opposite or pleasurable feelings are excited, there is a similar unconsciousness of painful feelings.

But it is now time that these important phenomena, connected with the vivifying action of morbific causes, should meet with some explanation.

I have before described the influence imparted by the brain and nerves to the sanguineous system. Hence the contractility of the involuntary fibres of the heart and blood-vessels, and the resistance which such fibres make to the dilating power of the blood, during the course of its circulation. Thus, when heat is partially applied to a blood-vessel, its first effect is to increase the dilatibility of the contained fluid, and with it, to give rise to a pleasurable feeling. But, up-

---

* Probably the frightful shapes of demons represented in ancient mysteries are here alluded to.

on the farther continuation of this cause of excitation, the contractility of vascular fibres is opposed to the expansile influence of the contained fluid, and a feeling of pain is the consequence. Arguing, then, by analogy, from the phenomenon of heat, Sir Humphrey Davy has supposed it probable, that "pleasurable feeling is uniformly connected with a moderate increase of nervous action; and that this increase, when carried to certain limits, produces mixed emotions or sublime pleasure, and beyond those limits absolute pain."*

Lately much countenance has been given to this opinion, by the publication of an experiment in which, from some idiosyncracy in the constitution of the individual who inhaled the nitrous oxide, a moderate dose of the gas was found to exert a most powerful action on the state of the mind. This effect was experienced by a student at Yale College in America. "A gentleman," says Professor Silliman, "about nineteen years of age, of a sanguine temperament and cheerful temper, and in the most perfect health, inhaled the nitrous oxide, which was prepared and administered in the usual dose and manner. Immediately his feelings were uncommonly elevated, so that (as he expressed it) he could not refrain from dancing and shouting! To such a degree was he excited, that he was thrown into a frightful delirium, and his exertions became so violent that he sunk to the earth exhausted; and, having there remained till he in some degree recovered

---

* Sir Humphrey Davy's Researches concerning the Nitrous Oxide, p. 552.

his strength, he again rose only to renew the most convulsive muscular efforts, and the most piercing screams and cries, until, overpowered by the intensity of the paroxysms, he again fell to the ground, apparently senseless, and panting vehemently. For the space of two hours these symptoms continued; he was perfectly unconscious of what he was doing, and was in every respect like a maniac : he states, however, that *his feelings vibrated between perfect happiness and the most consummate misery.* After the first violent effects had subsided, he was obliged to lie down two or three times from excessive fatigue, although he was immediately roused upon any one's entering the room. The effects remained in a degree for two or three days, accompanied by a hoarseness, which he attributed to the exertions made while under the influence of the gas."[*]

This is a very singular experiment; and is so far instructive, that the alternations of pleasure and pain, which indicate an extreme state of excitement, sufficiently well explain the mixed character of many of the visions of enthusiasts. St Teresa, for instance, of whom I have before spoken, had ecstacies, wherein the vividness of her ideas was so intense, that, like the American student, she often " vibrated between perfect happiness and perfect misery;" or, in other words, she had alternate prospects of heaven and of hell, of benignant spirits and of devils. She saw St Peter and St Paul, but she saw likewise foul fiends, whom

---

[*] Edinburgh Philosophical Journal for January 1, 1823, page 204.

she insulted by crossing herself, and by making signs of scorn, or whom she kept at bay, by sprinkling holy water on the ground. She had, afterwards, the felicity of seeing souls freed from purgatory, and carried up to heaven; but none, to her recollection, ever escaped the purifying flame, except Father Peter of Alcantara, Father Ivagnez, and a Carmelite friar.*

---

* Townsend's Tour through Spain, vol. ii. p. 100.

CHAPTER XVI.

WHEN CAUSES ACT ACUTELY UPON ORGANS OF SENSATION, AND ARE UNREMITTINGLY PROLONGED, THEY OCCASIONALLY CHANGE THE QUALITY OF THEIR ACTION; AS, FOR INSTANCE, FROM PAIN TO PLEASURE. IDEAS LIKEWISE PARTAKE OF THIS CHANGE OF EXCITEMENT.

> " The visage of a hangman frights not me:
> The sight of whips, racks, gibbets, axes, fires,
> Are scaffoldings by which my soul climbs up
> To an eternal habitation."—MASSINGER.

It has been shewn in the last chapter, that when sensations and ideas are stimulated conjointly, and to an excessive degree, an ecstacy may ensue which is alternately pleasurable and painful. An effect analogous to this may occur, when the organs of sensation alone are subjected to an acute excitement, as the following remarkable case, which is to be found in Dr Crichton's Dissertation on Mental Derangement, sufficiently well illustrates. It is a translation from the Gazette Literaire, published in France. " An extraordinary young man, who lived at Paris, and who was passionately fond of mechanics, shut himself up one evening in his apartment, and bound not only his breast and belly, but also his arms, legs, and thighs, around with ropes, full of knots, the ends of which he fastened to hooks in the wall. After having passed a considerable part of the night in this situation, he wished to disengage himself, but attempted it in vain. Some neighbouring females, who had been early up, heard his cries, and calling the assistance of the patrol, they forced open the door of his apartment, where they found him swinging in the air, with only one arm extricated. He was immediately carried to the lieutenant-general of the police for examination, where he declared that he had often put similar trials into execution, as he experienced indescribable pleasure in them. He confessed that at first he felt pain, but that after the cords became tight, he was soon rewarded by the most exquisite sensations of pleasure."*

As this curious fact requires explanation, I shall again advert to the remark which was made in a preceding chapter, that an irritating cause, which primarily operates upon organs of sensation, may eventually influence the whole of the circulation,—to the varied conditions of which the general vividness of sensations and ideas holds a more immediate correspondence than to states of the nervous system. Again, it has been shewn, that an irritating cause, which excites to an intense degree organs of sensation, may change the quality of its operation, namely, from pain to pleasure. When, therefore, the same cause of irritation has so generally influenced the state of the circulating system, as to add to the influence of ideas of a similar

---

* Crichton on Mental Derangement, vol. i. p. 132.

pleasurable quality, we are entitled to expect that ecstatic illusions may ensue, such as have been described by the superstitious under the name of *beatific visions*.

This explanation may assist us, in accounting for some incidents relative to the spectral impressions of many individuals, who, in times of religious persecution, have been exposed to all the cruelties which intolerant power could devise. Thus it is recorded of Theodorus, that, in pursuance of the orders of Julian the Apostate, he was unremittingly tortured, even by a change of executioners, for an interval of ten hours. But at length the tyrant's engines of persecution ceased to have their wonted effect;—instead of inflicting pain, the sensations over which they had control imparted a grateful influence, which was eventually extended to the renovated feelings of the mind. The thoughts of this firm Christian had dwelt upon that blessed state of immortality, which was promised as a reward to those who were prepared to lay down their lives for the sacred cause they had espoused; and the indication of this state of mind was the subject of his illusions. For Theodorus has related, that while he was under the hands of the executioners, he was cheered by the aspect of a bright youth, conceived by him to be a messenger from heaven, who allayed his sufferings by wiping the perspiration from his body, and by pouring cool water upon his irritated limbs. At length, as he has likewise affirmed, he felt no pain at all. This confession has been supposed to afford a satisfactory explanation, why the sufferer continued on the scaffold, in the sight of all men, smiling, and even singing, until it was thought expedient to take him down. Ruffinus, to whom we are indebted for this narrative, remarks, that he had subsequently many conversations with Theodorus touching this supernatural interposition (for such it was readily conceived to be), and that the martyr uniformly assured him, that he was so comforted and confirmed by it in the faith, that he could not but regard the hours which he passed under the hands of the torturers as imparting exquisite delight rather than pain.

Such is the effect which may take place when causes of acute suffering are unremittingly prolonged, and when their influence, which has become grateful, is imparted to ideas.

An incident, similar to the foregoing, is recorded by La Trobe, in the history which he has given of the Moravians. He relates, " That about the year 1458, the Brethren in Lititz, founders of the Moravians, did not cease to send to all places to strengthen the persecuted in the faith, and to exhort them to patience. Among others, Gregory, nephew of Rokyzan, the archbishop of Prague, came to Prague; but upon his having just held a meeting, he was surprised on a sudden, and, together with some others, committed to prison by the judge or justice, with these affecting words:—' It is written, all that will live godly in Christ Jesus shall suffer persecution; therefore follow me, by command of the higher powers!' Under the rack he fell into a swoon; during which, it is said, he had a vision of the three men, who were, six years after, elected the first bishops of the Brethren. They appeared as the guardians of a blooming tree, on the fruit of which many lovely singing-birds were feeding."

But examples of this kind have been so frequently recorded, that poets have even attempted to dramatise them. Thus, Massinger, in his play of the Virgin Martyr:—

THEOPHILUS.
.... 'Tis not for life I sue for,
Nor is it fit that I, that ne'er knew pity
To any Christian, being one myself,
Should look for any; no, I rather beg
The utmost of your cruelty; I stand
Accountable for thousand Christian deaths;
And, were it possible that I could die
A day for every one, then live again,
To be again tormented, 'twere to me
An easy penance, and I should pass through
A gentle cleansing fire; but that denied me,
It being beyond the strength of feeble nature,
My suit is, you would have no pity on me.
In mine own house there are a thousand engines
Of studied cruelty, which I did prepare
For miserable Christians; let me feel,
As the Sicilian did his brazen bull,
The horrid'st you can find, and I will say,
In death, that you are merciful.

DIOCLESIAN.
            Despair not,
In this thou shalt prevail. Go fetch them hither:
Death shall put on a thousand shapes at once,
And so appear before thee; racks, and whips!—
Thy flesh, with burning pincers torn, shall feed
The fire that heats them; and what's wanting to

The torture of thy body, I'll supply
In punishing thy mind. Fetch all the Christians
That are in hold; and here, before his face,
Cut them in pieces.

THEOPHILUS.
　　　　　'Tis not in thy power:
It was the first good deed I ever did.
They are removed out of thy reach; howe'er
I was determined for my sins to die,
I first took order for their liberty,
And still I dare thy worst.

DIOCLESIAN.
　　　　　　Bind him, I say;
Make every artery and sinew crack:
The slave that makes him give the loudest shriek
Shall have ten thousand drachmas: wretch! I'll force thee
To curse the Power thou worship'st.

THEOPHILUS.
Never, never:
No breath of mine shall e'er be spent on him,
　　　　　　　　　[*They torment him.*
But what shall speak his majesty or mercy.
I'm honour'd in my sufferings. Weak tormentors,
More tortures, more:—alas! you are unskilful—
For Heaven's sake, more; my breast is yet untorn:
Here purchase the reward that was propounded.
The iron's cool,—here are arms yet, and thighs;
Spare no part of me.

MAXIMINUS.
　　　　　　He endures beyond
The sufferance of a man.

SAPRITIUS.
　　　　　　No sigh nor groan,
To witness he hath feeling.

DIOCLESIAN.

Harder, villains!

Enter DOROTHEA *in a white robe, a crown upon her head, led in by* ANGELO; ANTONINUS, CALISTA, *and* CHRISTETA *following, all in white, but less glorious;* ANGELO *holds out a crown to* THEOPHILUS.

THEOPHILUS.

Most glorious vision!—
Did e'er so hard a bed yield man a dream
So heavenly as this? I am confirm'd,
Confirm'd, you blessed spirits, and make haste
To take that crown of immortality
You offer to me. Death, till this blest minute,
I never thought thee slow-paced; nor would I
Hasten thee now, for any pain I suffer.
But that thou keep'st me from a glorious wreath,
Which through this stormy way I could creep to,
And, humbly kneeling, with humility wear it.
Oh! now I feel thee:—blessed spirits! I come;
And witness for me all these wounds and scars,
I die a soldier in the Christian wars.   [*Dies.*

But it is unnecessary to dwell longer upon such painful descriptions. All tormentors of human victims, whether residing among the savage wilds of the western continent, or within the walls of an European inquisition, but too well know, that if they would prolong the duration of their meditated inflictions, they must occasionally allow their victim a brief respite. It is indeed evident, that acute sensations of this kind, when assiduously and unremittingly inflicted, not only fail in their object, but occasionally prove grateful in their effects. Nor is the influence restricted to actual impressions ;—ideas partake of this pleasurable excitement, and become so stimulated as not unfrequently to induce ecstatic illusions.

These are all the remarks which I have to offer on the causes that give rise to such a general state of mental excitement as is productive of spectral illusions; and it will be now advisable to take a short review of the conclusions at which we have arrived in some of the last chapters.

It was considered, that in every ecstacy, or state of general excitement of the mind, either pleasurable feelings were excited and painful ones depressed, or, *vice versa*, painful feelings were excited, and pleasurable ones depressed.

A cause, then, which, by stimulating organs of sensation, extends its vivifying influence to the renovated feelings of the mind, may modify an ecstacy in three ways:

1*st*, It may impart a vivifying influence similar to that of any quality of feelings, pleasurable or painful, which is rendered intense, and may thus increase the force of the ecstacy.

2*dly*, It may impart a vivifying influence to any quality of feelings, pleasurable or painful, which is depressed; and by reducing this means, the intensity of the excited quality of feelings may shorten the duration of the ecstacy; or,

3*dly*, It may, if acutely and unremittingly prolonged, change the nature of its action, as from pleasure to pain, or from pain to pleasure, and thus, according to the circumstances under which it acts, either increase the force of the general excitement, or shorten its duration.

To all these varieties of effects, however, which result from morbific causes of general excitement, there must evidently, from various idiosyncracies of constitution, arise frequent exceptions. For, among the numerous individuals who, about twenty years ago, imbibed the nitrous oxide, there were few whom it affected entirely alike. Indeed, to some persons, pain instead of pleasure resulted from the inhalation.*

I have at length concluded my observations on what may be considered as the leading mental laws which are connected with the origin of spectral impressions.

The general inference to be drawn from them is,— that APPARITIONS ARE NOTHING MORE THAN MORBID SYMPTOMS, WHICH ARE INDICATIVE OF AN INTENSE EXCITEMENT OF THE RENOVATED FEELINGS OF THE MIND.

---

* One individual, after having imbibed the gas, experienced a pressure in all the muscles; a second, felt as if the bulk of the body was increased without its gravity; a third, as if a weight was pressing him to the ground; a fourth, complained of a prickling sensation in his stomach, but this soon gave way, and was succeeded by a lively delirium and laughter; a fifth, endured inexpressible uneasiness from a burning heat in the chest, and was afterwards thrown into a syncope of some minutes in duration.

PART V.

SLIGHT REMARKS ON THE MODIFICATIONS WHICH THE INTELLECTUAL FACULTY OFTEN UNDERGOES DURING INTENSE EXCITEMENTS OF THE MIND.

PART V.

SLIGHT REMARKS ON THE MODIFICATIONS WHICH THE INTELLECTUAL FACULTY OFTEN UNDERGOES DURING INTENSE EXCITEMENTS OF THE MIND.

> " Hark, amid the wond'ring grove,
>   Other harpings answer clear,
>   Other voices meet our ear,
> Pinions flutter, shadows move,
> Busy murmurs hum around,
> Rustling vestments brush the ground;
> Round, and round, and round they go,
> Through the twilight, through the shade,
> Mount the oak's majestic head,
> And gild the tufted mistletoe."
>
> MASON'S *Caractacus.*

In the last part of this treatise, the research, as I observed at the time, was of a novel kind. Since apparitions are ideas equalling or exceeding in vividness actual impressions, there ought to exist some important and definite laws of the mind which have given rise to this undue degree of vividness. It was, chiefly, therefore, for the purpose of investigating such laws that this dissertation was written.

But I have here entered into a perfectly new field of research, where far greater difficulties were to be encountered than I anticipated. The extent of these can only be estimated by the metaphysician.

The last object of this dissertation was to have established, that all the subordinate incidents connected with phantasms might be explained on the following general principle :—That, in every undue excitement of our feelings, (as, for instance, when ideas become more vivid than actual impressions,) the operations of the intellectual faculty of the mind sustain corresponding modifications, by which the efforts of the judgment are rendered proportionally incorrect. But here I must pause. In order to give a full rationale of the phenomena which we have been lately contemplating, certain principles of the mind, to which I have yet but slightly adverted, require the fullest consideration. I allude to the laws connected with the intellectual faculty, and to the obstacles which are opposed to the correctness of its operations, during the extreme degrees of intensity to which the states of the mind become liable from morbific causes.—But, can it be reasonably expected, that any individual would undertake an investigation of this kind, which demands the consideration of every phenomenon of the human mind as it is presented in health or disease, with the solitary object in view of explaining the subordinate incidents connected with apparitions? For such a purpose, it would be necessary to incorporate within this treatise a complete systematic view of the pathology of the human mind,—a mark of attention, which, to the bugbears of popular superstition, I am not inclined to pay. Yet, not to avoid the question altogether, I shall in preference quote the opinion of other authors upon the subject, rather than submit to the reader any remarks of my own. This plan I prefer, because the explanation of my own views would comprehend the notice of many other mental principles, besides those which will now be quoted, that might require an extensive discussion. To any pneumatologist, therefore, who has more inclination than myself to persist in an investigation of this kind—who has the spirit to exclaim, with one of Dryden's heroes,

> "I'll face these babbling demons of the air,
> In spite of ghosts I'll on,"

the slight remarks and illustrations which appear in this part of the work are, with due deference, submitted.

Dr Brown, in his Physiology of the Human Mind, remarks, "That the union of perception with conceptions that harmonize with it, does truly vivify those harmonizing conceptions, by giving a sort of mixed reality to the whole, is shewn by some of the most interesting phenomena of thought and emotion. It is, indeed, a law of the mind, which, though little heeded by metaphysical inquirers, seems to me far more important, and far more extensive, than many of those to which they have paid the greatest attention. Some of our most vivid emotions,—those of beauty, for example,—derive their intensity chiefly from this circumstance; and many of the gay or sad illusions of our hopes and fears are only forms of this very illusion. To the superstitious, in the loneliness of twilight, many wild conceptions arise, that impress them with awe, perhaps not with terror; but if, in the moment of such imaginations, their eye turn on any objects of indistinct outline, that give as it were a body to the phantasms of their own mind; the phantasms themselves, in blending with them, become immediately, with spectral reality, external and terrifying objects of perception. How often, in gazing on a dim and fading fire, do we see, in the mixture of light and shade that plays before us, resemblances of well-known shapes, that grow more and more like as we continue to gaze on them. There is at first, in such a case, by the influence perhaps of the slightest possible similarity, the suggestion of some form that is familiar to us, which we incorporate, while we gaze on the dim and shadowy film that flutters before us, till the whole seems one blended figure, with equal reality of what we conceive and what we truly see."

Such is the explanation which Dr Brown has given of some of the illusions that we have been just considering. Mr Coleridge, with no less acuteness, has adverted to the self-same principle, while proposing to account for Luther's apparitions. His words are the following:—" In aid of the present case I will only remark, that it would appear incredible to persons not accustomed to these subtle notices of self-observation, what small and remote resemblances, what mere hints of likeness from some real external object, especially if the shape be aided by colour, will suffice to make a vivid thought consubstantiate with the real object, and derive from it an outward perceptibility."*

This correct view cannot meet with a better illustration than in a German narrative, translated by Dr Crichton, to which I have before adverted. It is the case of a superstitious female, in whose mind the well-known morbid symptoms which precede a fit of epilepsy, such as the *aura epileptica*,—the luminous sensations that are well known to occasionally impress the vision,—the illusive impressions of touch felt on various parts of the body, suggested many remote resemblances connected with the angels and devils which formed the subject of her thoughts. These ideas had been recalled by the law of association, and having been rendered as intense as actual impressions, *consubstantiated* (to use Mr Coleridge's term) with the morbid impressions that were the result of her disease, and were intimately blended with them. " While the angels," says this female in the account which she has given of her illusions, " thus spoke to me, a light, like that reflected from the river Diele, seemed to shine in the apartment. It moved up and down, and then disappeared, upon which I felt as if some person had pulled out the hairs of my head. But the pain was to be borne. The light came again, and the pain left me entirely; it ceased to shine, and I felt as if the flesh on my back was torn from the bones by pincers. The light then returned, and I was better. It once more

---

* Friend, by S. T. Coleridge, Esq. vol. i. p. 246.

went away, and I felt as if my shoulder-blades were torn from each other; my heart also felt as if it were torn out of my breast, and laid between my shoulders, where it died. I thought these must be my last moments; and I then beheld the devil beside the young angel. He came from behind the bed, with his back foremost. All that I saw of him, however, was his arm, a tail about two spans thick, which resembled a serpent, and his neck, and the back part of his head. I had not time to examine him minutely, for the angel pushed him away with his elbow."

Other incidents, referable to a similar law of the mind, but which more particularly regard hearing, are likewise mentioned by Dr Brown. "The old proverb, which says, that ' As a fool thinketh so the bell clinketh,' is a faithful statement of a physical phenomenon of the same kind. When both the air and the words of any song are very familiar to us, we scarcely can refrain from thinking, while the melody is performed by any instrument without a vocal accompaniment, that the very words are floating in the simple tones which we hear. In like manner, if any one beat the time of a particular air, on a table or other sounding body that is incapable of giving the distinct tones, it may be difficult for a listener, however well acquainted with it, to discover the particular melody; but, as soon as it is named to him, he will immediately discover in the same sounds, not the time merely, but the very tones, that are only conceptions of his own mind, which, as they harmonize with the sounds that are truly external, seem themselves also to be external, and to convert into music what before was unworthy of the name. I might add many other illustrations of the same principle; for in the constitution of the mind, as I have said, there is scarcely a principle of more extensive influence. But the examples which I have already adduced, may be sufficient to shew the vivifying influence of perception on the conceptions that harmonize and unite with it, and to throw light also on the mode in which I conceive this vivifying effect to take place, by the diffusion of the felt reality of one part of a complex group to the other parts of it, which are only imaginary."

To the same phenomena, when modified by disease, Mr Coleridge alludes. After expressing a wish to devote an entire work to the investigation of such illusions as are connected with popular superstitions, he thus proceeds,—" I might then explain, in a more satisfactory way, the mode in which our thoughts, in states of morbid slumber, become at times perfectly dramatic, (for in certain sorts of dreams the dullest wight becomes a Shakspeare,) and by what law the form of the vision appears to talk to us in its own thoughts, in a voice as audible as the shape is visible; and this to do often-times in connected trains, and not seldom even with a concentration of power which may easily impose on the soundest judgment, uninstructed in the optics and acoustics of the inner sense, for revelations and gifts of prescience."

The best example of this view is, perhaps, to be found in the illusions of Tasso, as related by Mr Hoole. " At Bisaccio, near Naples, Manso had an opportunity of examining the singular effects of Tasso's melancholy, and often disputed with him concerning a familiar spirit which he pretended conversed with him; Manso endeavoured in vain to persuade his friend that the whole was the illusion of a disturbed imagination; but the latter was strenuous in maintaining the reality of what he asserted, and, to convince Manso, desired him to be present at one of the mysterious conversations. Manso had the complaisance to meet him next day, and while they were engaged in discourse, on a sudden he observed that Tasso kept his eyes fixed on a window, and remained in a manner immoveable: he called him by his name, but received no answer; at last Tasso cried out, 'There is the friendly spirit that is come to converse with me; look! and you will be convinced of the truth of all that I have said.'

"Manso heard him with surprise; he looked, but saw nothing except the sunbeams darting through the window; he cast his eyes all over the room, but could perceive nothing; and was just going to ask where the pretended spirit was, when he heard Tasso speak with great earnestness, sometimes putting questions to the spirit, sometimes giving answers; delivering the whole in such a pleasing manner, and in such elevated expressions, that he listened with admiration, and had not the least inclination to interrupt him. At last, the uncommon conversation ended with the departure of the spirit, as appeared by Tasso's own words, who, turning to Manso, asked him if his doubts were removed. Manso was more amazed than ever; he scarce knew what to think of his friend's situation, and waved any farther conversation on the subject."

It is with reluctance that I quit the notice of other similar cases. But to explain the laws that *give rise* to these illusions is one thing,—to explain the phenomena connected with them when they *do occur,* is another. An object of the last-mentioned kind cannot be attempted but in connexion with almost all the phenomena of the human mind. To pursue the subject, therefore, any farther, would be to make a dissertation on apparitions the absurd vehicle of a regular system of metaphysics.

But, in expressing these sentiments, I would not be mistaken. While I am merely alluding to the awkwardness of accompanying a theory of apparitions with a complete investigation of the laws of the human mind, I am very far from underrating any well-recorded phenomena of this kind, although they should not be immediately connected with the morbid origin of such illusions. It is, indeed, one of the leading objects of this dissertation to prove, that they are of the greatest importance in explaining the laws of the human mind, as they occur in health, and as they are modified by disease.

PART VI.

SUMMARY OF THE COMPARATIVE DEGREES OF FAINTNESS, VIVIDNESS, OR INTENSITY SUBSISTING BETWEEN SENSATIONS AND IDEAS, DURING THEIR VARIOUS EXCITEMENTS AND DEPRESSIONS.

PART VI.

INTRODUCTION.

SUMMARY OF THE COMPARATIVE DEGREES OF FAINTNESS, VIVIDNESS, OR INTENSITY SUBSISTING BETWEEN SENSATIONS AND IDEAS, DURING THEIR VARIOUS EXCITEMENTS AND DEPRESSIONS.

My last object is, for the sake of more complete elucidation, to give a summary of those phenomena relative to *consciousness*, which are manifested during the excitements and depressions to which the feelings of the mind are constantly subject.

The success of this investigation, however, must essentially depend upon a full statement of the proportional difference which subsists between sensations and ideas during their various transitions from faintness to intensity, or from intensity to faintness. But it is almost unnecessary to add, regarding a physiological inquiry of this kind, that it is a problem which can never be satisfactorily accomplished: yet if, after all, for the mere sake of greater perspicuity, I should be induced to attempt a sort of tabular view of the various degrees of vividness to which our mental feelings are liable, it can have no other claim to regard than as a formula which, in the language of mathematicians, is *empirical*, or purely experimental. It is, in fact, a result obtained by repeated trials, the effect of which is rather to give an artificial consistency to certain successions of mental phenomena, than to produce the conviction that the formula is in every respect agreeable to truth and to nature.

In reference, then, to the annexed tabular sketch of the various proportional degrees of vividness subsisting among sensations and ideas, no fewer than fifteen of such degrees are supposed to exist; these being represented on an ascending scale by horizontal lines. The lowest of such lines, marked 1, denotes the faintest state of our mental feelings, while the highest in the series, marked 15, represents the most excited condition of them.

The vertical lines by which the horizontal ones are intersected dispose the various degrees of vividness thus represented into eight columnar divisions, each of these including a distinct transition of the feelings of the mind from faintness to intensity, or from intensity to faintness.

These several transitions will be next described, though not in the exact order which is represented in the general table now given.

CHAPTER I.

THE VARIOUS EXCITEMENTS AND DEPRESSIONS CONNECTED WITH THE SLEEPING AND DREAMING STATES.

> " A pleasing land of drowsy-head it was,
> Of dreams that wave before the half-shut eye;
> And of gay castles in the clouds that pass,
> For ever flushing round a summer-sky."
> *Castle of Indolence.*

IN this chapter will be described the particular excitements and depressions connected with the sleeping and dreaming states; a reference being at the same time made to the general tabular view which I have given of the comparative degrees of faintness, vividness, or intensity, subsisting between sensations and ideas, during the various transitions to which they are subject.

SECTION I.

TRANSITION (marked the 1st in the Table)
From perfect Sleep to the common State of Watchfulness.

The first transition to be noticed is from perfect sleep to that cool and collected state which characterizes our common waking moments.

During intervals of deep slumber, sensations are

supposed to be more faint than ideas; none of these mental states are, however, vivid enough to be the subject of consciousness. Sensations are accordingly placed on the annexed scale at the lowest degree, marked 1, while ideas occupy the graduated line marked 3.

It is also assumed, that at each stage of excitement ideas increase less in vividness than sensations.

Keeping the foregoing proportional increase in view, the several stages of excitement which occur during this transition may, in the subjoined table, be readily traced.

TABULAR VIEW.

Sensations, from being more faint than ideas, become more vivid.

	Degrees of Vividness or Faintness.	Perfect Sleep.	1st Stage of Excitement.	2d Stage of Excitement.	3d Stage of Excitement.	4th Stage of Excitement.
Conscious and active states of watchfulness.	9	. . .	. . .	. . .	. . .	Sensations
	8	. . .	. ? .	. . .	. . .	. . .
	7	. . .	. . .	. . .	Sensations	Ideas
Muscles obey the will.	6	. . .	. . .	. . .	Ideas	. . .
Consciousness begins.	5	. . .	. . .	{Sensations Ideas*	. . .	. . .
	4	. . .	. . .	Ideas	. . .	. . .	. . .
Feelings so faint as not to excite consciousness.	3	Ideas	Sensations	. . .	. . .	. . .
	2	. . .	. . .	. . .	. . .	. . .
	1	Sensations	. . .	. . .	. . .	. . .

* When sensations and ideas are equally vivid there is no mental consciousness of them.

1st Stage of Excitement.

In the first stage of excitement, represented in the table, ideas are raised to degree 4, while sensations, which are more excitable, follow them so close as to stand at the degree 3. These mental states, however, are still so faint, that no consciousness of them ensues.

2d Stage of Excitement.

In the second stage, sensations and ideas, from their different excitabilities, each appear at the same degree of vividness. If they had proportionally differed in vividness, a mental consciousness of such states would have ensued. But, as I have remarked on a former occasion, (in part 4,) " when it is considered that the human mind can form no notion of the present and of the past, but from the comparative degree of vividness which, during our waking hours, subsists between sensations and ideas, and that the notion of present and past time enters into our definition of consciousness, it must follow, that when sensations arrive at the same degree of vividness as ideas, a state of mental unconsciousness must necessarily be the result."

Examples of this condition of our feelings are afforded in those moments which immediately precede our recovery from sound sleep.

3d Stage of Excitement.

In a third stage of excitement, sensations attain the 7th and ideas the 6th degree of vividness, the former becoming more vivid than the latter. The consciousness of the mind is now entire.

An important law of the mind is now called forth,

which may be thus briefly explained:—*When mental feelings of any description attain a certain degree of vividness, muscular motions obey the impulse of the will.** For, in the faint feelings of our common dreams, there is a decided volition, but no contractions of the muscles follow. The particular degree necessary for muscular motions is represented in the scale as the *sixth*. The effect induced is, however, but feeble:

> "The slumb'ring god, amazed at this new din,
> Thrice strove to rise, and thrice sunk down again:
> Listless he stretch'd, and gaping rubb'd his eyes,
> Then falter'd thus betwixt half words and sighs."

Another character may yet be mentioned, which distinguishes this stage of excitement. The vividness of ideas approaches so nearly to that of sensations, that recollected images of thought are often confounded with actual impressions. While, therefore, the various forms of fancy and of memory mingle together in confusion, a lethargic faintness increases the indistinctness, by imparting to the whole a dull and feeble gloom:

> "The landskip such, inspiring perfect ease,
> Where Indolence (for so the wizard hight)
> Close-hid his castle 'mid imbowering trees,
> That half shut out the beams of Phœbus bright,
> And made a kind of checker'd day and night." †

---

* Regarding this curious law I could say much, but am prevented by the limited nature of the present work.

† Thomson's Castle of Indolence.

4th Stage of Excitement.

In a fourth stage of excitement, sensations attain the 9th and ideas the 7th degree of vividness, the former now being more vivid than the latter.

This stage of excitement is particularly favourable for the operations of the reasoning powers. Actual impressions possess such a superior degree of vividness, that they are not easily confounded with the recollected images of thought. The attainment of a state of mind such as this, free from depressing or exciting passions, has been recommended by all moralists as indispensable for the discovery of truth. Thus the Roman writer Boethius:

> " Tu quoque si vis
> Lumine claro
> Cernere verum
> Tramite recto
> Carpere callem
> Gaudia pelle,
> Pelle Timorem,
> Nec dolor adsit,
> Spemque fugato.
> Nubila mens est,
> Vinctaque frenis
> Hæc ubi regnant."

Section II.

TRANSITION (marked the 4th in the Table) *From the common State of Watchfulness to perfect Sleep.*

A *second* transition is from the ordinary state of ou waking hours to perfect sleep.

It is unnecessary to dwell upon the phenomena of this depression of our mental feelings, which are the exact reverse of the stages of excitement just described. It is sufficient to state, that sensations, from being more vivid than ideas, become more faint.

A suitable opportunity occurs, however, for noticing such mental depressions of feelings as are referable to morbific causes. These, in fact, are to be traced in all the stages of reduced vividness incidental to a transition from the state of watchfulness to that of perfect sleep. But this view, which I have taken of the effects of depressing causes, will be rendered more explicit by the following table.

TABULAR VIEW.

States of the mind occurring from depressing causes of a morbific nature.

	Degrees of Vividness and Faintness.	Active State.	1st Lethargic State.	2dly, State during Catalepsy.	3dly, Fainting states.
Conscious and active states of watchfulness.	9	Sensations	. . .	. . .	. . .
	8	. . .	. . .	. . .	. . .
	7	Ideas	Sensations	. . .	. . .
Muscles obey the will.	6	. . .	Ideas	. . .	. . .
Consciousness begins.	5	. . .	. . . {	Sensations Ideas*	. . .
	4	. . .	. . .	. . .	Ideas . . .
Feelings so faint as not to excite consciousness.	3	. . .	. . .	. . .	Sensations Ideas
	2	. . .	. . .	. . .	. . .
		. . .	. . .	. . .	. . . Sensations

* When sensations and ideas are equally vivid, there is no consciousness of them.

1st, or *Lethargic State.*

The first state, arising from morbific causes of depression, is that which I have named the *lethargic.* It frequently results from paralytic affections of the nervous system, and is sometimes the consequence of intense thinking. After an undue mental excitement has been caused by the ardent study of the abstract sciences, the drowsy god then displays his benumbing influence:

> " No passions interrupt his easy reign;
> No problems puzzle his lethargic brain:
> But dull Oblivion guards his peaceful bed,
> And lazy fogs bedew his gracious head."[*]

But this tendency of intense study to produce stupor has been by no one better illustrated, than by Dr Crichton, in his valuable work on mental derangement. With one example, therefore, which he gives, I shall conclude my notice of the lethargic state induced by depressing causes.

" A young Swiss gentleman, for six months, had given himself up wholly to the intense study of metaphysics. An inertness of mind followed, which at last ended in a complete stupor. 'Without being blind,' it is said, ' he appeared not to see; without being deaf, he seemed not to hear; without being dumb, he did not speak. In other respects, he slept, drank, ate without relish and without aversion, without asking to eat, or without refusing to do so. This

---

[*] Garth's Dispensary.

state continued a whole year. At length a person read loudly to him, and it was noticed that he expressed symptoms of acute suffering; the experiment was tried again; and his hearing was re-established on a similar principle. Every other sense was successively excited on the same principle, and in proportion as he regained the use of it the stupidity appeared to be diminished."*

2d, *State occurring in Catalepsy.*

In a second, or still more reduced stage of depression, sensations and ideas are of equal degrees of vividness when a state of unconsciousness ensues. I have supposed that this mental condition may be found in a variety of the affection called *catalepsy*. For if sensations had differed from ideas in their relative degree of vividness, muscular contractions would have been excited; but as in this case they partake of an equal degree of vividness, no mental consciousness of such feelings can possibly ensue, and, consequently, no voluntary influence can arise to affect the motific nerves which communicate with and regulate muscular fibres. Hence the muscles, while contracting, easily yield to any external impulse, and retain any given position.†

A curious illustration of the state of the mental feel-

---

* See the case given on the authority of Zimmerman, by Dr Crichton, in his work on Mental Derangement, vol. ii. p. 35.

† This is but an imperfect explanation of a very important phenomenon, the rationale of which would be too long to investigate in this limited treatise.

ings during catalepsy is given by Dr Crichton, on the authority of Borellus.

" George Giokatzki, a Polish soldier, deserted from his regiment in the harvest of the year 1677. He was discovered, a few days afterwards, drinking and making merry in a common alehouse. The moment he was apprehended, he was so much terrified, that he gave a loud shriek, and immediately was deprived of the power of speech. When brought to a court-martial, it was impossible to make him articulate a word; nay, he then became as immoveable as a statue, and appeared not to be conscious of any thing which was going forward. In the prison to which he was conducted he neither ate nor drank. The officers and the priests at first threatened him, and afterwards endeavoured to sooth and calm him; but all their efforts were in vain. He remained senseless and immoveable. His irons were struck off, and he was taken out of the prison, but he did not move. Twenty days and nights were passed in this way, during which he took no kind of nourishment, nor had any natural evacuation; he then gradually sunk and died."

3d, or Fainting States.

States of syncope are nothing more than those of sleep, requiring, however, greater stimuli for their excitement.

SECTION III.

TRANSITION (the 5th in the Table)
From perfect Sleep to common Dreams and Somnambulism.

A *third* transition is from the state of perfect sleep to that of dreaming, or of somnambulism. Consistently with our view of the cause of sleep, the sensations of perfect repose have been considered as fainter than ideas. It is now of importance to remark, that when causes of undue excitement, such as are known to induce states of dreaming and somnambulism, affect the mind, they do not, as in other circumstances enumerated, cause sensations to increase more than ideas in vividness, but, on the contrary, excite them uniformly.

TABULAR VIEW.

The ideas and sensations of perfect sleep are excited uniformly.

	Degrees of Vividness and Faintness.	Perfect Sleep.	1st Stage of Excitement.	2d Stage of Excitement.	3d Stage of Excitement.	4th Stage of Excitement.
Muscles obey the will.	7	...	...	...	...	Ideas
	6	...	...	...	Ideas	...
Consciousness begins.	5	...	...	Ideas	...	Sensations
	4	...	Ideas	...	Sensations	...
Feelings so faint as not to excite consciousness.	3	Ideas	...	Sensations	...	...
	2	...	Sensations	...	...	...
	1	Sensations	...	...	...	...

1st Stage of Excitement.

In the first stage of excitement, ideas are to be found at the 4th and sensations at the 2d degree of vividness. Neither description of feelings is, however, sufficiently vivid to excite mental consciousness.

2d Stage of Excitement.

In the second stage of excitement, ideas attain the

5th degree of vividness, when a consciousness of them ensues. But the mind is not conscious of sensations, these being only found at the 3d degree.

The dreaming state now commences, confined, however, to ideas:

> "When Reason sleeps, our mimic fancy wakes,
> Supplies her part, and wild ideas takes
> From words and things ill-suited and misjoin'd,
> The anarchy of thought and chaos of the mind."

3d Stage of Excitement.

In the third stage, ideas appear at the 6th degree of vividness. That law of the mind, before alluded to, is now called into force, which is,—that when any mental feelings attain a certain degree of vividness, (at or about the 6th degree, as represented in the scale), muscular motions obey the impulse of the will. Yet at this degree, the actions of muscles are very feeble, so that no other phenomena are induced than those which are indicated by the low mutterings, or the startings of lively dreams. It may be observed of the sensations of this stage of excitement as of the last, that, rising no higher than the 5th degree, they are still too faint to excite consciousness.

4th Stage of Excitement.

The fourth stage of excitement is that of somnambulism, the ideas of which, being at the 7th degree of vividness, are as vivid as those of complete watchfulness. Accordingly, vigorous muscular motions obey the will. There is likewise a consciousness of sensations, which are to be found in the table, at the 5th degree of vividness.

I shall now illustrate this stage of excitement by a case given on the authority of Mr Smellie, in his Philosophy of Natural History, wherein it is perfectly clear that ideas were more vivid than sensations. The individual who walked in her sleep was a servant-girl residing near Edinburgh. It will be likewise evident from the ensuing narrative, that the fear of an imaginary bull, which the somnambulist supposed was about to attack her, had reduced to a state of extreme faintness every feeling which was not connected with the moral occasion that gave rise to her emotions. Hence, the infliction of wounds from a sharp-pointed instrument failed in producing sensations sufficiently vivid to be the object of mental consciousness.

" I examined her countenance," says Mr Smellie, " and found that her eyes, though open, wild, and staring, were not absolutely fixed. *I took a pin, and repeatedly pricked her arm, but not a muscle moved, not a symptom of pain was discoverable.* At last she became impatient to get out, and made several attempts to escape by the door, but that was prevented by the domestics. Perceiving her inability to force the door, she made a sudden spring at the window, and endeavoured to throw herself over, which would have been fatal to her. To remove every suspicion of imposture, I desired the people, with proper precautions to prevent harm, to try if she would really precipitate herself from the window. A seemingly free access was left for her escape, which she perceived, and instantly darted with such force and agility, that more than one-half of her body was projected before her friends were aware. They, however, laid hold of her, and prevented the dreadful catastrophe. She was again prevailed upon, though with much reluctance, to sit down. She soon resumed her former calmness, and freely answered such questions as were put to her. This scene continued for more than an hour. I was perfectly convinced, notwithstanding my original suspicions, that the woman was actuated by strong and natural impulses, and not by any design to deceive. I asked if any of the attendants knew how to awaken her. A female servant replied that she did. She immediately, to my astonishment, laid hold of Sarah's wrist, forcibly squeezed and rubbed the projecting bones, calling out, at the same time, Sarah, Sarah! By this operation Sarah awoke. She stared with amazement, looked around, and asked how so many people came to be in her own apartment at so unseasonable an hour? After she was completely awake, I asked her what was the cause of her restlessness and violent agitation? She replied, that she had been dreaming that she was pursued by a furious bull, which was every moment on the point of goring her."*

Section IV.

TRANSITION (named the 6th in the Table)

From common Dreams and Somnambulism to perfect Sleep.

A *fourth* transition is from somnambulism and common dreaming to perfect sleep. As this series of

---

* Smellie's Philosophy of Natural History, vol. ii. p. 393.

mental changes is indicated by phenomena, the exact reverse of the stages of excitement last described, they will be sufficiently explained by an inspection of the general table which I have given. It is sufficient for me to observe, that ideas and sensations are uniformly depressed to a low degree of faintness.

Section V.

TRANSITION (marked the 7th in the General Table)

From Sleep less complete to common Dreams and Somnambulism.

It is yet possible to conceive of other circumstances slightly differing from those just mentioned, under which common dreams and somnambulism may be induced. During the transition from watchfulness to perfect sleep, there is an intermediate period of less complete repose, in which the following effects, resulting from a cause of mental excitement, may ensue:—

TABULAR VIEW.

Ideas and sensations are excited uniformly.

	Degrees of Vividness and faintness.	Sleep less complete.	1st Stage of Excitement.	2d Stage of Excitement.	3d Stage of Excitement.
Muscles obey the will.	7	. . .	. . .	. . .	Ideas
	6	. . .	. . .	Ideas	Sensations
Consciousness begins.	5	. . .	Ideas	Sensations	. . .
	4	Ideas	Sensations	. . .	. . .
Feelings so faint as not to excite consciousness.	3	Sensations	. . .	. . .	. . .
	2	. . .	. . .	. . .	. . .
	1	. . .	. . .	. . .	. . .

1st *Stage of Excitement.*

In the first stage of excitement, ideas attain the 5th and sensations the 4th degree of vividness; in which case there is a consciousness of the former feelings only, and the ordinary state of dreaming is induced.

2d *Stage of Excitement.*

In the 2d stage, ideas attain the 6th and sensations the 5th degree of vividness. Muscular motions now slightly obey the will, and there is also a consciousness of actual impressions.

3d *Stage of Excitement.*

In the third stage, ideas are found at the 7th and sensations at the 6th degree of vividness. This change is characterized by all the phenomena of somnambulism.

I know of no other way in which this last stage of excitement can be illustrated, than by shewing that causes of mental excitement, when inducing somnambulism, may operate before perfect sleep is induced. Thus, in a case which Mr Smellie has recorded in his Philosophy of Natural History, relative to a somnambulist, it is said, that " his ordinary sleep, which is seldom tranquil when about to be seized with a fit of somnambulism, is uncommonly disturbed. While in this state he is affected with involuntary motions; his heart palpitates, his tongue falters, and he alternately rises up and lies down. On one of these occasions the gentleman remarked, that he soon articulated more distinctly, rose suddenly, and acted agreeably to the motives of the dream which then occupied his imagination."

Another instance, wherein sleep-walking took place before perfect sleep was induced, may be found in the 9th volume of the Philosophical Transactions of Edinburgh. The somnambulist, to whose case I have alluded in the 2d part of this work, was a servant-girl, affected not only with sleeping, but with waking visions. It is said, that "having fallen asleep, surrounded by some of the inhabitants of the house, she imagined herself to be living with her aunt at Epsom, and going to the races. She then placed herself on one of the kitchen-stools, and rode upon it into the room, with much spirit and a clattering noise, but without being wakened."

Section VI.

TRANSITION (marked the 8th in the General Table)

From Somnambulism and common Dreams to less complete Sleep.

This transition is the exact reverse of the last described. I shall therefore take no farther notice of it than by a reference to the general table which I have given.

CHAPTER II.

THE ORDER OF PHENOMENA OBSERVABLE IN EXTREME MENTAL EXCITEMENTS, WHEN SENSATIONS AND IDEAS ARE CONJOINTLY RENDERED MORE VIVID.

> " To the magic region's centre
> We are verging it appears;
> Lead us right, that we may enter
> Strange enchantment's dreamy spheres."
> *Lord* F. GOWER's *Faust.*

THE transition next to be noticed, is from those medium degrees of vividness which characterize our ordinary waking moments, to the intense condition of mental feelings which gives rise to spectral illusions.

In the common state of watchfulness, ideas, as I just have pointed out, are supposed to be less vivid than sensations; at the end of this excitement, however, they are rendered more intense.

But a readier explanation of these phenomena will be afforded when they are arranged in a tabular form.

SUMMARY OF MENTAL

TRANSITION

From the ordinary tranquil State of Watchfulness to a State of extreme mental Excitement.

Ideas, from being less vivid than sensations, become more intense.

	Degrees of Vividness or Intensity.	Watchfulness.	1st Stage of Excitement.	2d Stage of Excitement.	3d Stage of Excitement.	4th Stage of Excitement.
Intense excitations necessary for spectral impressions.	15	. . .	. . .	. . .	. . .	Ideas
	14	. . .	. . .	. . .	. . .	. . .
	13	. . .	. . .	. . .	Ideas	Sensations
	12	. . .	. . .	. . .	Sensations	. . .
Vividness of ordinary emotions.	11	. . .	. . . {	Sensations Ideas *	. . .	. . .
	10	. . .	Sensations	. . .	. . .	. . .
Medium states of the mind.	9	Sensations	Ideas	. . .	. . .	. . .
	8	. . .	. . .	. . .	. . .	. . .
	7	Ideas	. . .	. . .	. . .	. . .

* When sensations and ideas are of the same degree of vividness, there is no mental consciousness of them.

After these general remarks, I shall proceed to describe the several stages of excitement which occur during this transition of the feelings of the mind.

1st Stage of Excitement.

In the first stage sensations are to be found at the 10th and ideas at the 9th degree of the table, the comparative vividness of the former not increasing so much as that of the latter.

This comparative degree of intensity finds an illustration in our ordinary mental emotions. The vividness of ideas approaches too near that of sensations, so that the proper distinction which ought to subsist between them is less easily discerned; and hence the reason why mental emotions do not allow of the decisions of cool judgment. The effect, likewise, of a vivifying influence, which acts in a particular manner upon ideas, is to give them, when compared with sensations, an undue prominence in our thoughts. A farther consequence, therefore, of this action, is,—that relations of comparison, such as subsist among all our varieties of feeling, are suggested in a much greater number and variety than when the mind is cool and tranquil. New resemblances, differences, forms, or positions, unexpectedly arise, and, in the same unlooked-for manner, connect the recollected images of the mind with the external objects by which we are surrounded. Should no calmer reference then be made for the correctness of such relations to actual circumstances, we enter the wild realms of Phantasy, where sober deliberations, which have truth for their object, are exchanged for the reveries of fanatics, of poets, or of philosophical theorists:

> "Fledg'd with the feathers of a learned muse,
> They raise themselves unto the highest pitch,
> Marrying base earth and heaven in a thought."*

When individuals labour under an evident defici-

---

* Old comedy of Lingua.

ency of the judging faculties, and when, at the same time, morbific causes impart a permanent influence to the too vivid state of ideas, then arises that distracted state of the thoughts, where little distinction is made between actual impressions and the renovated feelings of the mind. This variety of Amentia is happily illustrated by Pinel in the case which he has given of one of his own countrymen, who had been educated in all the prejudices of the ancient noblesse. " His passionate and puerile mobility was excessive. He constantly bustled about the house, talking incessantly, shouting, and throwing himself into great passions for the most trifling causes. He teased his domestics by the most frivolous orders, and his neighbours by his fooleries and extravagancies, of which he retained not the least recollection for a single moment. He talked with the greatest volatility of the court, of his periwig, of his horses, of his gardens, without waiting for an answer, or giving time to follow his incoherent jargon."

It is worthy of note, that the energy of muscular actions often keeps pace with this stage of mental excitement. This is happily illustrated in the effect which a variety of the Amanita Muscaria produces when used as an intoxicating ingredient by the inhabitants of the north-eastern parts of Asia. In a very interesting history of this fungus, lately drawn up by Dr Greville of Edinburgh, particular mention is made of its influence on the movements of the muscles. This writer observes, that " one large, or two small fungi, is a common dose, when intended to produce a pleasant intoxication for the whole day ;" he then adds, " it renders some persons remarkably active, and proves highly stimulant to muscular exertion : with too large a dose, violent spasmodic effects are produced. So very exciting to the nervous system in many individuals is this fungus, that the effects are often very ludicrous. If a person under its influence wishes to step over a straw or small stick, he takes a stride or a jump sufficient to clear the trunk of a tree ; a talkative person cannot keep silence or secrets ; and one fond of music is perpetually singing."*

The last remark which I shall make on this stage of mental excitement is, that no other mental impressions of a spectral nature are experienced, than such as may be corrected by a slight examination of the natural objects to which they owe their origin. Illusions of sound are such as have been described after the following manner by Mr Coleridge:—" When we are broad awake," says this writer, " if we are in anxious expectation, how often will not the most confused sounds of nature be heard by us as articulate sounds? For instance, the babbling of a brook will appear for a moment the voice of a friend, for whom we are waiting, calling out our own names." Illusions of vision are of the same nature as those which I took occasion to describe, when animadverting on the vivifying effects of Hope and Fear. The leading features of some images of the mind, which, if present, would, from moral causes, create emotion, may be traced in such outlines of light and shade as in part compose the figures that are actually impressing the visual organs.

---

* Wernerian Transactions, vol. iv. p. 344.

2d Stage of Excitement.

In this stage of excitement, sensations and ideas, from being excited in different proportions, each attain the same degree of vividness. (*See degree* 11 *in the following table.*) At the same time, as I have more than once explained, all knowledge of present and past time, which necessarily results from the comparative degrees of vividness that subsist been sensations and ideas, must totally cease; and with it, of course, all mental consciousness.

TABULAR VIEW.

	Degrees of Intensity.	1st Stage of Excitement.	2d Stage of Excitement.
Ordinary Mental Emotions.	11	. . .	Sensations Ideas*
	10	Sensations	
	9	Ideas	

* When sensations and ideas are of the same intensity there is no consciousness of them.

This momentary state of unconsciousness is not unfrequently induced by violent emotions of the mind. Accordingly, in the descriptions which poets have given us of the effects of various exciting passions, illustrations of such an incident will be commonly met with. One of the *dramatis personæ*, for instance, in Dryden's tragedy of Aurengzebe, while expatiating on the more than ordinary intensity which had been imparted to his feelings by some source of enjoyment or other, very philosophically adds,

> " Nature
> Gives all she can, and, lab'ring still to give,
> Makes it so great, we can but taste and live;
> So fills the senses that the soul seems fled,
> *And thought itself does for the time lie dead.*"

By the same poet, this stage of mental excitement has been described as a sort of lethargy:

> " Thus long my grief has kept me dumb,
> Sure there's *a lethargy in mighty woe.*"

And in the Conquest of Granada:

> Ev'n while I speak and look, I change yet more;
> And now am nothing that I was before.
> I'm numb'd and fix'd, and scarce my eyeballs move;
> I fear it is *the lethargy of love !*

This momentary unconsciousness is likewise attended with a corresponding cessation of all muscular motions, but more particularly of those which are concerned with vocal utterance. Thus, Shakspeare speaks of " the grief that does not speak."* But Dryden, in his translation of Ovid, has more particularly described this peculiar affection:

---

* Give sorrow words; the grief that does not speak,
Whispers the o'er-fraught heart, and bids it break.
Macbeth, Act 4, *Scene* 3.

> "She thus essay'd to speak; her accents hung,
> And, falt'ring, dy'd unfinish'd on her tongue,
> Or vanish'd into sighs: with long delay
> Her voice return'd, and found the wonted way."

In violent ebullitions of passion, feelings occasionally arise of which we are alternately conscious and unconscious. The following tabular view will probably afford a rationale of this phenomenon, which depends upon our mental feelings undergoing a sort of vacillation between the first and second stages of excitement which I have described.

	Degrees of Vividness.	Feelings of Consciousness.	Momentary Unconsciousness.	Consciousness returned.
Ordinary Emotions,	11	. . .	Sensations Ideas*	. . .
	10	Sensations	. . .	Sensations
	9	Ideas	. . .	Ideas

* When sensations and ideas are of the same degree of vividness, there is an unconsciousness of them.

Alternate transitions of this kind, from one stage of excitement to another, have been alluded to by Rowe, in his admirable drama of the Fair Penitent:

> "At first her rage was dumb, and wanted words;
> But when the storm found way, 'twas wild and loud.
> Mad as the priestess of the Delphic god,
> Enthusiastic passion swell'd her breast,
> Enlarg'd her voice, and ruffled all her form."

I shall next remark, that the second stage of excitement, thus characterized by a temporary unconsciousness, has been in a striking manner illustrated by the effects resulting from the inhalation of the nitrous oxide. When Sir Humphry Davy had respired six quarts of nitrous oxide, the operation of which was not so rapid as usual, he remarked, " The thrilling was very rapidly produced. The objects around me were perfectly distinct, and the light of the candle was not, as usual, dazzling. The pleasurable sensation was at first local, and perceived in the lips and about the cheeks. It gradually, however, diffused itself over the whole body, and in the middle of the experiment was for a moment so intense and pure as to absorb existence. *At this moment, and not before, I lost consciousness;* it was, however, quickly restored."*—But sometimes, when ideas arrive at the same degree of intensity as sensations, our feelings do not shew a tendency to increase in vividness ; in which case, a much longer state of unconsciousness subsists. Accordingly, this happened to another inhaler of the nitrous oxide, spoken of in Sir Humphry Davy's Researches. " I was *for some time,*" he remarks, " *unconscious of existence.*"

But a more permanent state of unconsciousness may be brought on by morbific excitements ; on which occasion a variety of catalepsy may be induced, differing from that which I have lately described. (See page 400). For, in the case already adduced, there was a more feeble excitement of the mind, and at the same time sensations and ideas acquired a similar degree of vividness. The vivifying influence, therefore,

---

* Davy's Researches concerning the Nitrous Oxide, p. 492.

which stimulated muscles, notwithstanding the absence of all mental consciousness, only caused very faint contractions of them. But in a greater stage of excitement, such as that which we are now considering, the more vivid condition of mental feelings induces vigorous muscular actions. Yet, as long as there is no consciousness of the present and the past, the muscles maintain the same state of rest or motion which they had acquired *previous* to the excitement.* A recent example of this variety of catalepsy may be found in Dr Good's work on the study of medicine.† It is the case of a student of Gray's Inn, about nineteen years of age. " Having been attacked," says this author, " with a fit of catalepsy while walking, within a few minutes after having left his chambers, he continued his pace insensibly, and without the slightest knowledge of the course he took. As far as he could judge, the paroxysm continued for nearly an hour, through the whole of which time his involuntary walking continued ; at the end of this period he began a little to recover his recollection, and the general use of his external senses. He found himself in a large street, but did not know how he got there, nor what was its name. Upon inquiry, he learned that he was at the further end of Piccadilly, near Hyde-Park-Corner, to which, when he left his chambers, he had no intention of going. He was extremely frightened, very much

---

* This is a very curious fact. It will be more particularly noticed in a separate investigation, which has for some time occupied my attention.

† See Good's Study of Medicine, vol. iii. p. 580.

EXCITEMENTS AND DEPRESSIONS. 419

exhausted, and returned home in a coach. *He was not conscious of any particular train of ideas that had passed in his mind during the fit.**

3d Stage of Excitement.

In a *third* stage of excitement, ideas are to be found at the 13th and sensations at the 12th degree of vividness. Spectral impressions now occur, ideas being more vivid than the actual impressions with which they are accompanied, and far more intense than the undisturbed and cool sensations of our proper waking hours.

The momentary unconsciousness just described, occurs as the prelude of spectral impressions,—conveying the notion that surrounding objects are vanishing, or melting into air, when, in fact, it is sensations themselves which are sinking into faint states of

---

* As I am on the subject of catalepsy, some of my readers may perhaps expect me to notice the case adduced by Martin, in his Treatise on the Second-sight of the Highlands, who has stated, that " there was one in Sky, of whom his acquaintance observed, that when he sees a vision, the inner part of his eyelids turn so far upwards, that after the object disappears, he must draw them down with his fingers, and he sometimes employs others to draw them down, which he finds to be the much easier way." From this circumstance, Dr Ferriar has conceived that the vision of the seer was connected with catalepsy. But this inference is a dubious one:

> " While thus the lady talk'd, the knight
> Turn'd th' outside of his eyes to white;
> As men of inward light are wont
> To turn their opticks in upon't."

unconsciousness. Immediately, however, this apparent evanescence is succeeded by ideas so intensely vivified, that the semblance is excited of a transmutation of tangible objects into the fantastical images of a visionary world. "I thought," said Arise Evans, an accredited seer of the year 1653, "in a vision that I had presently after the King's death, that I was in a great hall like the King's hall, or the castle in Winchester, and there was none there but a judge that sat upon the bench and myself; and as I turned to a window to the north-westward, and looking into the palm of my hand, there appeared to me a face, head, and shoulders, like the Lord Fairfax's, and presently it vanished. Again, there arose the Lord Cromwell, and he vanished likewise; then arose a young face, and he had a crown upon his head, and he vanished also; and another young face arose with a crown upon his head, and he vanished also; and another young face arose with a crown upon his head, and he vanished in like manner; and as I turned the palm of my hand back again to me and looked, there did appear no man in it. Then I turned to the judge, and said to him, there arose in my hands seven, and five of them had crowns; but when I turned my hand, the blood turned to its veins, and these appeared no more."*

---

* This vision, which, as Dr Ferriar has well remarked, resembled the royal shadows in Macbeth, was interpreted by Arise Evans after the following manner :—" The interpretation of this vision is, that, after the Lord Cromwell, there shall be kings again in England, which thing is signified unto us by them that arose after him, who were all crowned; but the generations to come may look for a change of the blood, and of the name in the royal seat, after

But a transition of this kind, when real objects become evanescent and are succeeded by phantasms, I have endeavoured to explain by the following

TABULAR VIEW.

	Degrees of Vividness.	Previous Mental States while contemplating real Objects.	States of Feeling while real Objects are vanishing.	States of Feeling which induce Spectral Impressions.
Intense Excitements.	13	...	...	Ideas
	12	...	...	Sensations
Ordinary Emotions.	11	...	{ Sensations { Ideas *	...
	10	Sensations	...	...
	9	Ideas	...	...

* When sensations and ideas are of the same degree of vividness, there is no consciousness of them.

Again, an order of depression, the exact reverse of the excitement which is displayed in the foregoing table, will present us with the mode in which phantasms appear to vanish, and real objects again become manifest.

Sometimes spectral impressions are ushered in by a more permanent state of unconsciousness, which was considered of great importance by old pneumatologists. The temporary unconsciousness which preceded an ecstacy, was attributed to the apprehensive

---

five kings once passed," &c. &c. But enough of this: the interpretation is far more difficult to be admitted than the vision itself. (*See Jortin's Remarks on Ecclesiastical History, Appendix to vol. i.*)

faculties of sense having left the body for the purpose of supernaturally exploring every thing

" Within earth's centre or heaven's circle found."

As soon, therefore, as the senses had returned from their long journey, loaded with intelligence, the ecstacy of the seer commenced:

> " He therefore sent out all his senses
> To bring him in intelligences,
> Which vulgars, out of ignorance,
> Mistake for falling in a trance;
> But those that trade in geomancy,
> Affirm to be the strength of fancy."

But there are other phenomena to be considered incidental to spectral illusions.

When the feelings of the mind are under the influence of an irregular excitement, it is not uncommon for them to fluctuate in their degrees of vividness; or, in other words, ideas, from being more faint than actual impressions, become, in turns, more vivid. In this case, objects of sensation appear to vanish; spectral images rise up and melt into air; sensible objects re-appear; and thus there is a constant alternation of realities and phantasms, which, when rapidly induced, gives origin to a painful delirium.

But the mode in which realities and phantasms alternate with each other may find a readier explanation in the following

TABULAR VIEW.

Degrees of Intensity.	Previous State of the Feelings.	Real Objects vanish.	Spectral Impressions.	Phantasms vanish.	Real Objects return.
13	. . .	. . .	Ideas	. . .	. . .
12	. . .	. . .	Sensations	. . .	. . .
11	. . .	{ Sensations { Ideas*	. . .	{ Sensations { Ideas*	. . .
10	Sensations	. . .	. . .	. . .	Sensations
9	Ideas	. . .	. . .	. . .	Ideas

* When sensations and ideas are of the same degree of intensity, there is an unconsciousness of them.

An example of this alternation of realities and phantasms will be found in Dr Crichton's work on mental derangement. It is given on the authority of Bonnet. The case recorded is of a gentleman whose mental disorder had originated from some affection of the brain, aggravated by intense study. It is said, that " mansions arose suddenly before his eyes with all their external and appropriate decorations. At times, the appearance of the paper in his room seemed at once to be changed, and, instead of the usual figures which are on it, a number of fine landscapes appeared to his view. Some time after, not only all the landscapes and paper, but the furniture also, disappeared, and the bare walls presented themselves to his eyes."*

Occasionally the states of the mind fluctuate between the second and third stages of excitement, so that feelings of which we are unconscious, and spec-

---

* Crichton on Mental Derangement, vol. ii. p. 39.

tral impressions, are alternately produced. In this case, phantasms arise,—they vanish,—other illusions of the same sort take their place,—these again vanish, —and thus, there is a longer or shorter succession of spectral appearances, without the intervention of any impressions which may be suggested by natural objects.

These phenomena may be illustrated as before.

TABULAR VIEW,

Explanatory of the Mode in which Successions of Phantasms occur.

Degrees of Intensity.	Previous State of Feelings.	Real Objects vanish.	Spectral Impressions.	Phantasms vanish.	Other Phantasms appear.	Phantasms again vanish, &c.
13	. . .	. . .	Ideas.	. . .	Ideas.	. . .
12	. . .	. . .	Sensations.	. . .	Sensations.	. . .
11	. . .	{ Sensations Ideas*	. .	{ Sensations Ideas*	. .	{ Sensations Ideas*
10	Sensations.	. . .	. . .	. . .	. . .	. . .
9	Ideas.	. . .	. . .	. . .	. . .	. . .

* When sensations and ideas are of the same degree of intensity, there is an unconsciousness of them.

Cowley, in some lines which he has written on Fancy, has very well depicted a similar succession of illusions, which he attributes to the special operations of this assumed and personified principle of the mind:

" Here, in a robe which does all colours show,
Fancy, wild dame, with much lascivious pride,
By twin-cameleons drawn, does gaily ride.
Her coach then follows, and throngs round about,

> Of shapes and airy forms an endless rout.
> A sea rolls on with harmless fury there;
> Straight 'tis a field, and trees and herbs appear:
> Here in a moment are vast armies made,
> And a quick scene of war and blood display'd:
> Here sparkling wines and brighter maids come in
> The bawds for sense and living baits for sin:
> Here golden mountains swell the cov'tous place,
> And centaurs ride themselves a painted race."

An actual instance, however, of spectral impressions undergoing successive changes in the subject of them, is afforded in the ecstatic illusions which Cardan experienced. These are minutely related. "I saw," he observes on one occasion, " different figures, as of brazen substances. They seemed to consist of small rings, like links of mail (although I had never yet seen chain-armour), ascending from a low corner of my bed, moving from right to left in a semicircular direction, and then melting as into air. I descried the shapes of castles, of houses, of animals, of horses with their riders, of herbs, of trees, of musical instruments, of the different features of men and of their different garments. Trumpeters appeared to blow their trumpets, yet no voices or sounds were heard. I saw, moreover, soldiers, people, fields, and the form of bodies even to this day unknown to me; groves and woods, some things of which I have no remembrance, and a mass of many objects rushing in together, yet not with marks of confusion, but of haste."

4th Stage of Excitement.

I have again supposed a *fourth*, or extreme stage of

general mental excitement, where ideas attain the 15th and sensations the 13th degree of vividness, the former being still more intense than the latter. This stage is shewn in the following table.

TABULAR VIEW

Of the two different Degrees of Excitements necessary for the Production of Spectral Impressions.

	Degrees of Intensity.	3d Stage of Excitement.	4th Stage of Excitement.
Spectral impressions induced.	15	. . .	Ideas
	14	. . .	. . .
	13	Ideas	Sensations
	12	Sensations	. . .
Ordinary emotions.	11	. . .	. . .

On a former occasion, I shewed that morbific excitements did nothing more than impart an addition of vividness to feelings, which, from moral causes, were of themselves either pleasurable or painful; but that, when inordinate vivifying actions were induced, spectral impressions followed, the subjects of which were alternately of a pleasurable and painful quality.

This, then, is the peculiar character of the 4th and last stage of mental excitement, an illustration of which is afforded in the visions of Kotter, who, as Dr Ferriar has remarked, " was sincere in his enthusiasm, and was as much a seer as any second-sighted prophet of the Hebrides." In the year 1616 an angel appeared to this prophet, who ordered him to inform the civil powers that great evils were impending over Germany. He had, accordingly, many visions, which were supposed to have reference to the future, but they were not declared on oath to the magistrates before the year 1619. I shall pass over several of the phantasies he experienced, contenting myself with the notice of one ecstacy only, which was so extremely intense as to shew evident marks that it was alternately pleasurable and painful. Supposing himself to be attended by two angels, Kotter thus proceeds:—" On the 13th day of September," says he, " both the youths returned to me, saying, ' Be not afraid, but observe the thing which will be shewn to thee.' And I suddenly beheld a circle like the sun, red as it were bloody, in which were black and white lines, or spots, so intermingled, that sometimes there appeared greater number of blacks, sometimes of whites; and this sight continued for some space of time. And when they had said to me, ' Behold! attend! fear not! no evil will befall thee!' lo, there were three successive peals of thunder, at short intervals, so loud and dreadful, that I shuddered all over. But the circle stood before me, and the black and white spots were disunited, and the circle approached so near, that I could have touched it with my hand. And it was so beautiful, that I had never in my life seen any thing more agreeable; and the white spots were so bright and pleasant, that I could not contain my admiration. But the black spots were carried away in a cloud of darkness, in which I heard a dismal outcry, though I could see no one. Yet these words of lamentation were audible:—' Woe unto us who have committed ourselves to the black cloud, to be withdrawn from the circle covered with blood of Divine Grace, in which the grace of God, in his well-beloved Son, had enclosed us!'"*

I have at length concluded my account of the various degrees of vividness which our mental feelings undergo in a transition from the ordinary tranquil state of our waking moments to that extreme mental excitement, which gives rise to spectral impressions. It has been assumed, that ideas, from being more faint than sensations, become more intense.

Another transition remains to be briefly noticed, which is from the highest pitch of mental excitement to those medium states of the mind, which are characterized by coolness and tranquillity. But it is useless to dwell long upon this depression of mental feelings, as it presents phenomena the exact reverse of the last-described stages of excitement. Ideas, from being more intense than sensations, are, *first*, reduced to the same degree of vividness as actual impressions, when a mental unconsciousness, generally momentary, ensues; and, *lastly*, they become more faint than sensations.

---

* This vision I have quoted from Dr Ferriar's Illustrations. See his Theory of Apparitions, page 78.

CHAPTER III.

THE IMAGES OF SPECTRAL IMPRESSIONS DIFFER FROM THOSE OF DREAMS IN BEING MUCH MORE VIVID.

Videre somnia est à fortitudine imaginationis; sicut intelligere ea est à fortitudine intellectûs.   ABDALA.

In a former part of this work it was explained, that when ideas became more vivid than sensations, they were contemplated as present, or as actual impressions; while the least vivid feeling suggested the notion of past time. I then added, that the partial resemblance of spectral impressions to dreams would now perhaps be apparent; but that there was still a difference to be noticed in the circumstances under which they are severally produced. Before spectral impressions could arise, the vivid ideas of our waking hours must be raised to an unusually high degree of intensity; but during our moments of mental repose, a very slight degree of vividness imparted to the faint ideas of perfect sleep was sufficient to excite a similar illusion. Hence the images of spectral impressions differ from those of dreams, in being much more vivid.

It is then my object to illustrate, by a tabular view, the comparative degrees of vividness which subsist between the impressions of dreams and the illusive phantasms of our waking moments.

SUMMARY OF MENTAL

TABULAR VIEW,

Shewing the Comparative Degrees of Vividness which subsist between the Sensations and Ideas that severally belong to Dreams, and to the Spectral Impressions which occur during waking Excitements of the Mind.

	Degrees of intensity, vividness, or faintness.	Various mental states during common dreams.		Various mental states during somnambulism.				States of the mind during spectral impressions.	
Intense excitements of the mind necessary for the production of spectral illusions.	15	.	.	.	.	.	.	.	Ideas
	14	.	.	.	.	.	.	Ideas	Sensations
	13	.	.	.	.	.	.	Sensations	.
	12	.	.	.	.	.	.	.	.
Vividness of ordinary mental emotions.	11	.	.	.	.	.	.	.	.
	10	.	.	.	.	.	.	.	.
Medium states of the mind, forming the ordinary tranquil state of watchfulness.	9	.	.	.	.	.	.	.	.
	8	.	.	.	.	.	.	.	.
	7	.	.	.	Ideas	.	.	.	.
Degree at which muscular motions obey the will.	6	.	.	Ideas	Sensations	Ideas	.	.	.
Degree of vividness at which consciousness begins.	5	Ideas	.	Sensations	.	Sensations	Ideas	.	.
	4	.	Sensations	.	.	.	Sensations	.	.
Faintness of mental feelings so extreme as not to excite consciousness.	3	Sensations	.	.	.	.	.	.	.
	2	.	.	.	.	.	.	.	.
	1	.	.	.	.	.	.	.	.

I shall now give a few examples of those cases of spectral illusions, where an exciting cause has so gradually, yet powerfully, operated upon the ideas of dreams, as to make them more than usually intense. Dreams of this kind, after the impression has ceased, are often with difficulty recognised as sleeping or waking visions; nor can the difference be often well determined by any inquiry we may institute,—If the illusion supervened to a state of absolute repose, or of watchfulness? An instance of this uncertain species of phantasms is contained in a narrative translated by Dr Crichton, from the Psychological Magazine of Germany, (some extracts from which have been before given,) relative to a female who was subject to trances. She is the narrator of her own case; and, after describing some cruel usage she experienced from her husband, which much affected the quality of her spectral impressions, she thus proceeds:—" My sorrows increased, and I went to bed in tears. I awakened about four o'clock in the morning, and imagined myself in my father's house on the river Diele. I looked up into heaven, and saw a water-dog walking in the firmament. As soon as it passed by, the skies descended to me, and my eyes were changed on purpose to see new sights, for I saw many hundred thousand miles. The mansion of God stood in the centre, lightly enveloped in clear blue clouds, and surrounded with a splendour of such various colours as are unknown to the world below. In each colour stood some millions of men, enrobed in garments of the same colour with that in which they stood; for instance, those who stood in red were clad in red, and those in the yellow had robes of yellow; and the faces of all these men were turned to the mansion of the Almighty. And there came out of the mansion a most lovely female, clothed in the brightest lustre of heaven, and a crown on her head. She was accompanied by three angels, one on her right hand and one on her left, the third walked beside her, and pointed out the crowd who stood in the splendid colours.

" In a minute the heavens were closed, and again opened as formerly, but the woman and angels were not to be seen; but our blessed Saviour came out of the mansion, followed by a long train of attendants, and he descended through all the splendour I have described. The Lord and his attendants all looked smilingly upon me. They were dressed in white, and wherever they went was a clear white. When he approached me near enough, that I could touch his foot, I was frightened and awoke.* It was then half-past four o'clock; I arose, and considered that my present life was not to be compared with such joys."

With regard to the foregoing illusion, it is impossible to say whether it was a trance or a very vivid dream, particularly, as the same causes which contribute to the spectral impressions of a waking vision are calculated to produce an intense dream. Most probably, however, it was the latter.

Another authentic story, respecting which there is a doubt whether it is the narrative of a lively dream or of a waking illusion, is to be found in *Bovet's*

---

* The writer evidently means, that she *awoke* out of her trance, as she has before spoken of awakening from her sleep.

Pandæmonium, or the Devil's Cloyster. The writer first informs us, that, about the year 1667, " he was with some persons of honour in the house of a nobleman in the west country, which had formerly been a nunnery;" he then continues his narrative after the following manner:—" I must confess, I had often heard the servants and others, that inhabited or lodged there, speak much of the noises, stirs, and apparitions, that frequently disturbed the house, but had at that time no apprehensions of it; for the house being full of strangers, the nobleman's steward, Mr C., lay with me in a fine wainscot room, called my lady's chamber. We went to our lodging pretty early, and having a good fire in the room, we spent some time in reading, in which he much delighted; then having got into bed, and put out the candles, we observed the room to be very light by the brightness of the moon, so that a wager was laid between us, that it was possible to read written hand by that light upon the bed where we lay. Accordingly I drew out of my pocket a manuscript, which he read distinctly in the place where we lay. We had scarcely made an end of discoursing about that affair, when" [*here probably commenced a dream*] " I saw (my face being towards the door, which was locked) entering into the room, five appearances of very fine and lovely women. They were of excellent stature, and their dresses seemed very fine; they covered all but their faces with their light veils, whose skirts trailed largely on the floor. They entered in a file, one after the other, and in that posture walked round the room, till the foremost came and stood by that side of the bed where I lay, with my left hand over the side of the bed; for my head rested on that arm, and I determined not to alter the posture in which I was. She struck me upon that hand with a blow that felt very soft, but I did never remember whether it were cold or hot. I demanded, in the name of the blessed Trinity, what business they had there, but received no answer. Then I spoke to Mr C., 'Sir, do you see what fair guests are here come to visit us?' before which they all disappeared. I found him in some kind of agony, and was forced to grasp him on the breast with my right hand (which was next him underneath the bedclothes) before I could obtain speech of him. Then he told me, that he had seen the fair guests I spoke of, and had heard me speak to them; but withal said, that he was not able to speak sooner unto me, being extremely affrighted at the sight of a dreadful monster, which, assuming a shape between that of a lion and a bear, attempted to come upon the bed's foot. I told him I thanked God nothing so frightful had presented itself to me; but I hoped through his assistance, not to dread the ambages of hell."

It is clear, that the subject of these visions was suggested by the popular superstitions of the old manor-house, and little doubt can be entertained but that by fear, and perhaps by other physical causes, it was impressed on the mind during a dream. It appears that, during the next night, the companion of Bovet, from dread, forsook the haunted room, so that the hero was left by himself to encounter the apparitions. "I ordered," he adds, "a Bible and another book to be laid in the room, and resolved to spend my time by the fire in reading and in contemplation, till I found myself inclined to sleep; and accordingly, having taken leave of the family at the usual hour, I addressed myself to what I had proposed, not going into bed till past one in the morning. A little after I was got into bed I heard somewhat walk about the room, like a woman in a tabby-gown trailing about the room. It made a mighty rushelling noise, but I could see nothing, though it was near as light as the night before. It passed by the foot of the bed, and a little opened the curtains, and thence went to a closet-door on that side, through which it found admittance, although it was close locked. There it seemed to groan, and to draw a great chair with its foot, in which it seemed to sit, and turn over the leaves of a large folio, which, you know, made a loud clattering noise. So it continued in that posture, sometimes groaning, sometimes dragging the chair, and clattering the book, till it was near day. Afterwards I lodged several times in this room, but never met with any molestation."

Regarding this latter apparition, Dr Ferriar is inclined to think, that it did not occur during a dream, but that it was a proper waking illusion. This supposition is, however, very doubtful, as the spectral impression ensued after the ghost-seer had found himself inclined to sleep.

Another instance, however, may be adduced, in which the mental illusions of a waking vision were erroneously conceived, after much debate on the subject, to be those of a dream. An able French writer, in a discourse which he published in the " Mercure Gallant" of the year 1690, describes a spectral impression that occurred to him after the following manner :—" I have already related to you one of my dreams, but must inform you of another, before explaining to you my thoughts more clearly upon the many pretended apparitions of souls and spirits, which are found in good as well as bad authors. I was sent very young to a town at a distance of seven leagues from my native place, in order that I might be weaned from home, and learn to write. Having returned from thence at the expiration of five or six months, I was directed to repair to the house of one of my relatives, where my father, who was newly returned from the army, had arrived, and had sent for me. He examined my specimens of writing, and finding them good, failed not to express a suspicion of their being my own. As he was going out, therefore, one afternoon, along with the lady of the house, to pay a visit in the neighbourhood, he recommended me to write ten or twelve lines in order to remove his doubts. Immediately upon my father's departure, my duty prompted me to go up to the chamber that had been allotted for us, and having searched for all my writing materials, I knelt down (being then a little boy) before an arm-chair, upon which I placed my paper and ink.

" While engaged in writing, I thought I heard upon the staircase people who were carrying corn to granaries ; having therefore risen from the place where I was kneeling, I turned a corner of the tapestry, and saw a little room open,—and in this room my father seemed engaged in conversation with the lady of the house, being seated near her. As I had seen both one and the other get into a carriage, and set out from the château, I was much surprised at now perceiving them before me. Terror united itself to astonishment; I let go the tapestry, and, leaving the chamber, quickly descended the staircase.

"Upon meeting with the housekeeper, she remarked some alteration in my face, and asked me what was the matter. I told her all about it. She honestly assured me that I had been dreaming, and that the marchioness and my father would not return for more than an hour. I would fain have discredited her assurance, and stood fixed near the door of her room, until at length I saw them arrive. My trouble was not a little increased at the sight; for the present, however, I said nothing to my father; but when, after supper, he would have sent me to bed before him, all the self-collection which I could muster on the occasion was to allow myself to be conducted out of his presence. Yet I waited for him to accompany me into our chamber, for I was unwilling to re-enter it but along with him. He was astonished, therefore, upon retiring, to find that I had lingered. He failed not to ask me what was the cause of it; and, after some vain excuses, I confessed to him that I was terrified, because spirits had appeared in the chamber. He derided my fear, and demanded of me to whom I was indebted for such foolish tales. I then told him my adventure; which he no sooner heard, than, intent upon undeceiving me, I was conducted by him to the granaries, or rather to the garrets to which the staircase led. It was then made known to me that these garrets were not fit to be store-rooms for corn,—that there was actually none there, and that there never had been any. Upon my return, as I followed close to my father, he asked me to point out the place where I had lifted up the tapestry and seen the room open. I searched for it in all directions to shew him, but in vain. I could find no other door in the four walls of our chamber than that which led from the staircase.

"Events so opposite to what I had believed could be the case, alarmed me still more, and I imagined from what I had heard related of *goblins*,* that some of them had caused these illusions in order to abuse my senses. My father then insisted that such alleged freaks of spirits were mere fables,—more fabulous even than those of Æsop or of Phædrus, adding, that the truth was, I had slept while writing; that I had dreamt during my sleep all which I now believed I had heard and seen, and that the conjoined influence of surprise and fear having acted on my imagination, had caused the same effect upon it as would have been produced by truth itself. I had difficulty at the time to assent to this reasoning; but was obliged to acknowledge it in the end as very just.—Observe, however, how strong the impression of this dream was. I think candidly, that if the vision had not been falsified by all the circumstances which I have just noted, I should, even at this time, have received it for a truth."

The foregoing illusion scarcely requires comment.

---

* In the original, *esprits follets*.

There can be little doubt but that it was a proper waking impression, and not a dream, as the youth was reluctantly led to suppose by his father.

These remarks conclude my general view of the comparative degrees of vividness subsisting among sensations and ideas, during their successive states of excitement and depression.

The laws which we have been considering may, indeed, be applied to the solution of far more important questions than those which belong to the subject of spectral impressions. While a knowledge of them may materially assist the physician in his treatment of the mental afflictions to which our humanity is liable, the moral philosopher may likewise discover, in the same laws, certain very important principles influencing human actions and conduct, upon which doctrines of the highest value to the science of ethics may be securely built.

NOTES.

Ancient Sculpture at Hulme-Hall, Lancashire. From a Drawing by Captain Jones, 29th Regiment.

" Begone, chimeras, to your mother clouds !".

Œdipus.

NOTES.

Note 1, p. 4.

The Devils seen by Benvenuto Cellini.—Extract from Mr Roscoe's Translation of his Life.

"It happened, through a variety of odd accidents, that I made acquaintance with a Sicilian priest, who was a man of genius, and well versed in the Latin and Greek authors. Happening one day to have some conversation with him, when the subject turned upon the art of necromancy, I, who had a great desire to know something of the matter, told him, that I had all my life felt a curiosity to be acquainted with the mysteries of this art. The priest made answer, 'That the man must be of a resolute and steady temper who enters upon that study.' I replied, 'That I had fortitude and resolution enough, if I could but find an opportunity.' The priest subjoined, 'If you think you have the heart to venture, I will give you all the satisfaction you can desire.' Thus we agreed to enter upon a plan of necromancy. The priest one evening prepared to satisfy me, and desired me to look out for a companion or two. I invited one Vincenzio Romoli, who was my intimate acquaintance: he brought with him a native of Pistoia, who cultivated the black art himself. We repaired to the Colosseo, and the priest, according to the custom of necromancers, began to draw circles upon the ground with the most impressive ceremonies imaginable: he likewise brought hither assafœtida, several precious perfumes, and fire, with some compositions also which diffused noisome odours. As soon as he was in readiness, he made an opening to the circle, and having taken us by the hand, ordered the other necromancer, his partner, to throw the perfumes into the fire at a proper time, intrusting the care of the fire and the perfumes to the rest; and then he began his incantations. This ceremony lasted above an hour and a half, when there appeared several legions of devils, insomuch that the amphitheatre was quite filled with them. I was busy about the perfumes, when the priest, perceiving there was a considerable number of infernal spirits, turned to me and said, ' Benvenuto, ask them something.' I answered, ' Let them bring me into the company of my Sicilian mistress, Angelica.' That night we obtained no answer of any sort; but I had received great satisfaction in having my curiosity so far indulged. The necromancer told me, it was requisite we should go a second time, assuring me, that I should be satisfied in whatever I asked; but that I must bring with me a pure immaculate boy.

" I took with me a youth who was in my service, of about twelve years of age, together with the same Vincenzio Romoli, who had been my companion the first time, and one Agnolino Gaddi, an intimate acquaintance, whom I likewise prevailed on to assist at the ceremony. When we came to the place appointed, the priest having made his preparations as before, with the same and even more striking ceremonies, placed us within the circle, which he had likewise drawn with a more wonderful art, and in a more solemn manner, than at our former meeting. Thus having committed the care of the perfumes and the fire to my friend Vincenzio, who was assisted by Agnolino Gaddi, he put into my hand a pintaculo or magical chart,* and bid me turn it towards

---

* " The most exact writers call it pentacoli, a sort of magical preparation of card, stone, and metal, on which are inscribed words and figures, considered very efficacious against the power of demons. See Ariosto Orl. F. c. iii. st. 21."—(*Note of the Translator.*)

the places that he should direct me; and under the pintaculo I held my boy. The necromancer having begun to make his tremendous invocations, called by their names a multitude of demons, who were the leaders of the several legions, and questioned them by the power of the eternal uncreated God, who lives for ever, in the Hebrew language, as likewise in Latin and Greek; insomuch that the amphitheatre was almost in an instant filled with demons more numerous than at the former conjuration. Vincenzio Romoli was busied in making a fire, with the assistance of Agnolino, and burning a great quantity of precious perfumes. I, by the direction of the necromancer, again desired to be in the company of my Angelica. The former thereupon turning to me, said,—' Know, they have declared, that in the space of a month you shall be in her company.'

" He then requested me to stand resolutely by him, because the legions were now above a thousand more in number than he had designed; and, besides, these were the most dangerous; so that, after they had answered my question, it behoved him to be civil to them, and dismiss them quietly. At the same time the boy under the pintaculo was in a terrible fright, saying, that there were in that place a million of fierce men, who threatened to destroy us; and that, moreover, four armed giants of an enormous stature were endeavouring to break into our circle. During this time, whilst the necromancer, trembling with fear, endeavoured by mild and gentle methods to dismiss them in the best way he could, Vincenzio Romoli, who quivered like an aspen leaf, took care of the perfumes. Though I was as much terrified as any of them, I did my utmost to conceal the terror I felt; so that I greatly contributed to inspire the rest with resolution; but the truth is, I gave myself over for a dead man, seeing the horrid fright the necromancer was in.

The boy placed his head between his knees, and said,—' In this posture will I die; for we shall all surely perish.' I told him that all these demons were under us, and what he saw was smoke and shadow;* so bid him hold up his head and take courage. No sooner did he look up, but he cried out,—' The whole amphitheatre is burning, and the fire is just falling upon us;' so, covering his eyes with his hands, he again exclaimed, that destruction was inevitable, and he desired to see no more. The necromancer entreated me to have a good heart, and take care to burn proper perfumes; upon which I turned to Romoli, and bid him burn all the most precious perfumes he had. At the same time I cast my eye upon Agnolino Gaddi, who was terrified to such a degree that he could scarce distinguish objects, and seemed to be half-dead. Seeing him in this condition, I said,— ' Agnolino, upon these occasions a man should not yield to fear, but should stir about and give his assistance; so come directly and put on some more of these perfumes.' Poor Agnolino, upon attempting to move, was so violently terrified, that the effects of his fear overpowered all the perfumes we were burning. The boy hearing a crepitation, ventured once more to raise his head, when, seeing me laugh, he began to take courage, and said, ' That the devils were flying away with a vengeance.'

"In this condition we stayed till the bell rang for morning prayer. The boy again told us, that there remained but few devils, and these were at a great distance. When the magician had performed the rest of his ceremonies, he stripped off his gown, and took up a wallet full of books which he had brought with him. We all went out of the circle

---

* "This confirms us in the belief," says Mr Roscoe, "that the whole of these appearances, like a phantasmagoria, were merely the effects of a magic-lantern, produced on volumes of smoke from various kinds of burning wood."

together, keeping as close to each other as we possibly could, especially the boy, who had placed himself in the middle, holding the necromancer by the coat, and me by the cloak. As we were going to our houses in the quarter of Banchi, the boy told us that two of the demons whom we had seen at the amphitheatre, went on before us leaping and skipping, sometimes running upon the roofs of the houses, and sometimes upon the ground. The priest declared, that though he had often entered magic circles, nothing so extraordinary had ever happened to him. As we went along, he would fain persuade me to assist with him at consecrating a book, from which, he said, we should derive immense riches: we should then ask the demons to discover to us the various treasures with which the earth abounds, which would raise us to opulence and power; but that those love-affairs were mere follies, from whence no good could be expected. I answered, ' That I would readily have accepted his proposal if I understood Latin:' he redoubled his persuasions, assuring me, that the knowledge of the Latin language was by no means material. He added, that he could have Latin scholars enough, if he had thought it worth while to look out for them; but that he could never have met with a partner of resolution and intrepidity equal to mine, and that I should by all means follow his advice. Whilst we were engaged in this conversation, we arrived at our respective homes, and all that night dreamt of nothing but devils."

NOTE 2, p. 16.

Giant of the Broken.

THE following is the account given by a German traveller of the Giant of the Broken :—

" In the course of my repeated tours through the Harz,*

---

* " The Harz mountains are situated in Hanover."

I ascended the Broken twelve times; but had the good fortune only twice (both times about Whitsuntide) to see that atmospheric phenomenon, called the Spectre of the Broken, which appears to me worthy of particular attention, as it must no doubt be observed on other high mountains which have a situation favourable for producing it. The first time I was deceived by this extraordinary phenomenon, I had clambered up to the summit of the Broken very early in the morning, in order to wait for the inexpressibly beautiful view of the sun rising in the east. The heavens were already streaked with red: the sun was just appearing above the horizon in full majesty, and the most perfect serenity prevailed throughout the surrounding country, when the other Harz mountains in the south-west, towards the Worm mountains, &c. lying under the Broken, began to be covered by thick clouds. Ascending at that moment the granite rocks called the Tempelskanzel, there appeared before me, though at a great distance, towards the Worm mountains and the Achtermaunshohe, the gigantic figure of a man, as if standing on a large pedestal. But scarcely had I discovered it when it began to disappear, the clouds sunk down speedily and expanded, and I saw the phenomenon no more. The second time, however, I saw this spectre somewhat more distinctly, a little below the summit of the Broken, and near the Heinnichshohe, as I was looking at the sun rising, about four o'clock in the morning. The weather was rather tempestuous; the sky towards the level country was pretty clear, but the Harz mountains had attracted several thick clouds, which had been hovering round them, and which, beginning on the Broken, confined the prospect. In these clouds, soon after the rising of the sun, I saw my own shadow, of a monstrous size, move itself for a couple of seconds in clouds, and the phenomenon disappeared. It is impossible to see this phenomenon, except when the sun is at such an altitude as to throw his rays upon the body in a horizontal direction; for, if he is higher, the shadow is thrown rather under the body than before it. In the month of September last year, as I was making a tour through the Harz with a very agreeable party, and ascended the Broken, I found an excellent account and explanation of this phenomenon, as seen by M. Haue on the 23d of May, 1797, in his diary of an excursion to that mountain. I shall therefore take the liberty of transcribing it:

" ' After having been here for the thirtieth time,' says M. Haue, ' and, besides other objects of my attention, having procured information respecting the above-mentioned atmospheric phenomenon, I was at length so fortunate as to have the pleasure of seeing it; and perhaps my description may afford satisfaction to others who visit the Broken through curiosity. The sun rose about four o'clock; and, the atmosphere being quite serene towards the east, his rays could pass without any obstruction over the Heinnichshohe. In the south-west, however, towards the Achtermaunshohe, a brisk west-wind carried before it their transparent vapours, which were not yet condensed into thick heavy clouds. About a quarter past four I went towards the inn, and looked round to see whether the atmosphere would permit me to have a free prospect to the south-west, when I observed, at a very great distance towards the Achtermaunshohe, a human figure of a monstrous size. A violent gust of wind having almost carried away my hat, I clapped my hand to it by moving my arm towards my head, and the colossal figure did the same. The pleasure which I felt on this discovery can hardly be described; for I had already walked many a weary step in the hope of seeing this shadowy image without being able to satisfy my curiosity. I immediately made another movement by bending my body, and the colossal figure before me repeated it. I was desirous of doing

2 F

the same thing once more, but my colossus had vanished. I remained in the same position, waiting to see whether it would return, and in a few minutes it again made its appearance in the Achtermaunshohe. I paid my respects to it a second time, and it did the same to me. I then called the landlord of the Broken; and having both taken the same position which I had taken alone, we looked toward the Achtermaunshohe, but saw nothing. We had not, however, stood long, when two such colossal figures were formed over the above eminence, which repeated our compliment by bending their bodies as we did; after which they vanished. We retained our position, kept our eyes fixed upon the same spot, and in a little the two figures again stood before us, and were joined by a third. Every movement that we made by bending our bodies, these figures imitated; but with this difference, that the phenomenon was sometimes weak and faint, sometimes strong and well defined. Having thus had an opportunity of discovering the whole secret of this phenomenon, I can give the following information to such of my readers as may be desirous of seeing it themselves:— When the rising sun, and according to analogy the case will be the same at the setting sun, throws his rays over the Broken upon the body of a man standing opposite to fine light clouds floating around or hovering past him, he needs only fix his eye steadfastly upon them, and in all probability he will see the singular spectacle of his own shadow extending to the length of five or six hundred feet, at the distance of about two miles before him. This is one of the most agreeable phenomena I ever had an opportunity of remarking on the great observations of Germany.'"—*Philosophical Magazine*, vol. i. p. 232.

NOTE 3, p. 195.

Extract from Farmer on the Worship of Human Spirits in the ancient Heathen World.

"ALL religious worship among the Gentiles, and indeed among all other people, has ever been adapted to the opinion they formed of its object. Those Gentiles who, by the sole use of their rational faculties, formed just conceptions of the spirituality and purity of the Divine Being, thought that he was best honoured by *a pure mind.* Such of them as regarded the luminaries of heaven as beneficent and divine intelligences that governed the world, worshipped them with *hymns and praises*,* in testimony of their gratitude; or by *kissing the hand* and *bowing the head* † to them, in acknowledgment of their sovereign dominion. This seems to have been the only homage they received from mankind in the most early ages of the world. At least, no other is taken notice of in the book of Job, or in the writings of Moses. When dead men were deified, it became necessary to frame a worship adapted to please and gratify human ghosts, or rather such spirits as they were *conceived* to be. And I will here attempt to shew, that the established worship of the Heathens was built upon these conceptions, and that this circumstance points out the human origin of the more immediate objects of that worship.

"Before we enter upon this argument, we must imagine ourselves in the same situation as the ancient Heathens were, fill our minds with the same ideas they had, and recollect

---

* Mede's Works, p. 656.
† *If I beheld the sun, or the moon,—and my mouth hath kissed my hand.* Job xxxi. 26, 27. The Israelites are forbidden *to worship*, or, as the original word imports, *to bend* or *bow down* to the sun, moon, and stars. Deut. iv. 19.

more especially what were their notions of human ghosts, and of their future state of existence. On the correspondence of their worship to these notions the force of the argument depends.

"The obvious distinction between the soul and body of man, and the permanence of the former after the dissolution of the latter, could not but be admitted by all the nations that worshipped the dead. Happy would it have been had they gone no farther, except to assert a future state of retribution. But they gave an unbounded scope to their imaginations. They not only ascribed to separate spirits, as indeed they justly might, all their former mental affections,* but all the sensations,† appetites, and passions of their bodily state; such as hunger and thirst,‡ and the propensities founded upon the difference of sexes.§ Ghosts were thought to be addicted to the same exercises and employments as had

---

* Of the parental affection we have an amiable example in the ghost of Anchises. Virg. Æn. VI. 685. Proofs of the hatred ghosts bore to their enemies, both when living and after their deaths, are produced by Potter, B. 4. c. 8. p. 261. I shall add the following passage from Ovid, in ibidem, v. 139:—

——————— Nec mors mihi finiet iras,
Sæva sed in manes manibus arma dabit:
Tunc quoque cum fuero vacuas dilapsus in auras,
Exanimis manes oderit umbra tuos.

See also Horace, Carm. V. 5., Virg. Æn. IV. 384, and the very characteristic description of the ghost of Ajax, Homer, Odyss. XI. 542, and of the other ghosts in the same book.

† Hence that prayer, taken notice of above, that the earth might lie light or heavy on the dead.

‡ This appears from their being provided, as it will be shewn they were, with the means of gratifying these appetites.

§ Hercules, though he feasted with the immortal gods, was wedded to Hebe. Homer, II. XI. 602. Some have thought that ghosts could assume a human body.

been their delight while men.* And though they could not be felt and handled† like bodies of flesh, and were of a larger size,‡ yet they had the same lineaments and features. Being an original part of the human frame, they were wounded whenever the body was, and retained the impression of their wounds.§

"Their idea of men's future state of existence was formed upon the model of our present condition. They lent money in this world upon bills payable in the next.‖ Between both worlds there was thought to be an open intercourse, departed spirits bestowing favours upon their survivors, and receiving from them gifts and presents. These gifts were sometimes supposed to be conveyed into the other world in their own natural form: for they put into the mouth of a dead man a piece of money, to pay Charon for his passage over Styx; and a cake, of which honey was the principal ingredient, to pacify the growling Cerberus.¶ Those things, whose natural outward form was destroyed, did not altogether perish, but

---

* Pars in gramineis exercent membra palæstris, &c.
Virg. Æn. VI. 642.

———————— Quæ gratia currûm
Armorumque fuit vivis, quæ cura nitentis
Pascere equos, eadem sequitur tellure repostos.
Id. ib. v. 653.

Multo magis rectores quondam urbium recepti in cœlum curam regendorum hominum non relinquunt. Macrobius, in Somn. Scip. l. i. c. 9.

† Homer, Odyss. XI. 205.

‡ Et nunc magna mei sub terras ibit imago. Virg. Æn. IV. 654.

§ Homer, Odyss. XI. 40. Virg. Æn. VI. 495.

‖ This is related of the Celts or Gauls. Pecunias mutuas, quæ his apud inferos redderentur, dare solitos. Pythagoras approved the custom: for our author adds, Dicerem stultos, nisi idem braccati sensissent, quod palliatus Pythagoras credidit.
Valerius Maximus, lib. 2. c. 6. § 10.

¶ Bos. Gr. Antiq. p. 410.

passed into the other world. The souls of brutes survived the dissolution of their bodies; and even inanimate substances, after they were consumed by fire, still, in some degree, subsisted! images flying off from them, which as exactly resembled them as a ghost did the living man. Hence it was, that, upon the funeral piles of the dead, they were accustomed to throw letters, in order to their being read by their departed friends.* And being able, as they imagined, to transmit to the dead whatever gifts they pleased, in one form or other; food, † and raiment, ‡ and armour, § were either deposited in their graves, or consumed in the same fire with their own bodies, together with their wives and concubines, ‖ their favourite slaves, ¶ and brute animals, **

---

* Diodorus Siculus, l. v. p. 352, relates this circumstance of the Gauls.

† See below, under Sacrifices.

‡ Solon (according to Plutarch, vit. Solon, p. 90. C.) made a law to prevent the burying with the dead more than three garments. This law was afterwards adopted by the Romans, and inserted in the 12 tables. Sumtum minutio; tria, si volet, ricinia adhibeto. The clothes of the dead were sometimes thrown upon the funeral pile. Bos. p. 422. Kennett, Rom. Antiq. p. 357.

§ The arms of soldiers were thrown upon their pyre.
Bos. ch. 22. p. 422.

‖ This is still a custom in some parts of the East, and it is of great antiquity. Evadne (by Ovid called Iphias) threw himself upon the funeral pile of Capaneus, uttering this prayer: *Accipe me, Capaneu.* Ovid. Ars. Am. l. 3. v. 21. Statius, Thebaid. l. 12. v. 801. Propertius, l. 15, 21.

¶ Servi et clientes, quos ab iis dilectos esse constabat, justis funeribus confectis una cremabantur. Cæsar, B. C. l. 6. c. 18. It was the same both in Mexico and Peru: on the death of the emperors and other eminent persons, many of their attendants were put to death, that they might accompany them into the other world, and support their dignity. See Robertson's Hist. of North America, v. 3. p. 211, 259.

** Cæsar, ubi supra. At the funeral of Patroclus, four horses and nine favourite dogs were thrown upon the pyre. Homer, Il. 23, v. 171.

and whatever else had been the object of their affection in life.*

"Accordingly we find the parrot of Corinna, after his death, in Elysium.† Orpheus, when in the same happy abode, appears in his sacerdotal robe, striking his lyre; and the warriors were furnished with their horses, arms, and chariots, which Virgil calls *inanes, empty, airy,* and *unsubstantial,* being such shades and phantoms of their former chariots as the ghosts themselves were of men.‡ In a word, whatever was burnt or interred with the dead, their ghosts were thought to receive and use. It is observable, that, as the ghosts appeared with the wounds made in them before their separation from the body, so the arms that had been stained with blood before they were burnt appeared bloody afterwards; § and, in like manner, the money-bills, and letters that had been consumed in the flames, were certainly thought to retain the impression of what had been written in them.

"Such notions of separate spirits can indeed for the most part be considered only as the childish conceptions of untutored minds, in the infancy of the world, or in ages of gross ignorance. Nevertheless, being consecrated to the purposes of superstition, and in length of time becoming venerable by their antiquity, they maintained their credit in more enlightened ages amongst the multitude, and, through policy, were patronized even by those who discerned their absurdity.

"This general view of the notions which the Heathens

---

* Moris fuerat, ut cum his rebus homines sepelirentur quas dilexerant vivi. Servius on Æn. X. 827. See also Caesar, L. 6. 18.
† Psittacus has inter, nemorali sede receptus,
  Convertit volucres in sua verba pias.
                                           Ovid, Amor. l. II. el. 6 v. 57.
‡ Virg. Æn. VI. 645—655.
§ Homer, Od. XI. 41.

entertained of human spirits, may prepare us to receive the farther account that will be given of them, and thereby of the ground of that particular kind of worship that was paid them. And, if the same worship was paid to the gods as to human spirits, and for the same reasons, it will appear highly probable, that both were of the same nature originally, though there was a difference of rank between them." *

NOTE 4, p. 217.

Prophetic Character of the Second-sight in the Highlands.

It has been often supposed, but with the greatest incorrectness, either that the second-sight boasted of by the Highlanders was a gift comparatively unknown to other tribes of Europe, or that it was a faculty which exclusively pointed to the divination assumed by the ancient priests of the Celts, who were well known under the name of *Druids*. Neither view, however, is exactly correct. In the first place, there is scarcely a people of Europe by whom a divining power of seeing objects invisible to all other eyes has not at one time or other been assumed; and, secondly, the faculty of the Highland seer more agrees in its superstitious character with one that was familiar to the northern tribes of Europe, who were either of a Teutonic stock, or were allied to the Fins. Indeed I have often considered that most of the superstitions of the Highlands, particularly of the western districts of Scotland, north of the Clyde, may be more successfully traced to the Norwegian than to the Gaelic progenitors of this people. Entertaining, therefore, this view, I shall give some extracts from a work of the 17th century, viz.—Scheffer's History of the Laplanders, in which a remarkable correspondence may be found to subsist between the spectral impressions of this people and those of the Highlanders.

---

* See Farmer on the Worship of Human Spirits, &c. p. 417, &c.

" The melancholic constitution of the Laplanders," says Scheffer, " renders them subject to frightful apparitions and dreams, which they look upon as infallible presages made to them by the Genius of what is to befall them. Thus they are frequently seen lying upon the ground asleep, some singing with a full voice, others howling and making a hideous noise not unlike wolves."——

" Their superstitions may be imputed partly to their living in solitudes, forests, and among the wild beasts; partly to their solitary way of dwelling separately from the society of others, except what belong to their own families, sometimes at several leagues distance. Hereafter it may be added, that their daily exercise is hunting, it being observed that this kind of life is apt to draw people into various superstitions, and at last to a correspondence with spirits. For those who lead a solitary life being frequently destitute of human aid, have oftentimes recourse to forbidden means, in hopes to find that aid and help among the spirits, which they cannot find among men; and what encourages them in it is impunity, these things being committed by them, without as much as the fear of any witnesses; which moved Mr Rheen to allege, among sundry reasons which he gives for the continuance of the impious superstitions of the Laplanders, this for one: Because they live among inaccessible mountains, and at a great distance from the conversation of other men. Another reason is, the good opinion they constantly entertain of their ancestors, whom they cannot imagine to have been so stupid as not to understand what God they ought to worship; wherefore they judge they should be wanting in their reverence due to them, if, by receding from their institutions, they should reprove them of impiety and ignorance."——

" The parents are the masters who instruct their own sons in the magical art: Those, says Tornæus, who have attained to this magical art by instructions receive it either from their parents, or from some body else, and that by degrees, which they put in practice as often as an opportunity offers. Thus they accomplish themselves in this art, especially if their genius leads them to it. For they don't look upon every one as a fit scholar; nay, some are accounted quite incapable of it, notwithstanding they have been sufficiently instructed, as I have been informed by very credible people. And Joh. Tornæus confirms it by these words: As the Laplanders are naturally of different inclinations, so are they not equally capable of attaining to this art. And in another passage, they bequeath the demons as part of their inheritance, which is the reason that one family excels the other in this magical art. From whence it is evident, that certain whole families have their own demons, not only differing from the familiar spirits of others, but also quite contrary and opposite to them. Besides this, not only whole families, but also particular persons, have sometimes one, sometimes more spirits belonging to them, to secure them against the designs of other demons, or else to hurt others. Olaus Petri Niurenius speaks to this effect, when he says,—They are attended by a certain number of spirits, some by three, others by two, or at least by one. The last is intended for their security, the other to hurt others. The first commands all the rest. Some of those they acquire with a great deal of pains and prayers, some without much trouble, being their attendants from their infancy. Joh. Tornæus gives us a very large account of it. There are some, says he, who naturally are magicians; an abominable thing indeed. For those who the devil knows will prove very serviceable to him in this art, he seizes on in their very infancy with a certain distemper, when they are haunted with apparitions and visions, by which they are, in proportion of their age, instructed in the rudiments of this art. Those who are a second time taken with this distemper, have more apparitions coming before them than in the first, by which they receive much more insight into it than before. But if they are seized a third time with this disease, which then proves very dangerous, and often not without the hazard of their lives, then it is they see all the apparitions the devil is able to contrive, to accomplish them in the magical art. Those are arrived to such a degree of perfection, that without the help of the drum,* they can foretel things to come a great while before; and are so strongly possessed by the devil, that they foresee things even against their will. Thus, not long ago, a certain Laplander, who is still alive, did voluntarily deliver his drum to me, which I had often desired of him before; notwithstanding all this, he told me in a very melancholy posture, that though he had put away his drum, nor intended to have any other hereafter, yet he should foresee every thing without it, as he had done before. As an instance of it, he told me truly all the particular accidents that had happened to me in my journey into Lapland; making at the same time heavy complaints, that he did not know what use to make of his eyes, those things being presented to his sight much against his will.

"Lundius observes, that some of the Laplanders are seized upon by a demon, when they are arrived to a middle age, in the following manner:—Whilst they are busie in the woods, the spirit appears to them, where they discourse concerning the conditions, upon which the demon offers them his assistance, which done, he teaches them a certain song, which they are obliged to keep in constant remembrance. They must return the next day to the same place, where the same spirit appears to them again, and repeats the former song, in case he takes a fancy to the person; if not, he does not ap-

---

* An instrument intended for the purpose of conjuration.

pear at all. These spirits make their appearances under different shapes, some like fishes, some like birds, others like a serpent or dragon, others in the shape of a pigmee, about a yard high; being attended by three, four, or five other pigmees of the same bigness, sometimes by more, but never exceeding nine. No sooner are they seized by the Genius, but they appear in a most surprising posture, like madmen, bereaved of the use of reason. This continues for six months; during which time they don't suffer any of their kindred to come near them, not so much as their own wives and children. They spend most of this time in the woods and other solitary places, being very melancholy and thoughtful, scarce taking any food, which makes them extremely weak. If you ask their children, where and how their parents sustain themselves, they will tell you, that they receive their sustenance from their Genii. The same author gives us a remarkable instance of this kind in a young Laplander called Olaus, being then a scholar in the school of Liksala, of about eighteen years of age. This young fellow fell mad on a sudden, making most dreadful postures and outcries, that he was in hell, and his spirit tormented beyond what could be expressed. If he took a book in hand, so soon as he met with the name of Jesus, he threw the book upon the ground in great fury, which after some time being passed over, they used to ask him, whether he had seen any vision during this ecstacy? He answered, that abundance of things had appeared to him, and that a mad dog being tied to his foot, followed him wherever he stirred. In his lucid intervals he would tell them, that the first beginning of it happened to him one day, as he was going out of the door of his dwelling, when a great flame passing before his eyes and touching his ears, a certain person appeared to him all naked. The next day he was seized with a most terrible headach, so that he made most lamentable outcries, and broke every thing that came under his hands. This unfortunate person's face was as black as a coal, and he used to say, that the devil most commonly appeared to him in the habit of a minister, in a long cloak; during his fits he would say that he was surrounded by nine or ten fellows of a low stature, who did use him very barbarously, though at the same time the standers-by did not perceive the least thing like it. He would often climb to the top of the highest fir-trees, with as much swiftness as a squirrel, and leap down again to the ground, without receiving the least hurt. He always loved solitude, flying the conversation of other men. He would run as swift as a horse, it being impossible for anybody to overtake him. He used to talk amongst the woods to himself no otherwise than if several persons had been in his company.

"I am apt to believe, that those spirits were not altogether unknown to the ancients, and that they are the same which were called by Tertullian Paredri, and are mentioned by Monsieur Valois, in his Ecclesiastical History of Eusebius.

"Whenever a Laplander has occasion for his familiar spirit, he calls to him, and makes him come by only singing the song he taught him at their first interview; by which means he has him at his service as often as he pleases. And because they know them obsequious and serviceable, they call them Sveie, which signifies as much in their tongue, as the companions of their labour, or their helpmates. Lundius has made another observation, very well worth taking notice of, viz.—That those spirits or demons never appear to the women, or enter into their service; of which I don't pretend to allege the true cause, unless one might say, that perhaps they do it out of pride, or a natural aversion they have to the female sex, subject to so many infirmities."*

---

* History of Lapland, written by John Scheffer, Professor of Law, &c. at Upsal in Sweden. English translation, published A. D. 1704.

Such is the remarkable similarity subsisting between the second-sight of the Highlanders and of the Laplanders, which, again, is like that of the Norwegians.

But, before dismissing this subject, I shall remark, that one of the latest proofs of the prophetic character of the second-sight is afforded by Dr Ferriar in his Theory of Apparitions. "A gentleman," says this author, "connected with my family, an officer in the army, *and certainly addicted to no superstition*,* was quartered early in life, in the middle of the last century, near the castle of a gentleman in the north of Scotland, who was supposed to possess the second-sight. Strange rumours were afloat respecting the old chieftain. He had spoken to an apparition, which ran along the battlements of the house, and had never been cheerful afterwards. His prophetic visions excited surprise even in that region of credulity; and his retired habits favoured the popular opinion. My friend assured me, that one day, while he was reading a play to the ladies of the family, the chief, who had been walking across the room, stopped suddenly, and assumed the look of a seer. He rang the bell, and ordered the groom to saddle a horse; to proceed immediately to a seat in the neighbourhood, and to inquire after the health of Lady ———. If the account was favourable, he then directed him to call at another castle, to ask after another lady whom he named.

"The reader immediately closed his book, and declared that he would not proceed till these abrupt orders were explained, as he was confident that they were produced by the second-sight. The chief was very unwilling to explain himself, but at length he owned that the door had appeared to

---

* Dr Ferriar might with much advantage have spared the remark which I have inserted in italics.

open, and that a little woman, without a head, had entered the room; that the apparition indicated the death of some person of his acquaintance; and the only two persons who resembled the figure were those ladies after whose health he had sent to inquire.

" A few hours afterwards the servant returned with an account that one of the ladies had died of an apoplectic fit, about the time when the vision appeared.

" At another time the chief was confined to his bed by indisposition, and my friend was reading to him in a stormy winter night, while the fishing-boat belonging to the castle was at sea. The old gentleman repeatedly expressed much anxiety respecting his people; and at last exclaimed, " My boat is lost!' The colonel replied, ' How do you know it, sir?'—He was answered, ' I see two of the boatmen bringing in the third drowned, all dripping wet, and laying him down close beside your chair. The chair was shifted with great precipitation; in the course of the night, the fisherman returned with the corpse of one of the boatmen."

It is perhaps to be lamented, that such a narrative as this should have been *seriously* quoted in Dr Ferriar's philosophic work on Apparitions. I have lately seen it advanced, on the doctor's authority, as favouring the vulgar belief in apparitions, and introduced in the same volume with the story of Mrs Veal!

NOTE 5, p. 237.

Illustration of the Mode in which the Narrative of a Case of Spectral Impressions, although published by and occurring to a medical Man, may be distorted by superstitious Fears and vulgar Prejudices.

IN the London Magazine, for the year 1765, (page 234,) we find an extraordinary account, under the signature of Josephus, of a young man, a student of an academy in Devonshire, who dreamt that he was paying a visit to his father's house in Gloucestershire, about a hundred miles distant; that, on his arrival there, "he first attempted to go in at the fore-door,—but, finding it fast, then went round to the back-door, where he gained an easy admission. Finding the family a-bed, he made the best of his way to the apartment where his father and mother lay. When he had entered the room, he first went to the side of the bed where his father was, whom he found fast asleep; on which, without disturbing him, he went round to the other side of the bed, where he found his mother, as he apprehended, broad awake; to whom he addressed himself in these words: ' Mother! I am going a long journey, and am come to bid you good b'w'ye.' On which she answered, in a fright, as follows:—' O, dear son, thou art dead!' Immediately on which the undersigned awoke, and took no further notice of the affair than he would have done of any other ordinary dream. But, in a few days, that is, as soon as the post could possibly reach him, he received a letter from his father, informing him that his mother had heard him such a night trying the doors of the house, and repeating precisely all the particulars of his dream as having been likewise exactly represented to her, while awake, in a spectral impression." The remark here made is,—" Such is the son's dream, and such the vision of the mother. This latter being a kind of counter-part to the former,—on which, however, nothing extraordinary turned up on either side."

This idle account, given under a fictitious signature, would be unworthy the least comment, were it not for the attempted explanations to which it gave rise,—but more particularly for the illustrations with which such explanations were accompanied. A correspondent of the Magazine (credulous soul!) having called upon his fellow-contributors to afford some key to the mystery, a *physician*, (proh pudor!)

Dr J. Cook, relates the following account of some apparitions which occurred to his observation, having first appealed for the truth of them " to the living God, before whom he must be severely judged, if he told a falsity, or intended thereby to deceive any one:"—

" Ever since I was three and twenty years of age," continues the superstitious doctor, who certainly laboured very long under genuine spectral impressions, " I have had an invisible being, or beings, attend me at times, both at home and abroad, that has by some gentle token or other given me warning and notice that shortly I should certainly lose a particular friend or a patient. It began and continued from our marriage till the decease of my first wife, in May 1728, and her infant daughter. After that they came seldom, but so gentle, civil, and familiar, that I chose rather to have them about my house than not, and would not, if I was to sell it, part with the same without some extraordinary consideration upon that very account; and I really hope they will never leave me as long as I live, though my spouse wishes otherwise, to whom they are not so agreeable.

" I may be reckoned by several to be a whimsical visionary, or what not,—but I know I am far from it, being neither superstitious, enthusiastic, nor timorous; and I am certain, too, I am not deceived by others, we all having had many and various impressions from invisible agents; and I myself, by no fewer than three of my senses, and those so often repeated, that they became quite easy and familiar, without any terror or amazement. I take the hint at once, and wait for the certain and infallible issue. I have spoke to it often, but never received any answer, and think I have courage enough to stand a private conference.

" Sometimes we have had these hints frequent and close together; at other times but seldom, and at a great distance

2 G

of time. But this I have observed, that rarely any patient, or friend, that I respected, or that valued me, departs hence, but I have some kind of sensible notice or warning of it;—but yet so discreet and mild, as never to flutter or frighten me. This notice, which is either by seeing, feeling, or hearing, is not fixed to any certain distance of time previous to their deaths,—but I have had it a week, a month, and more, before their decease, and once only three days.

" At first, in 1728, I kept a book of account, where I entered every notice or warning, with the particular circumstances attending, and the event that succeeded such notices; but they were then so frequent and numerous, that I grew quite weary in writing them down,—so left off that method, resolving to take them for the future just as they came. The very last hint I had was on Saturday night, the 6th of July, 1765, in my chamber, about eleven o'clock, as I was walking to my bed, being from home attending a patient I was that morning sent for to, and which I lost the 20th day of the same month. For the first five days I saw no danger, yet doubted the event; but, when I have more than one patient dangerously ill at a time, the issue only determines the case; and, though I lay no stress upon such notices so as to affect my practice, yet I fear the most; and, though the use of means is then to no purpose, yet it renders me the more diligent for conscience sake.

" To relate the particular circumstances of the several notices intimated on this or any other occasions, would be here entirely useless, as only affording matter of mirth to the light and unthinking, and those who know nothing of the matter. But this I again solemnly declare, that I have many times, even above a hundred, I believe, been made sensible of the existence of a different kind of beings from us, subtle and volatile inhabitants, as I take it, of the air, who see and know our worldly affairs here below, and have a concern for us and our welfare. Twice only have I seen spectres, but heard and felt them times innumerable.

"Angels they cannot be, those high and glorious beings being too grand and noble for such low offices, and are much better employed above. Devils they are not, as owing no good service at all to the lapsed race of mankind; and departed souls have no more business here, but are gone to their place.

"That there are innumerable inferior spiritual beings in our atmosphere, was the opinion of the ancients, of Milton, and the moderns; and I think they solve all difficulties attending this abstruse subject at once, and may remove the foolish fear so generally attending such odd stories. As no created space is absolutely void of all being, why should our gross atmosphere be without such inhabitants as are most suitable to such an element,—who may be, as it were, the lowest step of the spiritual scale, and the first gradation of a superior order?

"All histories of this sort, both divine and profane, by ancients and by moderns also, cannot be without some foundation; and the learned Whiston and Le Clerc both say the opinion of spectres is neither unreasonable nor unphilosophical, but may very well exist in the nature of things.

"In short, I could write a whole volume on the subject; but that I know it would be but to little purpose, and could serve none but such as are, like myself, in the secret; therefore it need never be expected. Yet I shall be ready, at any time, to satisfy the curiosity of all sober, sensible, and inquisitive people, by private letters, if desired; and solemnly protest I have no selfish end, interest, design, nor deceit herein; but the truth I must credit, and always speak, though but three people alive believe me; and yet I am as much averse to the many idle stories of hobgoblins, and the like vain and villanous impositions, as any man living. But yet the abuse of a thing is no good argument against the use of it, be it either in practice or knowledge.

"Nay, what is more wonderful still, besides my seeing these aerial shades in such vehicles, or something like them, which once I did in my own house at noonday, directed thereto by the barking of my little dog at the same, who saw it first,—I once heard one of them pronounce very audibly and articulately, but most emphatically and pathetically, in my chamber, just as I had put out my candle, and was laid down in my bed, these words: '*I am gone.*' My second cousin, a visitor, died on the Monday morning following, the fourth day after, who was seemingly well till two days before her decease. My spouse was fast asleep by me, so missed being witness of that notice, though she often is, and some of my sons too, and many others.

"But some will say, *cui bono*, of what use is all this? Suppose we could not resolve the question; what then? Can we, poor, dull, finite beings of a day, pretend to account for all phenomena about us? nay, can we exactly account for any?—Yet I will humbly offer my thoughts about it, and tell to what good use you may apply them; and then their intimations may not be altogether in vain.

"Look, as I do, upon all such uncommon impressions from invisible powers as a sensible proof, and manifest demonstration of another and future state of existence after this, and that the present is the first and lowest of all we are successively to pass through.—Betake yourself earnestly to prayer," &c. &c., "and let such secret impressions, items, and hints, be no longer matter of laughter, but of serious meditation," &c., &c., &c. "J. Cook, M.D."

[*Dated*] "*Leigh, Sept.* 18, 1765."

This strange narrative, as we might expect, provoked the replies of many commentators. The first of these, under the signature of W., calls his case "a discrasy of the brain, occasioned, perhaps, by an uncommon concern for his patients, and anxiety for their welfare." A second critic, in the course of a very learned metaphysical stricture on Dr Cook's illusions, thinks it is very probable that one of the ghosts which visited him was of Irish extraction, and certainly no grammarian; for, "once, indeed," he adds, "you heard the spiritual agent form an articulate voice, and utter these words,—'I am gone;' which you say was fulfilled by the sudden death of your cousin's daughter three days after.— A vain mortal should not presume to dictate expressions to a nobler being; but certainly his meaning had been less ambiguous, less mysteriously oracular, had he plainly said, 'Your cousin's daughter is going.' For no good reason can, I think, be given, why spirits, if they use our language, should not be as much confined as men in the articles of grammar and good sense, if they hope for any respect in this world."

I cannot spare room to notice Dr Cook's reply to these letters, nor to advert to the remarks of other commentators; but it appears from several contributions of his to the periodical journals, that he was often in an infirm state of health, arising from attacks of the gout. To this morbid source then we must probably look for the production of his phantasms. With regard to the doctor's family being joint witnesses of his ghostly visitants, a *moral* rather than a medical explanation may afford a key to this assertion.

HAMLET.
"Do you see yonder cloud, that's almost in shape of a camel?
POLONIUS.
By the mass, and 'tis like a camel indeed.
HAMLET.
They fool me to the top of my bent."

Addition to Note 5.

With the foregoing narrative may be compared one which I received, since the first edition of this work was published, from a respectable individual of Edinburgh, who has favoured me with his name and address. The writer, after making me acquainted with the fanciful impressions of his infancy, the subject of which was derived from the wonderful stories to be found in treatises on demonology, as well as from the popular traditional stories of Scotland, then relates the course of studies by which, in a more mature age, he escaped from the trammels of superstition. This discipline led him to regard, as a mere mental illusion, an incident which others would have considered as supernatural.

" About a dozen of years ago," remarks my correspondent, " a gentleman, with whom I had been long and intimately acquainted, died very suddenly. The information of his decease reached me soon after, and produced no slight emotion in my mind, which, although banished by the business in which I was employed, was occasionally renewed by the conversation of those with whom I associated. At dinner the subject was talked of in my family. I again pursued my vocation; and being more than usually busy, if it occurred again, it was only for a moment, and the feeling far less intense. About nine in the evening I went up stairs, and joined my family; the circumstance was not again mentioned by any one, we being engaged in talking over some family-matters in which we were interested. After supper, according to my usual custom, I went down stairs to take a walk in the court behind my house. This court was a parallelogram, and mostly paved, from thirty to forty feet in length; its breadth more than half as much; in part it was bounded by extensive open gardens, from which it was divided by a low parapet-wall, surmounted with a light railing; the extremities at both ends were the walls of offices belonging to the house. The sky was clear, and the night serene; and there was no light from my window which could either fall or produce any shadow in the court. (You will instantly perceive my reason for relating these minute particulars.)

"When I went down stairs, I was musing on a subject by no association of ideas connected with my deceased friend, and for several hours did not note him in my mind. My entrance to the court was at an angle; and I had proceeded at a slow pace, nearly half-way across, still pursuing my ruminations, when the figure of my departed friend seemed suddenly to start up right before me, at the opposite angle of the court. I do not at this moment see the pen in my hand, nor the paper on which I am writing, more visibly and distinctly, than he appeared to me; so that I could at a glance discern his whole costume. He was not in his usual dress, but in a coat of a different colour, which he had for many months left off wearing; I could even remark a figured vest, which he had also worn about the same time; also a coloured silk handkerchief around his neck, in which I had used to see him in a morning; and my powers of vision seemed to become more keen as I gazed on the phantom before me. It seemed to be leaning in the angle with its back to the wall, and gave me a bow, or rather a familiar nod of recognisance, making a slight motion with the right hand. I acknowledge that I started, and an indescribable feeling, which I shall never forget, shot through my frame; but after a pause of, I suppose, from twenty to thirty seconds, I became convinced that it was either an optical deception, or some sudden and temporary hallucination of the mind. I recovered my fortitude; and, keeping my eye intently fixed on the spectre, walked briskly up to the spot.

It vanished, not by sinking into the earth, but by seeming insensibly to melt into viewless air. I brought my hand in contact with the wall on which it seemed to lean, felt nothing, and the illusion was vanished for ever.

"There is no doubt that all this happened in consequence of the previous strong excitement of my feelings, and the deep impression left on my mind; but I have never been able to comprehend how it should have occurred, after the subject had been banished from my memory, and when my thoughts were employed on a very different subject; nor can I conceive how the external organs of sight should so readily be united with imagination, in producing the extraordinary illusion, especially with one who was so decidedly sceptical on the subject.*

"I have talked over this strange occurrence with friends, but have never heard a satisfactory solution, either physical or philosophical, of what could produce this temporary alienation of the reasoning faculties. One clerical friend, who, although otherwise not a weak-minded man, endeavoured to convince me, not only of the possibility, but even of the probability, that it was a real apparition which had so suddenly appeared before me. To this I replied, 'If so, to what purpose did it appear? or what good was promoted by its unexpected appearance? It neither reprimanded me for the past, nor admonished me for the future. The intrusion produced no consequences, except a momentary alarm, and some subsequent musings on how little I knew of my own frame, either physical or intellectual.'"

---

* I would remark, to my intelligent correspondent, who had not at the time seen my work, that these truly pertinent questions are frequently discussed in the course of this dissertation, but more particularly in some chapters of the Fourth Part of the present edition, commencing at page 224, and ending at page 304.

S. H.

NOTE 6, pp. 331 and 332.

In page 331, &c., I made a remark, that many narratives of ghosts may be found in various biographies, where they have only found a place because a fortuitous coincidence with the subject of the phantasm and subsequent events has served to countenance the popular views entertained regarding the sacred mission of apparitions. This remark, of course, applies no less to the phantasms of dreams than to those of waking impressions.

Since committing this passage to paper, however, I have met with the publication of a case of an opposite kind, and it is really the only one which I know of that has been recorded. It is to be found in an able letter addressed to a friend of the writer, " on the Vanity of Dreams, and upon the Appearance of Spirits," which was published in " Le Mercure Gallant," for January, 1690.

" The last proof, my dear friend," says the writer, " which I can give on the vanity of dreams, is my surviving after one that I experienced on the 22d of September, 1679. I awoke on that day at five o'clock in the morning, and having fallen asleep again half an hour after, I dreamt that I was in my bed, and that the curtain of it was undrawn at the foot (two circumstances which were true), and that I saw one of my relations, who had died several years before, enter the room, with a countenance as sorrowful as it had formerly been joyous. She seated herself at the foot of my bed, and looked at me with pity. As I knew her to be dead, as well in the dream as in reality, I judged by her sorrow that she was going to announce some bad news to me, and perhaps death; and foreseeing it with sufficient indifference, —' Ah well!' said I to her, ' I must die then?' She replied to me, ' It is true.'—' And when?' retorted I. ' Immediately?'—' To-day,' replied she. I confess to you the time appeared short; but, without being concerned, I interrogated her further, and asked her 'in what manner?' She murmured some words which I did not understand, and at that moment I awoke. The importance of a dream so precise made me take notice of my situation, and I remarked, that I had lain down upon my right side, my body extended, and both hands resting upon my stomach. I rose to commit my dream to writing, for fear of forgetting any part of it; and, finding it accompanied by all the circumstances which are attributed to mysterious and divine visions, I was no sooner dressed, than I went to tell my sister-in-law, that, if serious dreams were infallible warnings, she would have no brother-in-law in twenty-four hours. I told her afterwards all that had happened to me, and likewise informed some of my friends, but without betraying the least alarm, and without changing in any respect my usual conduct, resigning myself to the entire disposal of Providence.

"Now, if I had been weak enough to give up my mind to the idea that I was going to die, perhaps I *should* have died, and it would have happened to me, as to those men, of whom Procopius, the Greek historian, has spoken, who, when the plague prevailed, were struck with this scourge from God, for having only dreamt that demons touched them, or said to them that they would be soon in the tomb. I likewise should have paid by the shortening of my days for yielding up my belief to these dreams, and violating the law of God, which forbids such a superstition. At least it is certain, that a Canadian would not have escaped; for he would have even had recourse to precipices, or to his own hands, in order that his dream might not be a futile one. For the people of that country are absolutely persuaded, that they cannot dream of any thing which ought not to happen as a matter of course."

Note 7, p. 335.

There is not a more frequent subject of marvellous narrations, whether true or false, than the ghost of some departed friend appearing to an individual in fulfilment of a previous compact made before death. But the writer in " Le Mercure Gallant," of the year 1690, whom I have before quoted, though uttering his sentiments in a superstitious age and country, has not hesitated to express some doubts on the subject.

" Souls do not take flight from their bodies to return to them, the tarrying-place being too indifferent for such spirits, however delightful it may be in young persons. If it was otherwise, I should have seen Plusside since her death. This beauty, of whom you have heard me say so much, had sworn to me, in the strength of our affections, one day in Easter, at the foot of the altar, that if she died before me, she would come and see me, and tell me all the news of the other state. I also made her the same promise, and sanctified it with an oath. Nevertheless, many years have elapsed since she has paid the debt of nature, without having accomplished what she owed to friendship and to her word. "

THE END.